WITH CHRIST

*An Anthology of the Writings of
Blessed Columba Marmion*

WITH CHRIST

*An Anthology of the Writings of
Blessed Columba Marmion*

Compiled by
Dom Raymund Thibaut, O.S.B.

Angelico Press reprint edition, 2013
This Angelico Press edition is a republication
of the work originally published by
The Newman Press, Westminster, MD, in 1952

No part of this book may be reproduced or transmitted,
in any form or by any means, without permission

For information, address:
Angelico Press, 4619 Slayden Rd. NE
Tacoma, WA 98422
www.angelicopress.com

ISBN 978-1-887593-25-0 (pbk: alk. paper)

Cover Design: Cristy Deming

Image Credit: James Tissot (French, 1836–1902).
The Procession Nearing Calvary (*Le cortège arrivant au calvaire*), 1886–1894.
Opaque watercolor over graphite on gray wove paper, image:
8 11/16 x 11 1/2 in. (22.1 x 29.2 cm). Brooklyn Museum,
purchased by public subscription, 00.159.286.

To Mary
who
having become our Mother
at the foot of the Cross
understands all our sufferings
and takes upon herself
all our woes

CONTENTS

Preface [i]

Dom Columba Marmion [9]

PART I

Jesus Christ and His Work of Redemption

The Person of Christ [15]

The Place of Christ in the Divine Plan—Christ was Constituted our High Priest and our Mediator from the Moment of the Incarnation—The Name "Jesus Christ" Signifies His Mission and Characterizes His Work

Christ's Work of Redemption [24]

How Christ Began His Sacrifice from the Moment of His Birth—The Greatness and the Fecundity of the Hidden Life of Christ—The Love of Christ for His Fellow Men During His Public Life—The Passion of Jesus, Culmination of His Redemptive Work—"That the World May Know That I Love the Father"—"He Loved Me and Delivered Himself Up for Me"—"He Delivered Himself Up Because He Himself Wanted It"—The Fulness of the Sacrifice of Christ—From the Pretorium to Calvary—Through His Death, Christ, Our Head, Sanctifies the Church, Which Has Become His Mystical Body—The Continuance of the Sacrifice of Christ in Heaven—The Association of the Virgin Mary in the Redemptive Work of Her Son

PART II

We Co-operate in Christ's Work of Redemption by Sharing in His Passion

The Christian is Called to Co-operate in the Redemptive Work of Christ [85]

Basic Dispositions of the Soul Which Wants to Co-operate Worthily [91]

Silent Patience—Generous Love—Filial Abandonment

How to Produce These Interior Dispositions Within Ourselves [121]

Contemplation of the Suffering Christ—Prayer—Offering Ourselves to the Father in Union with Christ Immolated on the Altar—Uniting Ourselves to Christ in Holy Communion

PART III

On Human Misery and Some Forms of Trial and Suffering

Seeing the Mercy of God in our Trials [147]

Human Misery and Divine Mercy—Taking Our Miseries Upon Himself, Christ Became the Most Miserable of Men—"...In Order That the Strength of Christ Might Dwell in Me"—Sickness—Temptation—Hardships and Trials in the Fulfilling of Our Duties of State—Humiliations—Interior Sufferings

PART IV
The Fecundity of Suffering Accepted in a Christian Spirit

How Suffering Leads to Life [191]

Christianity is a Doctrine of Life—Suffering Purifies and Frees the Soul—Submission to God in Suffering is a Source of Peace—Christian Acceptance of Suffering Honours God, Draws Down Grace upon Souls and the Church, the Mystical Body of Christ

PART V
Facing Death, the Supreme Trial

Life is Not Taken Away, but Transformed [207]

PART VI
Our Sharing in the Eternal Glory of Christ

We Shall be Glorified with Christ [215]

Glorification Follows upon the Passion of Jesus—The Everlastingness of Our Glory—The Measure of Our Eternal Happiness—The Resurrection of the Body

A Parting Word [226]

Preface

SUFFERING is a world-wide fact. No man escapes it. It waits for every man to enter into the world and it walks him to the grave. It smites every man and grasps the whole of him: body and soul, heart and mind. It stalks him over the entire breadth of his being and of the multiple powers he bears within himself.

Like the Cross, its loftiest and most meaningful symbol, suffering is scandal for some, folly for others. For others still, it is the acid test of faithfulness, the golden key to perfection and union with Christ, the fertile seed of glory.

Living faith and love determine our reaction to suffering. On instinct most men repulse it violently like a foe—which it is, in fact, if they see it from only the natural point of view. Some welcome it with a smile as the bearer of grace. Thus suffering, for some, remains sterile; for others, it becomes dangerous; and for others, it makes atonement and merits redemption.

It is most important, then, to know how to accept suffering; and surely the supreme work of mercy is that difficult science, that delicate art, of teaching men to carry their cross. Not everyone can excel in this art or teach this exalted science effectively, but only he who has a great heart and the supernatural experience of sorrow.

Those two qualities characterize the moral makeup of Dom Columba Marmion. Great heart—that he was. To his clear, probing intellect, to his captivating simplicity, to his candid good nature, to his uprightness, we must add that most winning feature: extreme goodness, all-embracing and active goodness. He had an exquisite sense of goodness and a will for it. A friend of Cardinal Mercier's said of Dom Marmion, "He had a heart as big as a cathedral"—a figure we could follow through by saying that the cathedral was always open to anyone who came and the flame in the sanctuary burned unceasingly.

Wholly surrendered to the love of Christ, he wanted only to give

Christ to souls and souls to Christ. His fervent love, his utter devotion, his forgetfulness and gift of self, his life of union with God opened all hearts to him. He was one of those of whom it is said that their face radiates love and that they are "witnesses to the friendly presence of God in our midst." For those who knew him, his name evokes an atmosphere of light, confidence and spiritual joy. Wherever he goes, he sheds light; he lends a helping hand; he calms and comforts; he inflames hearts, strengthens wills, and sanctifies souls. This overflowing charity, this beneficent zeal, as well as the ring of conviction in his faith and the authority acquired from experience in guiding souls—all these made his words singularly persuasive. Those who spoke to him, even only casually, on spiritual matters sensed that accent which comes from holiness alone and which is far more touching than all manner of eloquence. The words of a saint penetrate even to the marrow of our bones because they are the clear echo of the Divine Word.

The influence which clung to Dom Marmion's spoken word clings also, we might say, to his ascetical writings. They have an extraordinarily wide audience, and for many they have become bedside books.[1]

The helpful, heartwarming quality of Dom Marmion's doctrine appears especially in moments of trial and suffering. It is precisely then that his ascendancy over souls, even over those who know him only through his books, is particularly effective.[2] Considering that one frequent result of suffering is the shutting up of the soul within itself and the blocking off of all avenues of approach, how can we explain his influence over those whose innermost heart is buried in grief?

The only explanation is the fact that, besides the all-pervading goodness that animates him, his writings are human in the full and noble sense of the word. That is why they move us. He has a wide knowledge of human sorrow. He can speak of suffering because he has known it in all its forms. But he could truthfully say, "I try to

---

1. For further information on all these points see Dom Raymund Thibaut, *Abbot Columba Marmion: A Master of the Spiritual Life* (St. Louis, MO: B. Herder Book Co., 1949), chapters XIV and XV.
2. This statement has been proved by many testimonies.

Preface

greet all vexations with a smile." There is heroism in that constant smile. Cardinal Mercier, who chose Dom Marmion as his confessor and honored him as a friend, said of him: "He accepted all his trials with a filial and supernatural submission to the Father." Thus, while Dom Marmion wrote to those who confided in him, his mind and heart evoked and sympathized with the pains, the difficulties and the sorrows of his correspondents. With his whole heart he pitied them and wanted to find a helping word for each of them.

As his good friend, Archbishop Goodier, S.J., of Hierapolis, said in the Preface to *Union with God, According to the Letters of Direction of Dom Marmion:* "[Those who read his books] know they are reading the teaching, not of a master but of one who himself has toiled and laboured, not as one above them but as one of themselves." Then the Archbishop continues: "He saw the bright side of every one and of every thing, he would not allow it to be dimmed. A soul might be depressed, but he would not leave it in depression; troubles might come from the outside, but he would always see in them the hand of God."

His teaching was efficacious, in fact, because it started from, and led to, "the Father of light," "the Father of mercies," and "the God of all consolation." His words and his letters make crosses, trials, and sorrows return to their starting point, transformed into powerful staffs of strength. Dom Marmion is interested, not in "things" as such, but in their spiritual value. At his touch, everything is elevated; from the narrowness of the material universe everything reaches the level of supernatural grandeur. His counsels are the overflow of a soul which feeds only on the healthful air of the mountaintops. His works, then, are salutary to the soul that suffers, because they bathe it in the divine light, restore or strengthen confidence, bestow peace and stabilize the soul in the supreme security of abandonment to God.

Though the subtle perfume of his goodness and the gentle unction of that soothing balm emanate from every page of Dom Marmion's writings, it has seemed useful to select from the major works of this ascetical master passages written especially for souls in the throes of suffering. Even with that purpose in mind, we found the field so rich that we had to impose severe limits on ourself. We have dwelt chiefly on a few most characteristic theses of his spirituality.

True to his thought, we have first of all placed before the soul—in the whole of Part I—the divine figure of Christ. That is essential. Christ Jesus, who was the great passion of Dom Marmion's entire life, is also at the center of his entire ascetical work. There the figure of the Incarnate Word appears in bright light and bold relief. "We must contemplate Jesus," he wrote. "He is God revealing Himself to us. Through a humble faith in Him we have the solution to all our difficulties. When we want to penetrate into the sanctuary of the divine secrets, God says to us, 'This is my well-beloved Son; hear ye him. . . .' If we contemplate Him, we do not find it hard to understand that God is love."

Dom Marmion was in the habit of considering Christ as "the Man of sorrows." His devotion to the Passion of Jesus is well known. He knew from experience that nothing so touches the soul, so draws and binds it to the Cross as does the sight of the God-Man entering into our lives, accepting our poverty and our need, our wretchedness and our suffering, freely taking our place through love and accepting to die engulfed in an ocean of grief in order to redeem our sinful race. Like His soothing power, the magnetic attraction of our crucified Love is infinite. Did not Jesus Himself prophesy: "When I am lifted up from the earth, I will draw all things to myself"? Did He not compare Himself to the brazen serpent which Moses set up in the wilderness and which the snake-bitten Israelites had but to look upon in order to be healed and to live? Thus will it be with all those who believe in Jesus the Son of God raised aloft on the Cross. That is why Dom Marmion so often repeated with Saint Paul: "Looking on Jesus, the author and finisher of faith, who, having joy set before him, endured the cross, despising the shame, and now sitteth on the right hand of the throne of God. For think diligently upon him that endured such opposition from sinners against himself: that you be not wearied, fainting in your minds."[3]

3. Hebrews 12:2–3.

Preface

Dom Marmion knew also that nothing is so fruitful as union with the source of living water which flows from Calvary and gives every trial and suffering a sovereign virtue and an indefinite power to purchase redemption for the entire world.

Just as Dom Marmion urges us to keep the image of Christ crucified uppermost in our minds during times of anguish, so he requires of the soul at grips with suffering the same dispositions which filled the Heart of Christ during His Passion—silent patience, burning love, and filial abandonment to the will of God (Part II). We shall see how strongly he insists on this last disposition, which is the crowning point of love.

In the matter of producing or cultivating these dispositions and showing how to apply them to various kinds of trials and sufferings (Part III), or of strengthening the soul in the face of death, the supreme trial (Part V), this master always leads us to Christ as to the sole source of all light and strength.

Finally, if the fecundity of suffering even here below seems so marvelous to him (Part IV) and the glory which it gains above so dazzling (Part VI), it is only because they are the necessary prolongation of the fecundity and glory of Christ, the Head of the Mystical Body.

Thus it is that these selected passages, like the great ascetical works that yielded them, are stamped with the strong unity which derives from the central role Dom Marmion assigned to the Person of Christ.

Most of the extracts which make up this book are, naturally, taken from Dom Marmion's basic trilogy: *Christ, the Life of the Soul; Christ in His Mysteries;* and *Christ, the Ideal of the Monk.*

To this we have added, especially from Part II on, copious quotations from his letters as they appear in *Union with God, According to the Letters of Direction of Dom Marmion.* The doctrine in them is ever the same, not less profound or less penetrating, but more direct and spontaneous in expression, more vivid and familiar. Dom Marmion's deeply human heart shines through more clearly in them: we see him moved by the distress of souls and exhorting himself while encouraging them.

We have not hesitated to have recourse to a third source: the master's personal notes on his own spiritual life. They are so plentiful that they form, so to say, the weft of his biography.[4] We felt all the more justified in using these notes because, as has been remarked, it is rare that life and doctrine are so perfectly fused in a soul. The strictest unity binds man and doctrine. Set side by side with the more didactic pages, these intimate notes illustrate them graphically and make them more attractive and forceful.

Though gathered from such a variety of sources,[5] the teaching in this anthology is perfectly consistent because it is always drawn from the unique principle of all light: the eternal wisdom of the Incarnate Word. Though the tone of these extracts is sometimes quite varied, they all have the same deep ring, at once severe and human, the timbre of a soul which has lived in uninterrupted union with the Spirit of consolation and which, at the same time, remains close to us in his radiant goodness.

Perhaps it would be better here to summarize Dom Marmion's doctrine on suffering. But that might mean giving a mere cold précis, devoid of the lively faith, the ardent charity, and the incomparable, penetrating unction with which his writings, and especially his let-

---

4. Dom Raymund Thibaut: *op. cit.* The five books mentioned in this section are published by B. Herder Book Co., St. Louis, MO.

5. In addition to these five sources, we must also mention *Sponsa Verbi* and *Mélanges Marmion,* from which we have quoted to some extent.—We have tried not to cut up these extracts excessively. More than once we have printed the entire text because the thoughts, though diverse, were bound together logically. Splitting the text would have weakened the thought. As a result, some passages are long and others short. Also, as in any anthology of this kind, a certain amount of overlapping and repetition is inevitable. We have disregarded it; for, apart from the fact that these repetitions reveal the dominant ideas in Dom Marmion's mind, eliminating them would have destroyed the harmonious development and lessened the persuasive power of his reasoning. References to scriptural quotations have been omitted since they may be found in the works from which these passages have been quoted.

Preface

ters, are filled. The reader, besides, will find that doctrine for himself, luminous and profound, throughout the course of this book.

Furthermore, it goes without saying, Dom Marmion's philosophy of suffering is in line with purest Christian Faith, which is based on Sacred Scripture. As always, he plunges into the fullness of supernatural light and bids us follow him. Like Saint Paul, who was his favorite author and whose most personal thoughts and sentiments he assimilated, he sees in death, of which suffering is but the prelude and foretaste, the wages of sin.

But, through the grace of Christ, we are victors over sin and death and pain. Through love, Christ, the Strength of God, became the worker of our redemption by taking upon Himself our woes, our weaknesses, and the burden of our sins in order to destroy sin by His ignominious death upon the Cross.

Divinized in the Person of Christ, our miseries and sufferings, death itself, will become for us, by the merits and power of Christ and His grace, marvelous titles to the mercy of His Father, incomparable means of personal holiness, the secret of a vivific shining forth of redemption in the Church, and the seed of eternal glory.

In the divine plan, which stretches like a great arch from eternity to eternity, suffering appears in its true light, with its transitory character and relative value. It fits into this divinely wise plan only as a step, necessary but provisional, whereby the soul may attain, following the example of Christ, to the kingdom of undying splendor and unchanging peace. Only when viewed from the perspective of eternity can suffering have any meaning and become acceptable.

Consequently, Dom Marmion will not give suffering first place in the spiritual life. For him, as for Saint Paul, the first place goes to charity. Charity alone has absolute value. Although suffering gives love an opportunity to manifest itself with more force and magnificence, love alone can crown suffering with a diadem of grace and glory, help it realize its full value, and transform its innate bitterness into spiritual joy. And when suffering has fulfilled its austere divine mission here below, love, which welcomed it in order to assure its fecundity and reap its fruits, will perpetuate its merits eternally.

That is why Dom Marmion always brings the soul back to the spirit of holy abandonment, the acme of love, in union with Christ, who has become our elder Brother and our traveling companion on the road to eternity. All along that road Jesus repeats to us what He told the disciples as they walked toward Emmaus on the night of the resurrection: "Was it not necessary that the Christ should suffer and so enter into his glory?"—words of light and life that inflamed the hearts of His disciples.

We trust that these pages, filled as they are with Christ, His spirit, and His love, will be for souls in the grip of suffering pages of light, comfort, and peace.

DOM RAYMUND THIBAUT

Maredsous
May 29, 1941

Dom Columba Marmion
(†1923)

JOSEPH MARMION was born in Dublin in 1858 of an Irish father and a French mother. At the end of his secondary schooling, he was received at the seminary of Clonliffe. Having finished his priestly studies in Rome, he was ordained there in 1881, and was named assistant at Dundrum and, later, professor of philosophy at the seminary of Clonliffe. A visit to Maredsous on his return from Italy was the occasion of his calling to the monastic life. In 1886 he returned to the Belgian abbey and asked to be admitted as a novice. Once professed, he was assigned to various posts: he was soon made professor of philosophy; then, in 1899, he was sent to Mont-César at Louvain as Prior and professor of theology, positions which he filled for ten years. In 1909 he was made Abbot of Maredsous, where he died on January 30, 1923, leaving behind him the memory of a great monk with an intense interior life, of a consummate theologian, and of a contemplative and an apostle of indefatigable zeal.

His spiritual conferences have been published in three volumes: *Christ, the Life of the Soul*, which first appeared at the end of 1917; *Christ in His Mysteries*, 1919; and *Christ, the Ideal of the Monk*, 1922. Rated among the classics of Christian spirituality,[1] these books have led theologians and spiritual writers of various schools to call the author of them "Master" and even "Doctor" of the spiritual life. Bishops and princes of the Church have confirmed this praise. Benedict XV, who, in his own words, "made use of them for his spiritual life," said to Archbishop Szepticky of Lemberg: "Read this: it is the pure doctrine of the Church." As could be expected, these works achieved wide circulation in an extremely short time.

This "unanimous acclaim on the part of Catholics"[2] is fully justi-

---

1. Joseph de Guibert, S.J., in *Revue d'ascétique et de mystique*, April, 1930, p. 204.
2. Paul Doncoeur, S.J.

fied by the fact that these volumes exhibit a blend of qualities which one rarely finds united to such a degree of excellence. Dom Marmion's work is based entirely on Catholic dogma and theology, of which it is an organic and living synthesis. And just as Christian doctrine and piety center around the Person and the work of Christ, so did Dom Marmion wish only one thing: to make the divine figure of the Incarnate Word shine forth in all Its splendor.

To this end, he constantly has recourse to the Scriptures. Or, rather, we may say that the Holy Bible itself is the source whence spring the harmonious development and the fruitful application of his teaching. The Bible too supplies the incense of prayer that arises from his books. Cardinal Mercier used to say that Dom Marmion "makes us touch God." He plunges us into the supernatural, into an atmosphere of prayer. Hence he bestows light, security, peace. and joy.

In addition to the trilogy we have discussed, there are two other important volumes to be considered: his biography, *A Master of the Spiritual Life*; and a collection of letters, *Union with God*. By enabling us to know this Doctor of the spiritual life more intimately, these books enhance his teaching with a new appeal and a new forcefulness.

Critics have said again and again that the biography is stirring, imparting as it does a deeper and fuller knowledge of Dom Marmion's interior life. We shall quote only one review: "This work, well composed, elegantly and soberly written, and packed with good doctrinal meat, compares favorably with many a treatise on Christian perfection."[3]

Crowning these works, the anthology of spiritual letters reveals still more spontaneously the soul of him whose life was really Christ. These pages, in which Dom Marmion appears primarily as an eminent spiritual director, are first and foremost a treasury of doctrine. They are eloquent of a profound spirituality which never belies itself and which wells up from the abundance of his heart and experience. That experience, joined at once to a singular psychological penetration and the sweetest, most comprehensive charity,

---

3. François Jansen, S.J., in *Nouvelle Revue Théologique*, 1930, p. 614.

helped him find the way to all hearts. Of that collection of letters Bernard Capelle has written: "Dom Marmion excelled in the difficult art of writing letters of spiritual direction. Since his doctrine was as simple as it was deep, his guidance established the soul firmly in certitude, light, and peace. This sheaf of letters will spread far and wide the good produced by his words. It admirably completes the *corpus asceticum* [of Dom Marmion's spiritual writings] which has already become a classic."[4]

---

4. In *Questions Liturgiques et Paroissiales,* February, 1934.

PART I

Jesus Christ and
His Work of Redemption

The Person of Christ

The Place of Christ in the Divine Plan

GOD CHOSE US in Christ "before the foundation of the world, that we should be holy and unspotted in His sight in charity. Who hath predestinated us unto the adoption of children through Jesus Christ unto Himself, according to the purpose of His will: unto the praise of the glory of His grace, in which He hath graced us in His beloved Son."[1]

These are the terms in which the divine plan is set forth by the Apostle St. Paul, who had been caught up to the third heaven, and was chosen by God to bring to light, as he himself says, the economy of the mystery which hath been hidden from all eternity in God.

Revelation has come to us, bringing its light.

It teaches us that there is an ineffable paternity in God. God is a Father: that is the fundamental dogma which all the others suppose, a magnificent dogma which leaves the reason confounded, but ravishes faith with delight and transports holy souls.

God is a Father. Eternally, long before the created light rose upon the world, God begets a Son to Whom He communicates His nature, His perfections, His beatitude, His life, for to beget is to communicate being and life: *Filius meus es tu, ego hodie genui te; ex utero ante luciferum genui te.* In God then, is life, life communicated by the Father, and received by the Son. This Son, like in all things to the Father, is the only Son of God: *Unigenitus Dei Filius.* He is so because He has,[2] with the Father, one same and indivisible divine nature, and both, although distinct from one another (on account

---

1. By the gift of a similar nature.
2. Strictly speaking, we should say that He *is* with the Father and the Holy Ghost one same divine nature. Creatures can only lisp when they speak of such mysteries.

of their personal properties "of being Father" and "of being Son"), are united in a powerful, substantial embrace of love, whence proceeds that Third Person, Whom Revelation calls by a mysterious name: the Holy Ghost.

Such is, as far as faith can know it, the secret of the inmost life of God; the fulness and the fruitfulness of this life are the source of the incommensurable bliss that the ineffable society of the three Divine Persons possesses.

And now God—not in order to add to His plenitude, but by it to enrich other beings—extends, as it were, His paternity. God decrees to call creatures to share this divine life, so transcendent that God alone has the right to live it, this eternal life communicated by the Father to the only Son, and by them to the Holy Spirit. In a transport of love which has its source in the fulness of Being and Good that God is, this life overflows from the bosom of divinity to reach and beatify beings drawn out of nothingness, by lifting them above their nature. To these mere creatures God will give the condition and sweet name of children. By nature God has only one Son; by love, He wills to have an innumerable multitude: that is *the grace of supernatural adoption.*

Realised in Adam from the dawn of creation, then crossed by the sin of the first of human kind, who drew after him into disgrace all his race, this decree of love is to be restored by a marvellous invention of justice and mercy, of wisdom and goodness. The Son of God, Who dwells eternally in the bosom of the Father, unites Himself in time to a human nature, but in so close a manner that this nature, while being perfect in itself, belongs entirely to the Divine Person to Whom it is united. The divine life, communicated in its fulness to this humanity, makes it the very humanity of the Son of God: that is the wonderful work of the *Incarnation*. It is true to say of this Man Who is called Jesus, the Christ, that He is God's own Son.

But this Son, Who by nature is the only Son of the Eternal Father, *Unigenitus Dei Filius*, appears here below only to become the firstborn of all who shall receive Him, after having been redeemed by Him: *Primogenitus in multis fratribus*. Alone born of the Father in eternal splendour, alone Son by right, He is constituted the head of a multitude of brethren, on whom, by His redeeming work, He will bestow the grace of divine life.

So that the same divine life which proceeds from the Father into the Son and from the Son into the humanity of Jesus, will circulate, through Christ in all who will accept it; it will draw them even into the bosom of the Father, where Christ has gone before us, after having paid, with His blood, the price of this divine gift.

Hence all holiness is to consist in this: to receive the divine life from Christ and by Christ, Who possesses its fulness and Who has been constituted the one Mediator; to keep this divine life and increase it unceasingly by an ever more perfect adhesion, an ever closer union with Him Who is its source.

Holiness, then, is a *mystery of divine life communicated and received*: communicated in God, from the Father to the Son by an ineffable generation; communicated by the Son to humanity, which He personally unites to Himself in the Incarnation; then restored to souls by this humanity, and received by each of them in the measure of their special predestination: *secundum mensuram donationis Christi*, so that Christ is truly the life of the soul because He is the source and giver of life.

Communication of this life will be made to men within the Church until the day fixed by the eternal decrees for the achievement of the divine work upon earth. On that day, the number of the children of God, of the brethren of Jesus, will have reached its perfection. Presented by Christ to His Father, the innumerable multitude of these predestined souls will surround the throne of God, to draw an endless beatitude from the fountains of life, and to exalt the splendours of the divine goodness and glory. Union with God will be eternally consummated, and "God will be all in all."

Such is the divine plan in its general outline.

When, in prayer, we consider this liberality and these advances towards us on the part of God, we feel the need of prostrating ourselves in adoration, and of singing a song of thanksgiving to the praise of the Infinite Being Who stoops towards us to give us the name of children. "O Lord, how great are Thy works; Thy thoughts are exceeding deep!" *Nimis profundae factae sunt cogitationes tuae.* "Thou hast multiplied Thy wonderful works, O Lord, my God; in Thy thoughts there is no one like to Thee." "In the works of Thy hands I shall rejoice." "I will sing to the Lord as long as I live, I will sing praise to my God while I have my being. Let my mouth be filled with praise that I may sing Thy glory!" *Repleatur os meum laude ut cantem tibi gloriam tuam.*

Christ, the Life of the Soul, Part I, chapter 1, section 1

Christ was Constituted our High Priest and our Mediator from the Moment of the Incarnation

It is especially in his Epistle to the Hebrews that St. Paul sets forth in broad and strong terms the ineffable greatness of Christ as High Priest: *De quo nobis grandis sermo, et ininterpretabilis ad dicendum.* We herein see His mission of Mediator, the transcendency of His priesthood and sacrifice above the priesthood of Aaron and the sacrifices of the Old Testament: the unique sacrifice, consummated on Calvary, of which the offering is continued with inexhaustible efficacy in the sanctuary of heaven.

St. Paul reveals to us this truth that Christ Jesus possesses His priesthood from the very moment of His Incarnation.

At this moment, the Word is made flesh. The Word is forever united, by an ineffable union, to our humanity. Through the Incarnation, the Word enters into our race, He becomes authentically one of ourselves, like unto us in all things, excepting sin. He can, then, become High Priest and Mediator, since being God and Man He can bind man to God: *Ex hominibus assumptus.*

In the Holy Trinity, the Second Person, the Word, is the infinite glory of the Father, His essential glory: *Splendor gloriae et figura substantiae ejus.* But, as Word, before the Incarnation, He does not offer sacrifice to His Father. Why is this? Because sacrifice supposes homage, adoration, that is to say, the acknowledgment of our own abasement in presence of the Infinite Being; the Word being in all things equal to His Father, being God with Him and like Him, cannot then offer Him sacrifice. Christ's priesthood could only begin at the moment when the Word was made flesh. At that moment when the Word became incarnate, He united in Himself two natures: the divine nature whereby He was able to say: *Ego et Pater unum sumus*: "I and the Father are one," one in the unity of the divinity, one in equality of perfections; the other, the human nature by reason of which He said: *Pater major me est*: "The Father is greater than I." It is therefore inasmuch as He is God-Man that Jesus is Pontiff.

Learned authors derive the word "pontiff" from *pontem facere*: "*to establish or build a bridge.*" Whatever be the value of this etymology the idea is just as applied to Christ Jesus. In *The Dialogue of St. Catherine of Siena*, we read that God the Father vouchsafed to explain to her how, by the union of the two natures, Christ threw a bridge over the abyss that separated us from heaven: "I would that thou shouldst look at the Bridge that I have built for thee in My only-begotten Son, and that thou shouldst see the greatness thereof, for it reaches from heaven to earth, that is, the greatness of the divinity is joined to the earth of your humanity.... That was necessary in order to restore the road which was broken and make it possible for man to pass through this world's bitterness and attain (eternal) life."

Moreover it is through the Incarnation itself that the humanity of Jesus was "consecrated," "anointed." Not with an outward anointing, as is done for simple creatures, but with an entirely spiritual unction. By the action of the Holy Spirit, Whom the liturgy calls *spiritalis unctio*, the divinity is poured out upon the human nature of Jesus, like an "oil of gladness": *Unxit te Deus oleo laetitiae prae consortibus tuis*. This unction is so penetrating, the humanity is so closely consecrated to God that no closer consecration could be possible, for this human nature has become the very humanity of a God, of the Son of God.

This is why at the moment of the Incarnation whereby the first Priest of the New Alliance was consecrated, a cry resounded in heaven: *Tu es sacerdos in aeternum*, "Thou art a priest for ever." St. Paul, whose gaze pierced so many mysteries, likewise reveals this one to us. Listen to what he says: "Neither doth any man take the honour (of priesthood) to himself, but he that is called by God...

thus Christ also did not glorify Himself, that He might be made a high priest; but He that said unto him: *Thou art My Son, this day have I begotten Thee.* As He saith also in another place: *Thou art a priest for ever....*"

So then, by the Apostle's testimony, it was from the Eternal Father Himself that Christ received the supreme priesthood, from this Father Who also said to Him: "Thou art My Son, this day have I begotten Thee." Christ's priesthood is a necessary and immediate consequence of His Incarnation.

He is the Christ, that is to say, the High Priest pre-eminently; "for it was fitting," says St. Paul, "that we should have such a high priest, holy, innocent, undefiled, separated from sinners, and made higher than the heavens." But His Father laid upon Him the sins of all mankind: *Posuit in eo iniquitatem omnium nostrum.* Jesus became, according to the energetic expression of St. Paul, "sin for us." Thereby the offering that Jesus made of Himself to His Father, at the moment of His Incarnation, embraced the poverty of the manger, the lowliness of the hidden life, the fatigues and conflicts of the public life, the terrors of the agony, the ignominies of the Passion, the torments of a bitter death.

Let us adore this holy, immaculate High Priest, Who is God's own Son; let us cast ourselves down before this Mediator Who alone, because He is at once God and Man, can fully realise His mission of salvation and render to us God's gifts by the sacrifice of His humanity; but let us likewise confide ourselves to His divine virtue which, also alone, was powerful enough to reconcile us with the Father.

Christ in His Mysteries, Part I, chapter 5, sections 1–3

The Name "Jesus Christ" Signifies His Mission and Characterizes His Work

Christ Jesus is the Incarnate Word appearing in the midst of us, at once God and Man, true God and true Man, perfect God and perfect Man. In Him two natures are inseparably united in one Person, the Person of the Word.

The Person of Christ

These traits constitute the very being of Jesus. Our faith and piety adore Him as our God while confessing the touching reality of His humanity.

If we would penetrate deeper into the knowledge of the Person of Jesus, we must begin by contemplating, for a few moments, His mission and His work. The Person of Jesus gives value to His mission and work; His mission and work complete the revelation of His Person.

And it is most noteworthy that the names which designate the very Person of the Incarnate Word declare at the same time His mission and characterize His work. These names are not, as is too often the case with ours, lacking in significance. They come from heaven and are rich in meaning. What are these names? They are many, but the Church, following St. Paul in this, has especially retained two of them: that of *Jesus*, and that of *Christ*.

As you know, *Christ* means one who is *anointed, sacred, consecrated*. Formerly, under the Ancient Alliance, kings were frequently anointed, prophets more rarely, and the high priest always. The name of Christ, like the mission of king, prophet and pontiff which it designates, was given to several personages in the Old Testament before being given to the Incarnate Word. But none save Himself could fulfil its signification in all its fulness. He is the Christ, for He alone is the King of Ages, the Prophet pre-eminently, the one supreme and universal High Priest.

He is King. He is so by His divinity, *Rex Regum et Dominus dominantium*; He rules over all creatures brought out of nothing by His almighty power: *Venite adoremus, et procidamus ante Deum. . . . Ipse fecit nos et non ipsi nos.*

He will be so likewise as the Incarnate Word. The sceptre of the world had been foretold to Jesus by His Father. The Messias says: "I am appointed king by Him over Sion, His holy mountain, preaching His commandment. The Lord hath said to Me: Thou art My Son, this day have I begotten Thee. Ask of Me, and I will give Thee the Gentiles for Thine inheritance, and the utmost parts of the earth for Thy possession."

The Word became Incarnate in order to establish "the kingdom of

God." This expression often occurs in the preaching of Jesus. In reading the Gospel you will have remarked an entire group of parables—the pearl of great price, the hidden treasure, the sower, the grain of mustard seed, the murderous vine-dressers, the guests invited to the wedding-feast, the tares, the servants awaiting their master, the talents, etc.—which group is intended to show the greatness of this kingdom, its origin, its development, its extension to the pagan nations after the reprobation of the Jews, its laws, its conflicts, its triumphs. Christ organises this kingdom by the election of the Apostles, and the foundation of the Church to which He entrusts His doctrine, His authority, His sacraments. It is a wholly spiritual kingdom wherein is nothing temporal or political such as was dreamt of by the carnal minds of most of the Jews; a kingdom into which every soul of good will enters; a wonderful kingdom of which the final splendour is altogether heavenly and the beatitude eternal.

St. John extols the magnificence of this kingdom. He shows us the elect falling prostrate before their Divine Head, Christ Jesus, and proclaiming that He has redeemed them in His Blood, out of every tribe and tongue and people and nation, and has made of them a kingdom to the glory of His Father: *Et fecisti nos Deo nostro regnum.*

Christ is to be Prophet. He is the prophet pre-eminently, because He is the *Word* in person, the "Light of the World," Who alone can truly enlighten every man here below. "God...spoke in times past...by the prophets," St. Paul said to the Hebrews, but "in these days [God] hath spoken to us by His Son." He is not a prophet who announces from afar off, to a small portion of the human race and under symbols, sometimes obscure, God's still hidden designs. He it is Who, living in the bosom of the Father, alone knows the divine secrets and makes the wondrous revelation of these secrets to mankind: *Ipse enarravit.*

You know that from the beginning of His public life, Our Saviour applied to Himself the prophecy of Isaias declaring "the Spirit of the Lord is upon Me. Therefore He hath *anointed* Me to preach the Gospel to the poor...to preach deliverance to the captives, and sight to the blind...to preach the acceptable year of the Lord, and the day of reward."

He is, then, the One sent, God's Legate Who proves, by miracles wrought by His own authority, the divinity of His mission, of His work, and Person. Thus we hear the multitude, after the miracle of the multiplication of loaves, cry out: "This is of a truth the prophet that is to come into the world."

It is above all in His capacity of *High Priest* and Mediator, supreme High Priest and universal Mediator, that the Word Incarnate realises the signification of this name of Christ.

But here we must unite the name of *Jesus* to that of *Christ*. The name of Jesus means Saviour: "Thou shalt call His name Jesus," says the Angel to Joseph, "for He shall save His people from their sins." This is His essential mission: *Venit salvare quod perierat.* Truly Jesus only fully realises the signification of His divine name by His sacrifice, in fulfilling His work as High Priest: *Venit Filius hominis dare animam suam redemptionem pro multis.* The two names therefore complete each other and are henceforward inseparable. "Christ Jesus" is the Son of God, established as the Supreme Pontiff Who, by His sacrifice, is the Saviour of all humanity.

We have seen that it is indeed by the Incarnation itself that Jesus was consecrated Pontiff, and that it was from the moment of His entrance into this world that He inaugurated His Sacrifice. All His existence bears the reflection of His mission of Pontiff and is marked with the characters of His sacrifice.

A profound unity knits all Christ's actions together: the sacrifice of Jesus, because it is His essential work, is the culminating point towards which all the mysteries of His earthly life converge, and the source whence all the states of His glorious life derive their splendour.

Christ in His Mysteries,
Part I, chapter 5, introductory remarks

Christ's Work of Redemption

How Christ Began His Sacrifice from the Moment of His Birth

THE SACRIFICE of this one Pontiff is on a par with His priesthood: it was likewise from the moment of His Incarnation that Jesus inaugurated it.

You know that in Christ, the soul, created like ours, was not, however, subject to the progressive development of the corporal organism for the exercise of the faculties proper to it, intelligence and will: His soul had, from the first moment of its existence, the perfection of its own life, as befitted a soul united to the divinity.

Now, St. Paul reveals to us the first movement of the soul of Jesus at the instant of His Incarnation.

In one and the same glance, it beholds the ages past, the abyss wherein humanity lies powerless to liberate itself, the multiplicity and fundamental insufficiency of all the sacrifices of the Old Law; for no creature, however perfect, can worthily repair the injury committed by sin against the Creator. Christ beholds the programme of immolation that God demands of Him in order to work out the world's salvation.

What a solemn moment for the soul of Jesus! What a moment too for the human race.

What does His soul do? With a movement of intense love, it yields itself to perfect the work, both human and divine, which alone can render glory to the Father in saving humanity. O Father, "sacrifice and oblation Thou wouldst not," they are not sufficiently worthy of Thee, "but a body Thou hast fitted to Me": *Corpus autem aptasti mihi*. And wherefore hast Thou given it to me? Thou requirest that I should offer it to Thee in sacrifice. "Behold I come. In the head of the book [of My life] it is written of Me that I should do Thy will, O

Christ's Work of Redemption

God": *Ecce venio, in capite libri scriptum est de me ut faciam, Deus, voluntatem tuam.*

With a perfect will, Christ accepted that sum of sorrows which began with the lowliness of the manger only to be ended by the ignominy of the Cross. From His entrance into this world, Christ offered Himself as Victim: the first action of His life was a sacerdotal act.

What creature is able to measure the love that filled this sacerdotal act of Jesus? Who is able to know its intensity and describe its splendour? The silence of adoration can alone praise it in some degree.

Never has Christ Jesus retracted this act, nor withdrawn anything from this gift. All His life was ordered in view of His sacrifice upon the Cross. Read the Gospel in this light and you will see how in every mystery and state of Jesus is found an element of sacrifice leading Him little by little to the height of Calvary, so much is the character of High Priest, Mediator, and Saviour essential to His Person. We shall never grasp the true physiognomy of the Person of Jesus unless we constantly have in view His redeeming mission by the sacrifice and immolation of Himself. This is why when St. Paul said that he summed up everything in the knowledge of the mystery of Jesus, he immediately added: "and Him crucified": *Non enim judicavi aliquid scire inter vos nisi Jesum Christum,* ET HUNC CRUCIFIXUM.

Christ in His Mysteries, Part I, chapter 5, section 2

The human nature of Jesus, the Son of God, is similar in everything to that of His brethren: *Debuit per omnia fratribus similari,* says St. Paul, excepting sin: *Absque peccato.* Jesus has not known sin, nor that which is the source and consequence of sin—ignorance, error, sickness, all things unworthy of His wisdom, His dignity, and His divinity.

But our Divine Saviour willed, during His mortal life, to bear our infirmities, all those infirmities compatible with His sanctity. The Gospel clearly shows us this. There is nothing in the nature of man that Jesus has not sanctified; our labours, our sufferings, our tears. He has made all these His own. See Him at Nazareth: during thirty years He spent His life in the obscure toil of an artisan, so that when He began to preach, His compatriots were astonished, for up to this time they had only known Him as the son of the carpenter: *Unde huic omnia ista? Nonne hic est fabri filius?*

Like us our Lord has felt hunger; after having fasted in the desert "He was hungry": *Postea esuriit.* He has suffered thirst: did He not ask the Samaritan woman to give Him to drink, *Da mihi bibere?* and upon the Cross did He not cry: "I thirst," *Sitio?* Like us He has felt fatigue; He was often fatigued by His long journeys throughout Palestine. When at Jacob's well, He asked for water to quench His thirst. St. John tells us that He was wearied; it was the hour of noon, and after having walked far and being wearied, He sat down on the side of the well: *Fatigatus ex itinere, sedebat sic supra fontem. Hora erat quasi sexta.* Thus then, in the words of St. Augustine in the wonderful commentary he has given us on this beautiful evangelical scene, "He Who is the very Strength of God is overwhelmed with lassitude": *Fatigatur Virtus Dei.* Slumber has closed His eyelids; He slept in the boat when the tempest rose: *Ipse vero dormiebat.* He really slept, so the Apostles, fearing to be engulfed by the angry waves, had to awaken Him. He wept over Jerusalem, His own city which He loved despite its ingratitude; the thought of the disasters that, after His death, were to fall upon it drew tears from His eyes: "If thou hadst also known... the things that are to thy peace!" *Flevit super illam.* He wept at the death of Lazarus, as we weep over those we cherish, so that the Jews who witnessed this sight, said to one another: "Behold how He loved him!" Christ shed tears because His Heart was touched; He wept for him who was His friend; the tears sprang from the depth of His Heart. Several times too it is said of Him in the Gospel that His Heart was touched with compassion.

Christ, the Life of the Soul, Part I, chapter 2, section 2

He burns to achieve His sacrifice: *Baptismo autem habeo baptizari, et quomodo* COARCTOR *usquedum perficiatur.*

There is in Jesus, if we may so speak, a kind of enthusiasm for His sacrifice. See again in the Gospel how our Divine Saviour begins to disclose to His Apostles, gradually in order to spare their weakness, the mystery of His sufferings. One day He tells them that He must go to Jerusalem, that He will suffer many things from His enemies, and will be put to death. Then Peter immediately taking Him aside says: "Lord, be it far from Thee." But Jesus answers: "Go behind me, Satan, thou art a scandal unto Me; because thou savourest not the things that are of God, but the things that are of men." In the midst of the splendours of His Transfiguration upon Tabor of what did the Saviour speak with Moses and Elias? Of His coming Passion.

Christ thirsted to give to His Father the glory which His sacrifice was to procure for Him: *Iota unum aut unus apex non praeteribit a lege, donec omnia fiant.* He wishes to fulfil everything to the last iota, that is to say, to the least detail.

Christ in His Mysteries, Part I, chapter 5, section 2

Still more than this, He has felt sadness, heaviness, and fear: *Coepit pavere et taedere, et maestus esse*; in His agony in the Garden of Olives, His soul is overwhelmed with sorrow: *Tristis est anima mea usque ad mortem*; anguish penetrated His soul to the point of wringing from it "a strong cry and tears." All the mockeries, all the outrages with which He was saturated in His Passion, the being buffeted and spit upon, all these insults, far from leaving Him insensible, caused Him intense suffering. His nature being more perfect, His sensibility was the greater and more delicate. He was plunged in an abyss of suffering. Lastly, after having shown Himself to be truly man, like to us in all things, He willed to endure death like all the sons of Adam: *Et inclinato capite tradidit spiritum.*

Christ, the Life of the Soul, Part I, chapter 2, section 2

Finally upon Calvary, He consummates His immolation, and is able to say, before drawing His last breath, that He has entirely fulfilled all that His Father had given Him to do: *Consummatum est*. This last cry of the Divine Victim upon the Cross corresponds to the *Ecce venio* of the Incarnation in the Virgin's bosom.

Christ in His Mysteries, Part I, chapter 5, section 2

The Greatness and the Fecundity of the Hidden Life of Christ

Out of a life of thirty-three years, He Who is Eternal Wisdom chose to pass thirty of these years in silence and obscurity, submission, and labour.

Herein lies a mystery and teaching of which many souls, even pious souls, do not grasp all the meaning.

He Who is infinite and eternal, one day after centuries of waiting, humbles Himself to take a human form: *Semetipsum exinanivit, formam servi accipiens . . . et habitu inventus ut homo*. Although He is born of a spotless Virgin, the Incarnation constitutes an incommensurable abasement for Him: *Non horruisti virginis uterum*. And why does He descend into these abysses? To save the world, in bringing to it the divine Light.

Now—excepting those rays granted to a few privileged souls: the shepherds, the Magi, Simeon, and Anna—this Light is hidden; it remains voluntarily, during thirty years, "under a bushel," *sub modio*, to be at last manifested only for the duration of scarcely three years.

Is not this mysterious; is it not even disconcerting for our reason? If we had known the mission of Jesus, should we not have asked Him, as many of His kinsfolk did later, to manifest Himself to the world? *Manifesta teipsum mundo*.

But God's thoughts are not our thoughts, and His ways are higher than our ways. He Who comes to redeem the world wills to save it first of all by a life hidden from the eyes of the world.

Until He is thirty years old, Jesus, Who is God and comes to redeem the human race, lives, in a poor workshop, a life of labour and submission and obscurity. [He Who is to teach humanity and draw it out of the abyss into which Adam's proud disobedience had plunged it chose to live in silence and obey two creatures in the performance of the most ordinary actions.]

In the sight of His contemporaries, the life of Jesus Christ at Nazareth then appeared like the ordinary existence of a simple artisan. We see how true this is. Later, when Christ reveals Himself in His public life, the Jews of His country are so astonished at His wisdom and His words, at the sublimity of His doctrine and the greatness of His works, that they ask each other: "How came this man by this wisdom and miracles? Is not this the carpenter's son? Is not His Mother called Mary?... Whence therefore hath He all these things?" *Unde huic sapientia haec et virtutes? Nonne hic est fabri filius? Nonne mater ejus dicitur Maria? Unde ergo huic omnia ista?* Christ was a stumbling block for them.

This mystery of the hidden life contains teachings which our faith ought eagerly to gather up.

First of all there is nothing great in the sight of God except that which is done for His glory, through the grace of Christ. We are only acceptable to God according to the measure in which we are like unto His Son Jesus.

Christ's divine sonship gives infinite value to His least actions; Christ Jesus is not less adorable nor less pleasing to His Father when He wields the chisel or plane than when He dies upon the Cross to save humanity. In us, sanctifying grace, which makes us God's adoptive children, deifies all our activity in its root and renders us worthy, like Jesus, although by a different title, of His Father's complacency.

The most precious talents, the most sublime thoughts, the most generous and splendid actions are without merit for eternal life if not vivified by sanctifying grace. The passing world may admire and applaud them; eternal life neither accepts them nor holds them of account. "What doth it profit a man," said Jesus, the infallible Truth, "if he gain the whole world, and suffer the loss of his own soul?"

What does it serve a man to conquer the world by the force of arms, by the charm of eloquence or the authority of knowledge, if, not having God's grace, he be shut out from the kingdom that has no end?

See, on the other hand, that poor workman who painfully gains his livelihood, this humble servant ignored by the world, this beggar disdained by all: no one heeds them. If Christ's grace animates them, these souls delight the angels, they are continual objects of love for the Infinite Being; they bear within them, by grace, the very features of Christ.

Sanctifying grace is the first source of our true greatness. It confers upon our life, however commonplace it may seem, its true nobility and imperishable splendour.

But this gift is hidden.

The kingdom of God is built up in silence; it is, before all things, interior, and hidden in the depths of the soul: *Vita vestra est abscondita cum Christo in Deo.* Undoubtedly grace possesses a virtue which nearly always overflows in works of charity, but the principle of its power is entirely within. It is in the depths of the heart that the true intensity of the Christian life lies, it is there that God dwells, adored and served by faith, recollection, humility, obedience, simplicity, labour, and love.

Our outward activity has no stability nor supernatural fruitfulness save insofar as it is linked to this interior life. We shall truly only bear fruit outwardly according to the measure of the supernatural intensity of our inner life.

What can we do greater here below than promote Christ's reign within souls? What work is worth so much as that? It is the whole work of Jesus and of the Church.

We shall, however, succeed in it by no other means than those employed by our Divine Head. Let us be thoroughly convinced that we shall do more work for the good of the Church, the salvation of souls, the glory of our Heavenly Father, in seeking first of all to remain united to God by a life of love and faith of which He is alone the object, than by a devouring and feverish activity which leaves us no leisure to find God again in solitude, recollection, prayer, and self-detachment.

Nothing favours this intense union of the soul with God like the hidden life. And this is why souls living the inner life, and enlightened from on high, love to contemplate the life of Jesus at Nazareth. They find in it a special charm and, moreover, abundant graces of holiness.

Truly, my Saviour, You are a hidden God: *Deus absconditus, Israel Salvator.* Doubtless, O Jesus, You grow "in wisdom, age and grace with God and men." Your soul possesses the fulness of grace from the first moment of Your entrance into this world, and all the treasures of knowledge and wisdom, but this wisdom and this grace are only manifested little by little. You remain a hidden God in the eyes of men. Your divinity is veiled beneath the outward appearance of a workman. O Eternal Wisdom Who, to draw us out of the abyss into which Adam's proud disobedience had plunged us, chose to live in a humble workshop and therein to obey creatures, I adore and bless You!

Christ in His Mysteries, Part II, chapter 9, section 4

The Love of Christ for His Fellow Men During His Public Life

One of the principal and most touching aspects of the economy of the Incarnation is the manifestation of the divine perfections made to men through the human nature of Jesus. God's attributes, His eternal perfections are incomprehensible to us here below, they surpass our understanding. But, in becoming man, the Incarnate Word reveals to the most simple minds the inaccessible perfections of His divinity, by the words which fall from His human lips and by the actions performed by His human nature. We are charmed and drawn to Him as He enables us to grasp these divine perfections by His visible actions: *Ut dum visibiliter Deum cognoscimus, per hunc in invisibilium amorem rapiamur.*

It is above all during the public life of Jesus that this economy full of wisdom and mercy is declared and carried into effect.

Of all the divine perfections, love is certainly the one that the Incarnate Word is most pleased to reveal to us.

The human heart needs a tangible love in order to realize something of infinite love, far deeper as it is than this tangible love and surpassing our understanding. Nothing, indeed, so much attracts our poor hearts as to contemplate Jesus Christ, true God as well as true Man, translating the eternal goodness into human deeds. When we see Him lavishly scattering around Him inexhaustible treasures of compassion and mercy, we are able to conceive something of the infinity of that ocean of divine kindness whence the Sacred Heart draws these treasures for us.

Let us dwell on some traits; we shall see with what condescension, at times surprising, our Saviour stoops towards human misery under every form, sin included. And never forget that, even when He stoops towards us, He remains the very Son of God, God Himself, the Almighty Being, Infinite Wisdom, Who, ordering all things in truth, does nothing save what is sovereignly perfect. This undoubtedly gives to the words of kindness that He utters, to the deeds of mercy that He performs, an inestimable value that infinitely enhances them, and especially wins our hearts by manifesting to us the profound charms of the Heart of our Christ, of our God.

You know the first miracle of the public life of Jesus: the water changed into wine at the marriage feast of Cana, at the prayer of His Mother. For our human hearts, what an unexpected revelation of the divine tenderness and delicacy! Some austere ascetics may be scandalized to see a miracle asked for or wrought in order to hide the temporal need of a poor household during a wedding banquet. And yet it is this that the Blessed Virgin does not hesitate to ask, it is this that Christ vouchsafes to work. Jesus allows Himself to be touched by the embarrassment in which these poor people were about to find themselves; so as to spare them, He works a great prodigy. And what His Heart herein reveals to us of human goodness and humble condescension is but the outward manifestation of divine goodness whence the other has its source. For, whatever the Son does, the Father does it also.

A short time afterwards, in the synagogue of Nazareth, Jesus, quoting from Isaias, appropriates to Himself these words unveiling the plan of His work of love: "The Spirit of the Lord is upon Me. Wherefore He hath anointed Me to preach the Gospel to the poor, He hath sent Me to heal the contrite of heart, to preach deliverance to the captives, and sight to the blind, to set at liberty them that are bruised, to preach the acceptable year of the Lord, and the day of reward."

"This day," Jesus adds, "is fulfilled this scripture in your ears."

And indeed Jesus reveals Himself to all as a King full of meekness and kindness. I should need to quote every page of the Gospel if I

Christ's Work of Redemption

would show you how misery, weakness, infirmity, and suffering have the gift of touching Him, and in so irresistible a manner that He can refuse them nothing. St. Luke is careful to note how He is "moved with compassion": *Misericordia motus*. The blind and the lame, the deaf and dumb, those with the palsy, lepers come to Him; the Gospel says that He "healed all": *Sanabat omnes*.

He welcomes them all too with unwearying gentleness. He allows Himself to be pressed on all sides, continually, even "after sunset"; one day He "could not so much as eat bread"; another time, on the shore of the Lake of Tiberias, He is obliged to enter into a ship so as to be more at liberty to distribute the divine word. Elsewhere the multitude throng into the house where He is, so that in order to enable a paralytic man lying upon his bed to come near to Him, there is no other resource save to let down the sick man through an opening made in the roof.

The Apostles themselves were often impatient. The Divine Master took occasion of this to show them His gentleness. One day they want to send away the children that are brought to Him. "Suffer the little children to come unto Me," Jesus says, "and forbid them not, for of such is the kingdom of God." And He stays to lay His hands upon them and bless them. Another time, the disciples, being angry because He had not been received in a city of Samaria, urge Him to allow them to "command fire to come down from heaven" to consume the inhabitants: *Domine, vis dicimus ut ignis descendat de caelo?* And Jesus immediately rebukes them: *Et conversus increpavit illos*: "You know not of what spirit you are. The Son of man came not to destroy souls, but to save."

This is so true that Jesus works miracles even to raise the dead to life. Behold how at Naim He meets a poor widow following the mortal remains of her only son. Jesus sees her, He sees her tears; His Heart, deeply touched, cannot bear this sorrow. "O woman, weep not!" *Noli flere*. And at once He commands death to give up its prey: "Young man, I say to thee, arise." The young man sits up, and Jesus restores him to his mother.

All these manifestations of the mercy and goodness of Jesus, which reveal to us the sensibility of His human Heart, touch the deepest fibres of our being; they reveal, under a form which we are able to grasp, the infinite love of our God. When we see Christ weeping at the tomb of Lazarus, and hear the Jews, who witnessed this sight, say to one another: "Behold how He loved him," our hearts comprehend this silent language of the human tears of Jesus, and we penetrate into the sanctuary of eternal love that they unveil: *Qui videt me, videt et Patrem.*

We see too how everything that Christ does condemns our selfishness, our harshness, our dryness of heart, our impulses of anger and revenge, our resentment towards our neighbour!... We too often forget those words of our Saviour: "As long as you did it to one of these My least brethren, you did it to Me."

O Jesus, Who hast said: "Learn of Me because I am meek and humble of Heart," make our hearts like to Thine. Following Thy example, may we be merciful so that we may "obtain mercy" for ourselves, but above all so that by imitating Thee, we may become like to our Father in Heaven.

Christ in His Mysteries, Part II, chapter 11, section 3

Christ Jesus is both God and Man; perfect God, perfect Man; that is the very mystery of the Incarnation. As "Son of Man," Christ has a Heart like ours, a Heart of flesh, a Heart that beats for us with the tenderest, the truest, the noblest, the most faithful love that ever was.

In his Epistle to the Ephesians, St. Paul told them that he earnestly besought God that they might be able to comprehend what is the breadth and length, and height and depth, of the mystery of Jesus, so much was he dazzled by the incommensurable riches that it contained. He might have said as much of the love of the Heart of Jesus for us; he did say so in fact when he declared that this love "surpasseth all knowledge."

And, indeed, we shall never exhaust the treasure of tenderness, of loveableness, of kindness and charity, of which the Heart of the Man-God is the burning furnace. We have only to open the Gospel and, on each page, we shall see shine out the goodness, the mercy, the condescension of Jesus towards men. I have tried, in pointing out some aspects of the public life of Christ, to show you how deeply human and infinitely delicate is this love.

This love of Christ is not a chimera, it is very real, for it is founded upon the reality of the Incarnation itself. The Blessed Virgin, St. John, Magdalen, Lazarus knew this well. It was not only a love of the will, but also a heartfelt love. When Christ Jesus said: "I have compassion on the multitude," He really felt the fibres of His human Heart moved by pity; when He saw Martha and Mary weeping for the loss of their brother, He wept with them; truly human tears were wrung from His Heart.

Christ in His Mysteries, Part II, chapter 19, section 2

Christ loved to give pleasure. The first miracle of His public life was to change water into wine at the marriage feast of Cana, so as to spare His hosts any confusion when the wine failed. We hear Him promise to refresh all who labour and are burdened and come to Him. And how well He has kept His promise! The Evangelists often repeat that it is because He is "moved with compassion," *Misericordia motus,* that He works His miracles; it is from this motive He cures the lepers and raises the son of the widow of Naim. It is because He has compassion on the multitude who, having unweariedly followed Him during three days, now suffer hunger, that He multiplies the loaves: *Misereor super turbam.* Zacheus, a chief of the publicans, one of that class of Jews looked upon as sinners by the Pharisees, ardently wishes to see Christ. But, on account of his short stature, he cannot succeed in doing so, for the multitude surrounds Jesus on every side. Therefore Zacheus climbs up into a tree along the road where Jesus is about to pass, and our Lord anticipates this publican's desire. Having come close up to him, He tells him to come down for He wills to be his guest that very hour, and Zacheus, full of joy, and at the height of his wishes, receives Him into his house.

Christ, says St. Paul, who loves to employ this term, is the very kindness of God appearing upon earth; He is a King, but a King full of meekness, Who bids us forgive and proclaims those blessed who, following His example, are merciful. St. Peter, who had lived with

Him three years, says that everywhere He went about doing good: *Pertransiit benefaciendo.* Like the Good Samaritan, whose charitable action He so wonderfully describes, Christ has taken humanity into His arms, He has taken its sorrows into His soul: *Vere languores nostros ipse tulit, et dolores nostros ipse portavit.* He comes "for the destruction of sin," which is the supreme evil, the only true evil; He drives out the devil from the bodies of the possessed; but, above all, He drives him out from souls, in giving His own life for each one of us: *Dilexit me et tradidit semetipsum pro me.*

What greater mark of love is there than this? There is none. *Majorem hac dilectionem nemo habet ut animam suam ponat quis pro amicis suis.*

Christ, the Life of the Soul, Part II, chapter 11, section 3

Christ Jesus does not change. He was yesterday, He is today: His Heart remains the most loving and most loveable that could be met with. St. Paul tells us explicitly that we ought to have full confidence in Jesus because He is a compassionate High Priest Who knows our sufferings, our miseries, our infirmities, having Himself espoused our weaknesses—saving sin. Doubtless, Christ Jesus can no longer suffer: *Mors illi ultra non dominabitur;* but He remains the One Who was moved by compassion, Who suffered and redeemed men through love: *Dilexit me et tradidit semetipsum pro me.*

Christ in His Mysteries, Part II, chapter 19, section 2

The Passion of Jesus, Culmination of His Redemptive Work

Since Adam's fall, man can only return to God by expiation. St. Paul tells us in speaking of Christ that He is "a High Priest, holy, innocent, undefiled, separated from sinners": *Pontifex sanctus, innocens, impollutus et segregatus a peccatoribus.* Jesus, our Head, is infinitely far from all that is sin; and yet He has to pass through the sufferings of the Cross before entering into His glory.

You know the episode of Emmaus related by St. Luke. On the day of the Resurrection, two of Jesus' disciples set out to this town, a short distance from Jerusalem. They speak to one another of their disappointment caused by the death of the Divine Master, and the apparent downfall of all their hopes concerning the restoration of the kingdom of Israel. And behold, Jesus, under the guise of a stranger, joins them and asks them the subject of their discourse. The disciples tell Him the cause of their sadness. Then the Saviour, Who has not yet revealed Himself to them, says, in a tone of reproach: "O foolish and slow of heart to believe.... Ought not Christ to have suffered these things, and so to enter into His glory?": *Nonne haec oportuit pati Christum et ita intrare in gloriam suam?*

Why then "ought" Christ to have suffered? If He had so willed, could not God have universally forgiven sin without requiring expiation? Assuredly He could. His absolute power knows no limits; but His justice has exacted expiation, and, first of all, Christ's expiation.

The Word Incarnate, in taking human nature, substituted Himself for sinful man, powerless to redeem himself; and Christ became the Victim for sin. This is what our Lord gave His disciples to understand in telling them that His sufferings were necessary. Necessary, not only in their generality, but even in their least details: for if a single sigh of Christ would have sufficed, and far more than sufficed, to redeem the world, a free decree of the divine will, touching all the circumstances of the Passion, has accumulated therein an infinite superabundance of satisfaction.

Christ, the Ideal of the Monk, Part II, chapter 9, section 1

The Passion constitutes the "Holy of Holies" among the mysteries of Jesus. It is the crowning point of His public life, the summit of His mission here below, the work to which all the others converge or from which they draw their value.

Each year, during Holy Week, the Church commemorates in detail the various phases of the Passion; each day, in the Sacrifice of the Mass, she renews the remembrance and the reality of it in order to apply its fruits to us.

The Passion marks the culminating point of the work that Christ came to do here below. It is the hour wherein Jesus consummates the sacrifice that is to give infinite glory to His Father, to redeem humanity, and reopen to mankind the fountains of everlasting life. Moreover, our Lord Who, from the first moment of His Incarnation, delivered Himself up wholly to His Father's good pleasure, ardently desired to see arrive what He called "His hour." *Baptismo habeo baptizari, et quomodo coarctor usquedum perficiatur!* "I have a baptism whereby to be baptised—a baptism of blood—and how am I straitened until it be accomplished!" Jesus longed for the hour to come when He might be plunged in suffering and undergo death in order to give life to us.

Certainly, He will not advance this hour. Jesus is fully submissive to His Father's will. St. John more than once notes that the Jews try to take Jesus by surprise and put Him to death; our Lord ever escapes them, even by miracle, "because His hour was not yet come": *Nondum venerat hora ejus.*

But when it does come, Jesus delivers Himself up with the greatest ardour, although He knows in advance all the sufferings that He is to bear in body and soul: *Desiderio desideravi hoc Pascha manducare vobiscum antequam patiar.* "With desire I have desired to eat this Pasch with you, before I suffer." It has at last come, that hour so long awaited.

The Passion of Jesus is His essential work; nearly all the details of it were foretold. There is no other mystery of Jesus whereof the circumstances were announced with so much care by the Psalmist and prophets. And when we read, in the Gospel, the account of the Passion we are struck to see how attentive Christ Jesus is to "fulfil" what had been announced concerning Him. If He permits the presence of the traitor at the Last Supper, it is "that the Scripture may be fulfilled"; He tells the Jews who had come to lay hands upon Him that He delivers Himself up to them "that the Scriptures... might be fulfilled": *Ut adimplerentur Scripturae.* St. John relates how our Saviour upon the Cross calls to mind that the Psalmist had predicted of Him: "In My thirst they gave Me vinegar to drink." Then in order that this prophecy might be accomplished, Jesus cried: "I thirst": *Postea, sciens Jesus quia omnia consummata sunt,* UT *consummaretur Scriptura, dixit, Sitio.* Nothing, in this, is little or negligible, because all these details mark the actions of a God-Man.

Christ's Work of Redemption

Let us contemplate Jesus at this hour. The mystery of His Passion is ineffable, even to the smallest details, as, moreover, everything is in the life of the God-Man. Here especially we are on the threshold of a sanctuary where we can only enter with living faith and deepest reverence.

Christ in His Mysteries, Part II, chapter 14, introductory remarks and section 1; chapter 13, introductory remarks

"That the World May Know That I Love the Father"

The first act of the holy soul of Jesus in the Incarnation was to dart through the infinite space that separates the created from the divine. Resting in the bosom of the Father, His soul contemplates face to face His adorable perfections. We cannot picture to ourselves that this contemplation could be, if I may so express myself, only speculative. Far from it. As the Word, Christ loves His Father, in very deed, with an infinite love surpassing all comprehension.

But the humanity of Jesus is drawn into this impetuous current of uncreated love and the Heart of Christ burns with the most perfect love that could ever exist.

Christ, the Ideal of the Monk, Part II, chapter 12, section 9

The sacred humanity of Jesus so lives for the glory of the Word to Whom it is united that it surrenders itself to Him in absolute dependence and love until death. For, through that humanity, the Word possesses what He does not and cannot have in His divine opulence: the wherewith to atone for sin, to suffer and die for men. His humanity could say to Him from the first moment of their union: "Thou art espoused to me in blood"—*Sponsus sanguinum tu mihi es.* Yielded up to Him in order to carry out, with Him and in Him, the whole will of the Father, it never, throughout its entire existence, ceased tending toward that "baptism of blood" which was to consummate the marvellous and henceforth inexhaustible fecundity of that ineffable union.

Sponsa Verbi, chapter 2

A member of the human race through His Incarnation, Christ falls moreover under the great precept: "Thou shalt love the Lord thy God, with thy whole heart, and with thy whole soul, and with thy whole mind, and with thy whole strength." Jesus has perfectly fulfilled this commandment. From His first entering into the world, He yielded Himself up through love: *Ecce venio . . . Deus meus, volui et legem tuam in medio cordis mei.* I have placed, O Father, Thy law, Thy will "in the midst of My heart." His whole existence is summed up in the love for the Father.

But what form will this love take? The form of obedience: *Ut faciam, Deus, voluntatem tuam.* And why is this? Because nothing better translates filial love than absolute submission. Christ Jesus has manifested this perfect love and this full obedience from the moment of the Incarnation "even to the death of the Cross": *Usque ad mortem.*

Not only has He never for an instant hesitated to obey, but love draws Him, despite the sensible shrinking that He feels, towards the consummation of His obedience: "I have a baptism wherewith I am to be baptised: and how am I straitened until it be accomplished." It is with intense desire that He desires to eat the Pasch with His disciples, that Pasch which is to inaugurate the Passion.

Christ, the Ideal of the Monk, Part II, chapter 12, section 9

The sorrows and the ignominies of the Passion, even death itself, does not diminish this burning fervour of the Heart of Jesus for His Father's glory; quite the contrary. It is because in all things He seeks the will of the Father, as manifested by the Scriptures, that He delivers Himself, out of love, to the torments of the Cross: *Ut impleantur Scripturae.* The waters of a river do not rush towards the ocean with more majestic impetuosity than the soul of Jesus tended inwardly towards the abyss of suffering wherein the Passion was to plunge Him. "That the world may know that I love the Father; and as the Father hath given Me commandment, so do I": *Et sicut mandatum dedit mihi Pater, sic facio.*

Christ, the Ideal of the Monk, Part I, chapter 1, section 5

Christ's Work of Redemption

Christ's loving obedience is particularly noteworthy during His sufferings. Behold Christ during His agony. During three hours, weariness, sadness, sorrow, and anguish sweep over His soul like a torrent, and take possession of it to such a point that the blood escapes from His sacred veins. What an abyss of sorrow there is in this agony! And what does Jesus say to His Father? "Father, if Thou wilt, remove this chalice from Me." Is it, then, that Christ no longer accepts His Father's will? Certainly He does accept it. But this prayer is the cry of the sensitive part of poor human nature crushed by weariness and suffering. At this moment, Christ is above all *Vir sciens infirmitatem:* a Man of Sorrows. Our Lord feels the terrible burden of agony weigh upon His shoulders; He would have us know this, and therefore He thus prays.

Hear what He immediately adds: "But yet not My will, but Thine be done." This is love's triumph. Because He loves His Father, He places the will of His Father above all things, and He accepts to suffer everything. It is to be remarked that the Father, if He had so decreed in His eternal designs, could have lessened our Lord's sufferings and changed the circumstances of His death. He did not so will. In His justice, He exacted that, in order to save the world, Christ should yield Himself to every sorrow. Did this will diminish the love of Jesus? Certainly not; He does not say: My Father might have arranged things otherwise. No, He fully accepts all that His Father wills: *Non mea voluntas, sed tua fiat.*

Henceforward He will go to the very end in His sacrifice. Soon after His agony, at the moment of His arrest, when St. Peter wishes to defend Him and with his sword strikes one of those who come to seize his Master, what does the Saviour at once say to him? "Put up the sword into the scabbard. The chalice which My Father hath given Me, shall I not drink it?" *Calicem quem dedit mihi Pater, non bibam illum?*

Christ in His Mysteries, Part II, chapter 13, section 1

He is presently arrested as a malefactor; He could deliver Himself from His enemies who at a single word from Him are thrown to the ground; He could, if He so willed, ask His Father Who would have given Him "more than twelve legions of Angels," but He desires only that His Father's will, as manifested by the Scriptures, shall be fulfilled to the letter: *Sed ut adimpleantur Scripturae*, and therefore He gives Himself up to His mortal foes. He obeys Pilate because, although a pagan, the Roman governor represents the authority from above. He obeys His executioners; at the moment of expiring, in order to fulfil a prophecy, He cries out: "I thirst— *Postea, sciens Jesus quia omnia consummata sunt,* UT *consummaretur Scriptura, dixit: Sitio.* He does not die until all has been consummated by a perfect obedience: *Dixit: consummatum est, et inclinato capite, tradidit spiritum.* The *Consummatum est* is the most true and adequate expression of His whole life of obedience. It echoes the *Ecce venio* of the moment of His Incarnation. These two sentences are expressions of obedience, and the whole earthly existence of Jesus Christ revolves around the axis which rests upon these two poles.

Christ, the Ideal of the Monk, Part II, chapter 12, section 1

With all these actions of Jesus the Father is well pleased. He contemplates His Son with love, not only on Tabor when Christ is in the splendour of His glory; but likewise when Pilate shows Him to the multitude, crowned with thorns, and become the outcast of humanity; in the ignominies of His Passion as well as in the splendours of the Transfiguration: *Hic est Filius meus dilectus in quo mihi bene complacui.* And why?

During the Passion, Jesus honours and glorifies His Father in an infinite measure, not only because He is the Son of God, but also because He yields Himself up to all that His Father's justice and love demand of Him. If He could say, in the course of His public life, that He always did the things that pleased His Father: *Quae placita sunt ei facio semper,* it is especially true of those hours when, in order to acknowledge the rights of divine majesty outraged by sin, and to save the world, He delivered Himself up to death, and to the death of the Cross: *Ut cognoscat mundus quia diligo Patrem.* The Father loves Him with a boundless love because He gives His life for His sheep, and because by His sufferings, by His satisfactions, He merits for us all the graces that win back for us the friendship of His Father: PROPTEREA *me diligit Pater,* QUIA *ego pono animam meam.*

Christ in His Mysteries, Part II, chapter 14, section 1

How can we lack confidence when Christ, the Son of the Father, having become our Surety and the Propitiation for our iniquities, has expiated and paid off all? Why should we not draw near to this High Priest, Who, like unto us in all things, sin excepted, chose to experience all our infirmities, to drink of the chalice of all our sufferings, to find, in the experience of sorrow, the power of compassionating our miseries more deeply?

Christ, the Ideal of the Monk, Part I, chapter 2, section 2

"He Loved Me and Delivered Himself Up For Me"

Undoubtedly, love for His Father was the underlying motive power of every act in the life of the Incarnate Word. At the moment of completing His work, Christ declares to His Apostles that it is because He loves His Father that He is about to deliver Himself up: *Ut cognoscat mundus quia diligo Patrem.* In that wonderful prayer which He then makes, Jesus says that He has accomplished His work which was to glorify His Father upon earth: *Ergo et clarificavi super terram; opus consummavi quod dedisti mihi ut faciam.* Indeed at each instant of His life, He could say in all truth that He only sought the good pleasure of His Father: *Quae placita sunt ei facio semper.*

But His love for the Father is not the only love with which Christ's Heart beats; He loves us too and in an infinite manner.

Christ in His Mysteries, Part I, chapter 1, section 4

In loving us, it is His Father He loves; He sees us, He finds us in His Father: *Ego pro eis rogo . . . quia tui sunt.* These are His own words: "I pray for them . . . because they are Thine." Yes, Christ loves us, because we are the children of His Father, because we belong to His Father. He loves us with an ineffable love, surpassing all we can imagine, to such a point that each of us can say with St. Paul: *Dilexit me et tradidit semetipsum pro me*: "Who loved me, and delivered Himself for me."

Christ, the Life of the Soul, Part I, chapter 2, sections 2–3

It was veritably for us that He came down from heaven, in order to redeem us and save us from death: *Propter nos et propter nostram salutem*; it was to give us life: *Ego veni ut vitam habeant, et abundantius habeant*. He had no need to satisfy and to merit for Himself, for He is the very Son of God, equal to His Father, at Whose right hand He is seated in the heights of heaven; but it was for us that He bore everything. For us He became Incarnate, was born at Bethlehem, and lived in the obscurity of a life of toil; for us He preached and worked miracles, died and rose again; for us He ascended into heaven and sent the Holy Spirit; He still remains in the Eucharist for us, for love of us. Christ, says St. Paul, loved the Church, and delivered Himself up for her, that He might purify and sanctify her and win her to Himself.

Christ in His Mysteries, Part I, chapter 1, section 4

At the Last Supper, when the hour for achieving His oblation draws near, what does He say to His Apostles gathered around Him? "Greater love than this no man hath, that a man lay down his life for his friends": *Majorem hac dilectionem nemo habet, ut animam suam ponat quis pro amicis suis*. And this love which surpasses all love, Jesus is about to show forth to us, for, says St. Paul, "Christ died for all." He died for us when we were His enemies. What greater mark of love could He give us? None.

Christ in His Mysteries, Part II, chapter 13, section 1

Whence came this human love of Jesus, this created love? From the uncreated and divine love, from the love of the Eternal Word to which the human nature is indissolubly united. In Christ, although there are two perfect and distinct natures, keeping their specific

Christ's Work of Redemption

energies and their proper operations, there is only one Divine Person. As I have said, the created love of Jesus is only a revelation of His uncreated love. Everything that the created love accomplishes is only in union with the uncreated love, and on account of it; Christ's Heart draws its human kindness from the divine ocean.

Upon Calvary, we see Him die a man like unto ourselves, One Who has been a prey to anguish, Who has suffered, Who has been crushed beneath the weight of torments, heavier than any man ever bore; we understand the love that this Man shows us. But this love which, by its excess, surpasses our knowledge, is the concrete and tangible expression of the divine love. The Heart of Jesus pierced upon the Cross reveals to us Christ's human love; but beneath the veil of the humanity of Jesus is shown the ineffable and incomprehensible love of the Word.

Christ in His Mysteries, Part II, chapter 19, section 2

All the graces that adorn the soul and make it blossom forth in virtues have their inexhaustible source on Calvary: for this river of life gushed forth from the Heart and wounds of Jesus.

Can we contemplate the magnificent work of our powerful High Priest without exulting in continual thanksgiving: *Dilexit me et tradidit semetipsum pro me*: "Who loved me," says St. Paul, "and delivered Himself for me"? The Apostle does not say, although it be the very truth: *dilexit nos*: "He loved us"; but "He loved *me*," that is to say, His love is distributed to all, while being appropriated to each one of us. The life, the humiliations, the sufferings, the Passion of Jesus—all concern *me*. And how has He loved me? To love's last extremity: *in finem dilexit*.

O most gentle High Priest, Who by Thy Blood hast re-opened to me the doors of the Holy of Holies, Who ceaselessly dost intercede for me, to Thee be all praise and glory for evermore!

Christ, the Ideal of the Monk, Part I, chapter 2, section 2

"He Delivered Himself Up Because He Himself Wanted It"

That which completes the work of giving all beauty and fulness to the satisfactions and merits of Christ, is that He accepted His sufferings voluntarily and from love. Liberty is an essential element of merit, for the act is only worthy of praise if the one who accomplishes it is responsible: *Ubi non est libertas, nec meritum,* says St. Bernard.

This liberty covers the whole redeeming mission of Jesus. As Man-God, Christ accepted absolutely to suffer in His passible body. When on His entrance into this world He said to His Father: "Behold I come," *Ecce venio, ut faciam, Deus, voluntatem tuam,* He foresaw all the humiliations, all the sufferings of His Passion and death, and freely, from the depth of His Heart, out of love for His Father and for us, He accepted all: *Volui,* "I have willed." *Et legem tuam in medio cordis mei.*

Christ keeps intact this willingness to suffer, throughout His whole life. The hour of His sacrifice is always present to Him; He awaits it with impatience: He calls it "His hour" as if it were the only one that counted for Him in His earthly existence. He announces His death to His disciples, He traces out its details to them in advance, in such clear terms that they cannot be deceived. When St. Peter, deeply moved at the thought of seeing His Master die, wishes to set himself in opposition to the realisation of these sufferings, Jesus rebukes him: "Thou savourest not the things that are of God." But for Himself "He knows His Father," and through love for Him and charity for us, He goes to meet His Passion with all the ardour of His holy soul, but likewise with a sovereign liberty. His will is aglow with love, so that it burns in Him like a furnace: "I am come to cast fire upon the earth and what will I but that it be kindled? I have a baptism wherewith I am to be baptised," a baptism of blood, and yet no man has the power to take away His life; He lays it down of Himself. See how He manifests the truth of these words. One day, the inhabitants of Nazareth want to cast Him down headlong from the brow of the hill: Jesus passes through the midst of them with wonderful calmness. Another time, at Jerusalem, the Jews attempt to stone Him, because He affirms His divinity; He hides Himself and goes out of the temple: His hour is not yet come.

But when it does come, He yields Himself to them. See Him in the Garden of Olives on the eve of His death; the armed troops advance to take Him and lead Him to be condemned. "Whom seek ye?" He asks them. At their reply: "Jesus of Nazareth," He says to them simply: "I am He." This one word uttered by Him is enough to overthrow His enemies and make them fall to the ground. He could have kept them there; He could, as He said Himself, ask His Father, and He would send legions of angels to deliver Him. It is at this moment that He reminds these men that every day He sat with them in the temple and they did not lay hands on Him; the hour was not come, that is why He did not give them license to seize Him. Now the hour has struck when, for the salvation of the world, He is about to deliver Himself up to His executioners, who only act as the instruments of the powers of hell: *Haec est hora vestra et potestas tenebrarum*. The soldiery lead Him from tribunal to tribunal, He does not resist. However, before the Sanhedrin, the supreme tribunal of the Jews, He proclaims His rights as Son of God, then He abandons Himself to the fury of His enemies, until the moment when He consummates His sacrifice upon the Cross.

It is truly because He has willed it, that He is delivered to death: *Oblatus est* QUIA IPSE *voluit.* In this voluntary surrender of His entire self upon the Cross; by this death of the Man-God; by this immolation of a stainless victim, offering Himself through love and with absolute liberty—infinite satisfaction is paid to divine justice for us, inexhaustible merit is gained for us by Christ, while eternal life is restored to humanity. *Et consummatus, factus est omnibus obtem-perantibus sibi causa salutis aeternae.* "And being consummated, He became to all that obey Him *the (meritorious) cause of eternal salvation.*" Thus St. Paul could also say that in virtue of this will, we are sanctified by the oblation of the body of Jesus Christ once offered. *In qua voluntate sanctificati sumus per oblationem corporis Jesu Christi semel.*

It is for us all, for each one of us, that our Lord died: *Pro omnibus mortuus est Christus.* Christ has become the propitiation not only for our sins, but for the sins of the whole world: *Ipse est propitiatio pro peccatis nostris; non pro nostris autem tantum, sed etiam pro totius mundi,* so that He is the one Mediator between men and God: *Unus mediator Dei et hominum, homo Christus Jesus.*

Christ, the Life of the Soul, Part I, chapter 3, section 3

What infinitely enhances this love is the sovereign liberty wherewith Christ offered Himself: *Oblatus est quia ipse voluit.* These words tell us how spontaneously Jesus accepted His Passion. Did He not one day say, when speaking of the Good Shepherd Who gives His life for His sheep: "Therefore doth the Father love Me, because I lay down My life, that I may take it again [upon My Resurrection day]. No man taketh it away from Me: but I lay it down of Myself and I have power to lay it down; and I have power to take it up again"?

This freedom with which Jesus gives His life is entire. And this is one of the most admirable perfections of His sacrifice, one of the aspects that touch our human hearts most deeply. "God so loved the world, as to give His only begotten Son." Christ loved His brethren to this point that He spontaneously and entirely gave Himself up to save them.

Christ in His Mysteries, Part II, chapter 13, section 1

The Fulness of the Sacrifice of Christ

Let us for a few moments contemplate the sufferings that the Incarnate Word endured when the hour came for Him to expiate sin; we can hardly form any conjecture into what an abyss of agony and humiliation sin caused Him to descend.

Christ Jesus is God's own and only Son. In Him His Father is well pleased; all the work of the Father is to glorify Him: *Clarificavi et adhuc clarificabo;* for He is full of grace, grace superabounds in Him; He is "a high priest holy and innocent"; though He is like unto us, He however knows neither sin nor imperfection. "Which of you," said He to the Jews, "shall convince Me of sin?" "The prince of

Christ's Work of Redemption

this world (that is to say, Satan) ... in Me hath not anything." This is so true that it is in vain His most bitter enemies, the Pharisees, searched into His life, examined His doctrine, spied upon all His actions, as hatred knows how to do, and sought to ensnare Him in His speech. They could find no pretext to condemn Him; in order to invent one, they had to have recourse to false witnesses. Jesus is purity itself, the reflection of His Father's infinite perfections, "the brightness of His glory."

And behold how the Father dealt with His Son when the moment came for Jesus to pay in our place the debt due to justice for our sins; behold how the "Lamb of God" was stricken when He substituted Himself for sinners. The Eternal Father willed with that will which nothing can resist "to bruise Him in infirmity": *Voluit conterere eum in infirmitate.* A flood of sadness, weariness, fear, and languor enters even into the holy soul of Jesus till His immaculate body is bathed in a sweat of blood. He is so distressed and overwhelmed by the torrent of our iniquities that, in the repulsion felt by His sensible nature, He beseeches His Father that He may not drink the bitter chalice presented to Him: *Pater mi, si possibile est, transeat a me calix iste.* On the eve of His Passion at the Last Supper He had not spoken thus: *Volo Pater,* "I will," He then said to His Father, for He is His equal; but now, the sins of men which He has taken upon Himself cover Him with shame and it is as a culprit He prays: *Pater, si possibile est,* "Father, if it is possible...." But it is the hour of justice, the hour when the Father wills to deliver up His own Son to the power of darkness: *Haec est hora vestra et potestas tenebrarum.*

Betrayed by one of His Apostles, abandoned by the others, denied by their chief, Christ Jesus becomes an object of mockery and outrage in the hands of valets. Behold Him, the Almighty God, struck with blows, His adorable face, which is the joy of the saints, covered with spittle. He is scourged, a crown of thorns is pressed upon His head, a purple mantle is flung in derision over His shoulders, a reed is placed in His hand; then the soldiers bend the knee before Him in insolent mockery. What an abyss of ignominy for one before Whom the angels tremble! Contemplate Him, the Master of the universe, treated as a malefactor, and an impostor, placed on a level with an infamous robber whom the rabble prefers before Him! Behold

Him, outlawed, condemned, fastened to the Cross between two thieves; enduring the agony of the nails being dug in His hands and feet and the torture of thirst! He sees the people He has laden with benefits wag their heads in scorn; He hears the malicious sarcasms of His enemies: "He saved others, Himself He cannot save. Let Him come down from the cross and then, but only then, we will believe in Him."

Contemplate that picture of the sufferings of Christ traced long before, by the prophet Isaias: "There is no beauty in Him, nor comeliness, and we have seen Him, and there was no sightliness that we should be desirous of Him. Despised and the most abject of men, a man of sorrows and acquainted with infirmity; and His look was as it were hidden and despised, whereupon we esteemed Him not. Surely He hath borne our infirmities and carried our sorrows; and we have thought Him as it were a leper and as one struck by God and afflicted. But He was wounded for our iniquities, He was bruised for our sins.... The Lord hath laid on Him the iniquity of us all.... He shall be led as a sheep to the slaughter, and shall be dumb as a lamb before His shearer, and He shall not open His mouth.... He is cut off out of the land of the living: for the wickedness of My people have I struck Him ... and the Lord was pleased to bruise Him in infirmity...."

Is that enough? No, not yet. Our Divine Saviour has not yet sounded the lowest depth of sorrow. O my soul, behold thy God hanging on the Cross; He has no longer even the semblance of humanity, He has become "the outcast of the people": *Ego sum vermis et non homo, opprobrium hominum et abjectio plebis.* His body is but a single wound; His soul has melted away, as it were, under suffering and derision. And at this moment, the Gospel tells us, Jesus cried out: "My God, My God, why hast Thou forsaken Me?" Jesus is abandoned by His Father. We can never know what an abyss of suffering was this abandonment of Christ by His Father; it is an unfathomable mystery. Jesus abandoned by His Father! Yet throughout His life has not Jesus always done His Father's will? Has He not fulfilled the mission received by Him of manifesting the Father's name to the world: *Manifestavi nomen tuum hominibus?* Is it not through love—*Ut cognoscat mundus quia diligo Patrem*—that He delivers Himself up? Most certainly, yes. Then wherefore, O Eternal Father, dost Thou thus strike Thy well-beloved Son? "For the wickedness of My people": *Propter scelus populi mei percussi eum.* Christ having at this moment delivered up Himself for us, so as to give full and entire satisfaction for sin, the Father no longer sees in His Son anything except the sin which He has taken upon Himself to such a degree that this sin appears to be His own: *Eum qui non noverat peccatum, pro nobis peccatum fecit*; He is "made a curse for us": *Factus pro nobis maledictum;* His Father abandons Him and although, at the summit of His being, Christ retains the ineffable joy of the beatific vision, this abandonment plunges His soul in such profound sorrow that it wrings from Him this cry of infinite anguish; "My God, why hast Thou abandoned Me?" Divine justice giving itself free course to punish the sin of all mankind has fallen like an impetuous torrent on God's own Son: *Proprio Filio suo non pepercit Deus, sed pro nobis omnibus tradidit illum.*

If we want to know what God thinks of sin, let us look at Jesus in His Passion. When we behold God strike His Son, Whom He infinitely loves, with the death of the Cross, we understand a little what sin is in God's sight.

If we could only understand in prayer that for three hours Jesus begged the Father: "If it be possible, Father, let this chalice be removed from Me," *Pater, si possibile est, transeat a me calix iste*; that the Father answered "No"; that Jesus paid our debt with the very last drop of His blood; and that despite His "strong cry and tears," *cum clamore valido et lacrymis*, God did not spare Him—if only we could understand those things, we should have a holy horror of sin. What a revelation of the nature of sin is this heap of insults, outrages and humiliations with which Jesus is burdened. How great must be God's hatred for sin that He should afflict Jesus so without measure, that He should crush Him under suffering and ignominy.

One who deliberately commits sin brings his share to the sorrows and outrages which fell upon Christ. He has poured more bitterness into the chalice offered to Jesus in His agony. He was with Judas to betray Him; with the soldiery to spit into His divine face, to blindfold His eyes and strike Him; with Peter to deny Him, with Herod to turn Him into derision, with the rabble to clamour for His death, with Pilate cowardly to condemn Him by an iniquitous judgment; He was with the Pharisees to cover the dying Christ with the venom of their implacable hatred; with the Jews to mock and overwhelm Him with sarcasm. It was he who, at the supreme moment, gave Jesus gall and vinegar to assuage His thirst.... A soul who refuses to submit to the divine law causes the death of the only Son of God, Christ Jesus. If one day we have had the unhappiness to wilfully commit a single mortal sin, we were this soul.... We can say: "The Passion of Jesus was my work. O Jesus, nailed to the cross, You are the holy and immaculate High Priest, the innocent and spotless Victim—and I am a sinner...!"

Christ, the Life of the Soul, Part II, chapter 3, section 1

All is perfect in the sacrifice of Jesus: the love that inspires it, and the liberty with which He accomplishes it. Perfect, too, in the gift offered: Christ offers Himself: *Semetipsum tradidit.*

Christ offered the whole of Himself; His soul and body were bruised and broken by suffering; there is no suffering that Jesus has not known. If we read the Gospel attentively, we see that the sufferings of Jesus were ordered in such a way that no member of His sacred body was spared; there was no fibre of His Heart but was torn by the ingratitude of the multitude, by being forsaken by His own disciples, and by the sorrows of His Mother. He underwent all the outrages and humiliations wherewith a man can be oppressed. He fulfilled to the letter the prophecy of Isaias: "Many have been astonished at Thee, so shall His visage be inglorious among men.... There was no sightliness that we should be desirous of Him... and we have thought Him as it were a leper, and as one struck by God and afflicted...."

During the agony in the Garden of Olives, Christ, Who exaggerates nothing, reveals to His Apostles that His innocent soul is now oppressed with sadness so poignant and bitter that it is enough to cause His death: *Tristis est anima mea usque ad mortem.* What an abyss! A God, Infinite Power and Beatitude, is overcome by sadness,

Christ's Work of Redemption

fear and heaviness: *Coepit pavere, et taedere et moestus esse!* The Word Incarnate knew all the sufferings that were to fall upon Him throughout the long hours of His Passion. This vision awoke in His sensitive nature all the repulsion that a simple creature would thereby have experienced; in the divinity to which it was united, His soul saw clearly all the sins of mankind, all the outrages committed against God's holiness and infinite love.

He had taken upon Himself all these iniquities; He was, as it were, clad with them, He felt all the wrath of divine justice weigh upon Him: *Ego sum vermis, et non homo: opprobrium hominum et abjectio plebis.* He foresaw that for many men His blood would be shed in vain, and this sight brought the grief of His blessed soul to its climax. But, as we have seen, Christ accepted all.

He has truly drunk the chalice to the dregs, He has fulfilled to the last iota, that is to say, to the least detail, all that was foretold of Him. Thus, when all is accomplished, when He has exhausted to the depths every sorrow and every humiliation, He can utter His *Consummatum est.* Yes, all is consummated: He has now only to give up His soul to His Father: *Et inclinato capite, tradidit spiritum.*

When the Church, during Holy Week, reads us the account of the Passion, she interrupts herself at this place, in order to adore in silence.

Like her, let us fall down in adoration before the Crucified Who has just breathed forth His last sigh; He is truly the Son of God: *Deus verus de Deo vero.* Let us take part, on Good Friday, in the solemn adoration of the Cross, which, in the spirit of the Church, is intended to repair for the numberless outrages heaped upon the Divine Victim by His enemies upon Golgotha. During this touching ceremony, the Church places some moving reproaches upon the lips of the innocent Saviour. These literally apply to the deicide people; we can take them in an altogether spiritual sense: they will give birth in our souls to intense feelings of compunction: "O My people, what have I done to thee? or in what have I afflicted thee? Answer Me. What ought I to have done for thee that I have not done? I planted thee as My most beautiful vineyard, and thou art become to Me exceedingly bitter; for, in My thirst, thou hast given Me vinegar to drink, and with a spear hast thou pierced the side of thy Saviour.... For thy sake, I scourged Egypt with its firstborn;

and thou hast scourged Me.... I led thee out of Egypt, drowning Pharaoh in the Red Sea; and thou didst deliver Me up to the chief priests.... I opened a passage for thee in the midst of the sea, and thou didst open My side with a lance.... I went before thee as a pillar of fire, and thou didst lead Me to the judgment-hall of Pilate.... I fed thee with manna in the desert and thou didst strike Me with blows and scourges.... I gave to thee a royal sceptre and thou didst give to My head a crown of thorns.... I lifted thee up with great power, and thou didst hang Me on the gibbet of the Cross!"

Let our hearts be touched by these plaints of a God suffering for men; let us unite ourselves to this loving obedience which led Him to the immolation of the Cross: *Factus obediens usque ad mortem, mortem autem crucis.* Let us say to Him: "O Divine Saviour, Who suffered so much for love of us, we promise to do all that we can in order to sin no more; grant us by Your grace, O adorable Master, to die to all that is sin, attachment to sin and to the creature, and to live no longer save for You."

For, says St. Paul, the love that Christ showed us in dying for us "presseth us ... that they also who live, may not now live to themselves, but unto Him Who died for them": *Ut et qui vivunt, jam non sibi vivant, sed ei qui pro ipsis mortuus est.*

Christ in His Mysteries, Part II, chapter 13, section 2

From the Pretorium To Calvary

Devotion to the sufferings of Christ in the Way of the Cross is the one that is most closely linked to the Eucharistic Sacrifice; like the Mass, it continues to recall to us the death of Jesus: *Mortem Domini annuntiabitis donec veniat.*

In order to have the blood of Jesus applied to us as fully as possible, this is what must be done: Every morning unite yourself to Jesus, that with Him you may offer to the Father the blood of Christ to be offered in every Mass that day. But make this act with great intensity of faith and love: in this way you will partake as fully as possible in the chalice of Jesus, for His blood is offered in every Mass *pro nostra omniumque salute.*

Christ's Work of Redemption

Then, when you make the Way of the Cross, offer anew to the heavenly Father at each station the precious blood, that it may be applied to your soul.[3] This contemplation of the sufferings of Jesus is very fruitful. After the sacraments and liturgical worship I am convinced there is no practice more useful for our souls than the Way of the Cross made with devotion. Its supernatural efficacy is sovereign. The Passion is the "holy of holies" among the mysteries of Jesus, the pre-eminent work of our supreme High Priest; it is there above all that His virtues shine forth, and when we contemplate Him in His sufferings He gives us, according to the measure of our faith, the grace to practise the virtues that He manifested during these holy hours.

Abbot Columba Marmion, chapter 18

Never let us forget that Christ Jesus is not a dead and inert model; but, ever living, He supernaturally produces in those who draw near to Him in the right dispositions, the perfection that they contemplate in His Person.[4]

At each station, our Divine Saviour presents Himself to us in this triple character: as the Mediator Who saves us by His merits, the perfect Model of sublime virtues, and the efficacious Cause Who can, through His divine omnipotence, produce in our souls the virtues of which He gives us the example.

---

3. Faithful to this thought, he therefore habitually made the Way of the Cross after his thanksgiving. When he first entered Holy Cross College Father Gowan had inspired him with this devotion. Since then he had remained always faithful to the suggestion of this holy religious; it may be said that he never failed a single day to practise this devotion. During his last years, even when traveling and when most absorbed in the work of preaching, he took care to spare a few minutes to do so. During his last years he made this practice the object of a vow. He devoted a whole conference to it in his spiritual works, and when preaching a retreat he never failed to speak of it. On his death-bed he still endeavoured to make the Stations of the Cross, thus uniting his last sufferings to those which marked the supreme hours of the earthly life of Jesus.

4. See Part II of the present work, Section C, article 1, "Contemplation of the Suffering Christ."

It may be said that these characters are to be found in all the mysteries of Jesus Christ. This is true, but with how much more plenitude in the Passion!

This is why if, every day, during a few moments, interrupting your work, laying aside your preoccupations, and closing your heart to all outward things, you accompany the God-Man along the road to Calvary, with faith, humility, and love, with the true desire of imitating the virtues He manifests in His Passion, be assured that your souls will receive choice graces which will transform them little by little into the likeness of Jesus and of Jesus Crucified. And is it not in this likeness that St. Paul sums up all holiness?

It suffices, in order to gather the precious fruits of this practice, as well as to gain the numerous indulgences[5] with which the Church has enriched it, to visit the fourteen stations without notable interruption, to stay a while at each of them and there to meditate upon the Saviour's Passion. No formula of prayer is prescribed, no form of meditation is imposed, not even that of the subject suggested by the station. Full liberty is left to the attraction of each one and to the inspiration of the Holy Spirit.

Let us now make the Way of the Cross together; the considerations here presented at each station have no other end than to help

---

5. In an act of October 20, 1931, Pope Pius XI abrogated all the indulgences for the Way of the Cross that had been granted before him, and replaced them by the following: (1) a plenary indulgence each time the Stations are done; (2) another plenary indulgence when one communicates on the same day or communicates within a month of having done the Stations ten times; (3) an indulgence of ten years for each station, when one has been obliged to interrupt the devotion for a reasonable motive. The sick who are unable to make the Way of the Cross by going from station to station in a church, may obtain the same indulgences provided they hold in their hand a crucifix blessed for this purpose by a priest so empowered and recite the Our Father, the Hail Mary and the Glory be twenty times—that is, once for each station, five times in honor of the sacred wounds of Jesus, and once for the intentions of the Pope. If for a serious reason one cannot recite the twenty required for a plenary indulgence, one may gain an indulgence of ten years for each Our Father, Hail Mary and Glory be. The sick who, because of the extreme gravity of their illness, cannot recite the prayers may gain the above indulgences provided they kiss a crucifix blessed for this purpose, or simply look upon it with feelings of piety and contrition, and recite, if possible, some invocation in honor of the Passion and death of our Lord Jesus Christ.

us in our meditation. We can each take what we will, varying these considerations and affections, according to our aptitudes and the needs of our souls.

Before beginning, let us recall St. Paul's recommendation: "Let this mind be in you, which was also in Christ Jesus. . . . He humbled Himself, becoming obedient unto death, even to the death of the Cross." The more we enter into those dispositions that filled the Heart of Jesus as He passed along the Sorrowful Way—love towards His Father, charity towards men, hatred of sin, dispositions of humility and obedience—the more our souls will receive graces and lights, because the Father will behold in us a more perfect image of His Divine Son.

My Jesus, You followed this path for love of me in bearing Your Cross. I wish to follow it with You and like You; pour into my heart the sentiments which overflowed from Yours in those holy hours. Offer to Your Father for me the precious blood that You then shed for my salvation and sanctification.

Jesus Is Condemned to Death by Pilate

"And Jesus stood before the governor": *Stetit ante praesidem.* He stands, because, being the second Adam, He is the Head of all the race which He is about to redeem by His immolation. The first Adam has merited death by his sin: *Stipendia enim peccati mors.* Jesus, innocent, but laden with the sins of the world, is to expiate them by His sacrifice of blood. The chief priests, the Pharisees, His own nation, surround Him with furious clamours. Through these clamours our sins cry out and tumultuously demand the death of the Just: *Tolle, tolle, crucifige eum!* The cowardly Roman governor delivers the Victim up to His enemies that they may hang Him upon the Cross: *Tradidit eis illum ut crucifigeretur.*

Let us contemplate Jesus at this moment. If He stands because He is our Head; if, as St. Paul says, He gives testimony to the truth of His doctrine, to the divinity of His Person and of His mission, He yet humbles Himself in interior self-abasement before the sentence pronounced by Pilate in whom He acknowledges an authentic power: *Non haberes potestatem adversum me ullam, nisi tibi datum esset desuper.* In this earthly power, unworthy but legitimate, Jesus beholds the majesty of His Father. Therefore He rather delivers Himself up than He is delivered: *Tradebat judicanti se injuste.* He humbles Himself in obeying even unto death; for us He voluntarily accepts the sentence of condemnation, in order to restore life to us: *Oblatus est quia ipse voluit.* "As by the disobedience of one man, many were made sinners, so also by the obedience of one, many shall be made just."

We ought to unite ourselves to Jesus in His obedience, to accept all that our Heavenly Father lays upon us, through whomsoever it may be, even a Herod or a Pilate, from the moment that their authority becomes legitimate. Let us also, even now, accept death in expiation for our sins, with all the circumstances wherewith it shall please Providence to surround it; let us accept it as a homage rendered to divine justice and holiness outraged by our iniquities; united with the death of Jesus it will become "precious in the sight of the Lord."

My Divine Master, I unite myself to Your Sacred Heart in Its perfect submission and entire abandonment to the Father's will. May the virtue of Your grace produce in my soul that spirit of submission which will yield me unreservedly and without murmuring to the divine good pleasure and to all that it shall please You to send me at the hour when I must leave this world.

Jesus is Laden with His Cross

"Then therefore [Pilate] delivered Him to them to be crucified. And they took Jesus, and led Him forth ... bearing His own Cross": *Bajulans sibi crucem.*

Jesus had made an act of obedience; He had delivered Himself up to the will of the Father, and now the Father shows Him what obedience imposes upon Him; it is the Cross. He accepts it as coming from the Father's hands, with all that it brings with it of distress and ignominy. At that instant, Jesus accepted the increase of suffering that this heavy burden, laid upon His bruised shoulders, brought to Him, and the indescribable sufferings wherewith His sacred members were to be afflicted at the moment of the crucifixion. He accepted the bitter sarcasms, the malignant blasphemies, which His worst enemies, apparently triumphant, were about to heap upon

Him as soon as they should see Him hung upon the infamous gibbet; He accepted the three hours' agony, the being forsaken by His Father.... We shall never sound the depths of the abyss of afflictions to which our Divine Saviour consented in receiving His Cross. At this moment, too, Christ Jesus Who represented us all, and was going to die for us, accepted the Cross for all His members, for each one of us: *Vere languores nostros ipse tulit, et dolores nostros ipse portavit.* He then united to His own sufferings all the sufferings of His mystical body, causing them to find in this union their value and price.

Let us, therefore, accept our cross in union with Him, like Him, so that we may be worthy disciples of this Divine Head; let us accept it without reasoning, without repining. Although the Cross that the Father laid upon Jesus was of such weight, was His love, His confidence towards His Father diminished thereby? Quite the contrary. "The chalice which My Father hath given Me, shall I not drink it?" *Calicem quem dedit mihi Pater, non bibam illum?* Let it be the same with us. "If any man will come after Me let him . . . take up his cross and follow Me." Do not let us be of those whom St. Paul calls "enemies of the cross of Christ." Rather let us take up our cross, the one that God lays upon us. In the generous acceptation of this cross, we shall find peace. Nothing brings such peace to the soul that is in suffering as this utter self-surrender to God's good pleasure.

My Jesus, I accept all the crosses, all the contradictions, all the adversities that the Father has destined for me. May the unction of Your grace give me strength to bear these crosses with the submission of which You gave us the example in receiving Yours for us. May I never seek my glory save in the sharing of Your sufferings!

Jesus Falls the First Time Under the Cross

He shall be "a man of sorrows, and acquainted with infirmity": *Vir dolorum, sciens infirmitatem.* This prophecy of Isaias is fulfilled to the letter. Jesus, exhausted by His sufferings of soul and body, sinks under the weight of His Cross; He, the Omnipotent, falls from weakness. This weakness of Jesus is a homage to His divine power. By it He expiates our sins, He repairs the revolt of our pride, and raises up a fallen world, powerless to save itself: *Deus qui in Filii tui humilitate jacentem mundum erexisti....* Moreover, at that moment, He merited for us the grace to humble ourselves for our sins, to acknowledge our falls and sincerely confess them; He merited for us the grace of fortitude to sustain our weakness.

With Christ, prostrate before His Father, let us detest the risings of our vanity and ambition; let us acknowledge the extent of our frailty. As God casts down the proud, so the humble avowal of our infirmity draws down His mercy: *Quomodo miseretur pater filiorum ... quoniam ipse cognovit figmentum nostrum.* Let us then cry to God for mercy, in the moments when we feel that we are weak in face of the cross, of temptation, of the accomplishment of the divine will: *Miserere mei, quoniam infirmus sum.* It is when we thus humbly declare our infirmity that grace, which alone can save us, triumphs within us: *Virtus in infirmitate perficitur.*

O Christ Jesus, prostrate beneath Your Cross, I adore You. "Power of God," You show Yourself overwhelmed with weakness so as to teach us humility and confound our pride. O High Priest, full of holiness, Who passed through our trials in order to be like unto us and to compassionate our infirmities, do not leave me to myself, for I am but frailty. May Your power dwell in me, so that I fall not into evil: *Ut inhabitet in me virtus Christi.*

Jesus Meets His Holy Mother

The day has come for the Blessed Virgin whereon Simeon's prophecy is to be fulfilled in her: "Thy own soul a sword shall pierce." In the same way that she was united to Jesus when offering Him, in years gone by, in the Temple, so now in this hour when Jesus is about to consummate His sacrifice, she is to enter, more than ever, into His dispositions and share in His sufferings. She sets out towards Calvary where she knows that her Son is to be crucified. Upon the way she meets Him. What immense sorrow to see Him in this terrible state! Her gaze meets His, and the abyss of the sufferings of Jesus calls upon the abyss of His Mother's compassion. What is there that she would not do for Him!

This meeting was at once a source of sorrow and of joy for Jesus.

Christ's Work of Redemption

Of sorrow, in seeing the deep desolation wherein His suffering state plunged His Mother's soul; of joy, in the thought that His sufferings were to pay the price for all the privileges she had already received and for those yet to be lavished upon her.

This is why He scarcely lingers. Christ had the most tender Heart that ever beat. He shed tears at the tomb of Lazarus, He wept over the evils that were to fall upon Jerusalem. Never did son love his mother as He did; when He met her so desolate upon the road to Calvary, every fibre of His Heart must have been torn. And yet, He passes on, He continues His way towards the place of His execution, because it is His Father's will. Mary is one with Him in all that He feels, she knows that all things must be accomplished for our salvation; she takes her share in the sufferings of Jesus in following Him as far as Golgotha where she will become co-redemptress.

Nothing that is human should hold us back in our path towards God; no natural love should trammel our love for Christ; we must pass onwards so as to remain united to Him.

Let us ask the Blessed Virgin to associate us with her in the contemplation of the sufferings of Jesus, and to make us share in the compassion that she shows towards Him, that we may gain therefrom the hatred of sin which required such an expiation. It has at times pleased God to manifest sensibly the fruit produced by the contemplation of the Passion, by imprinting on the bodies of some saints, such as St. Francis of Assisi, the stigmata of the wounds of Jesus. We ought not to wish for these outward marks; but we ought to ask that the image of the suffering Christ may be imprinted upon our hearts. Let us implore this precious grace from the Blessed Virgin: *Sancta mater istud agas, crucifixi fige plagas cordi meo valide.*

O Mother, behold your Son; by the love that we bear towards Him, obtain for us that the remembrance of His sufferings may everywhere follow us; it is in His name that we ask this of you; to refuse it to us would be to refuse it to Himself, since we are His members. O Christ Jesus, behold Your Mother; for her sake, grant that we may compassionate Your sorrows so that we may become like unto You.

Simon the Cyrenean Helps Jesus to Carry His Cross

"And going out they found a man of Cyrene, named Simon, him they forced to take up His Cross."

Jesus is exhausted. Although He be the Almighty, He wills that His sacred humanity, laden with all the sins of the world, shall feel the weight of justice and expiation. But He wants us to help Him carry His Cross. Simon represents us all, and Christ asks all of us to share in His sufferings; we are His disciples only upon this condition: "If any man will come after Me, let him . . . take up his cross, and follow Me." The Father has decreed that a share of sorrow shall be left to His Son's mystical body, that a portion of expiation shall be borne by His members: *Adimplebo ea quae desunt passionum Christi in carne mea pro corpore ejus, quod est Ecclesia.* Jesus wills it likewise and it was in order to signify this divine decree that He accepted the help of the Cyrenean.

But at the same time, He merited for us the grace of fortitude wherewith to sustain trials generously. In His Cross He has placed the unction that makes ours tolerable; for in carrying our cross, it is truly His own which we accept. He unites our sufferings to His sorrow, and He confers upon them, by this union, an inestimable value, the source of great merits. Our Lord said to St. Mechtilde: "As My divinity drew to itself the sufferings of My humanity, and made them its own (it is the dowry of the bride), thus will I transport thy pains into My divinity; I will unite them to My Passion, and will make thee to share in that glory which My Father bestowed upon My sacred humanity in return for all its sufferings."

This it is that St. Paul gives us to understand in his Epistle to the Hebrews in order to encourage us to bear all things for the love of Christ: "Let us run by patience to the fight proposed to us; looking on Jesus, the author and finisher of faith. Who having joy set before Him, endured the cross, despising the shame, and now sitteth on the right hand of the throne of God. Think diligently upon Him Who endured such opposition from sinners against Himself; that you be not wearied, fainting in your minds."

My Jesus, I accept from Your hand the particles that You detach for me from Your Cross. I accept all the disappointments, contradictions, sufferings, and sorrows that You permit or that it pleases You to send me. I accept them as my share of expiation. Unite the little that I do to Your unspeakable sufferings, for it is from them that mine will draw all their merit.

A Woman Wipes the Face of Jesus

Tradition relates that a woman, touched with compassion, drew near to Jesus, and offered Him a linen cloth to wipe His adorable face.

Isaias had foretold of the suffering Jesus: "There is no beauty in Him, nor comeliness, and we have seen Him, and there was no sightliness, that we should be desirous of Him:" *Non est species ei, neque decor, nec reputavimus eum.* The Gospel tells us that during those terrible hours after His apprehension the soldiers had dealt Him insolent blows, that they had spat in His face; the crowning with thorns had caused the blood to trickle down upon His sacred countenance. Christ Jesus willed to suffer all this in order to expiate our sins; He willed that we should be healed by the bruises that His divine face received for us: *Livore ejus sanati sumus.*

Being our Elder Brother, He has restored to us, by substituting Himself for us in His Passion, the grace that makes us the children of His Father. We must be like unto Him, since such is the very form of our predestination: *Conformes fieri imaginis Filii sui.* How can this be? All disfigured as He is by our sins, Christ in His Passion remains the beloved Son, the object of all His Father's delight. We are like to Him in this, if we keep within us the principle of our divine similitude, namely, sanctifying grace. Again we are like to Him in practising the virtues that He manifests during His Passion, in sharing the love that He bears towards His Father and towards souls, His patience, fortitude, meekness, and gentleness.

O Heavenly Father, in return for the bruises that Thy Son Jesus willed to suffer for us, glorify Him, exalt Him, give unto Him that splendour which He merited when His adorable countenance was disfigured for our salvation.

Jesus Falls the Second Time

Let us consider our Divine Saviour again sinking under the weight of the Cross. God has laid all the sins of the world upon His shoulders: *Posuit Dominus in eo iniquitatem omnium nostrum.* They are our sins that crush Him. He beholds them all in their multitude and in their every detail. He accepts them as His own to the extent that He no longer appears, according to St. Paul's own words, anything but a living sin: *Pro nobis peccatum fecit.* As the Eternal Word, Jesus is all-powerful; but He chooses to feel all the weakness of a burdened humanity: this wholly voluntary weakness honours the justice of His Heavenly Father, and merits strength for us.

Never let us forget our infirmities; never let us give way to pride. However great may be the progress that we believe we have made, we always remain too weak of ourselves to carry our cross after Jesus: *Sine me nihil potestis facere.* The divine virtue that goes out from Him alone becomes our strength: *Omnia possum in eo qui me confortat;* but it is only given to us if we often ask for it.

O Jesus, become weak for love of me, crushed under the weight of my sins, give me the strength that is in You, so that You alone may be glorified by my works!

Jesus Speaks to the Women of Jerusalem

"And there followed Him a great multitude of people, and of women, who bewailed and lamented Him. But Jesus, turning to them, said: Daughters of Jerusalem, weep not over Me; but weep for yourselves and for your children. For behold the days shall come, wherein they will say: Blessed are the barren.... Then shall they begin to say to the mountains: Fall upon us.... For if in the green wood they do these things, what shall be done in the dry?"

Jesus knows the ineffable exigencies of His Father's justice and holiness. He reminds the daughters of Jerusalem that this justice and this holiness are adorable perfections of the Divine Being. Jesus Himself is "a high priest, holy, innocent, undefiled, separated from sinners." He does but substitute Himself for them; and yet see with what rigour divine justice strikes Him. If this justice requires of Him so extensive an expiation, what will be the rigour of the stripes dealt to the guilty who obstinately refuse to unite their share of expiation to the sufferings of Christ? *Horrendum est incidere in manus Dei viventis.* Upon that day, the confusion of human pride will be so great, so terrible will be the chastisement of those who wanted to do without God that these unhappy ones, outcast from God for ever, will gnash their teeth in despair; they will call upon the hills to cover them, as if the hills could hide them from the fiery darts of a justice of which they will clearly see the entire equity....

Let us implore mercy from Jesus for the dreadful day when He will come, no longer as a Victim bowed down under the weight of our sins, but as the Supreme Judge to Whom the Father has given all power.

O my Jesus, grant me mercy! O Jesus, True Vine, grant that I may remain united to You by grace and good works, so that I may bear fruit worthy of You. Grant that I may not become, through my sins, a dead branch, good for nothing but to be gathered up and cast into the fire.

Jesus Falls for the Third Time

"The Lord was pleased to bruise Him in infirmity," said Isaias, speaking of Christ during His Passion: *Dominus voluit conterere eum in infirmitate.* Jesus is crushed beneath the weight of justice. We shall never be able, even in heaven, to measure what it was for Jesus to be subject to the darts of divine justice. No creature has borne the weight of it in all its fulness, not even the damned have done so. But the sacred humanity of Jesus, united to this divine justice by immediate contact, has undergone all its power and all its rigour. This is why, as a Victim Who has delivered Himself out of love to all its action, He falls prostrate, crushed and broken beneath its weight.

O my Jesus, teach me to detest sin which obliges justice to require of You such expiation. Grant that I may unite all my sufferings to Yours, so that by them my sins may be blotted out and I may make satisfaction even here below.

Jesus is Stripped of His Garments

"They parted My garments amongst them; and upon My vesture they cast lots." This is the prophecy of the Psalmist. Jesus is stripped of everything and placed in the nakedness of utter poverty; He does not even dispose of His garments; for, as soon as He is raised upon the Cross, the soldiers will divide them among themselves and will cast lots for His coat. Jesus, moved by the Holy Spirit: *Per Spiritum sanctum semetipsum obtulit Deo*, yields Himself to His executioners as the Victim for our sins.

Nothing is so glorious to God or so useful to our souls as to unite the offering of ourselves, absolutely and without condition, to the offering which Jesus made at the moment when He gave Himself up to the executioners to be stripped of His raiment and fastened to the Cross, "that through His poverty, [we] might be rich." This offering of ourselves is a true sacrifice; this immolation to the divine good pleasure is the basis of all spiritual life. But in order that it may gain all its worth, we must unite it to that of Jesus, for it is by this oblation that He has sanctified us all: *In qua voluntate sanctificati sumus*.

O my Jesus, accept the offering that I make to You of all my being; join it to that which You made to Your Heavenly Father at the moment of reaching Calvary; strip me of all attachment to created things and to myself!

Jesus is Nailed to the Cross

"They crucified Him, and with Him two others, one on each side, and Jesus in the midst." Jesus delivers Himself up to His executioners "dumb as a lamb before his shearer." The torture of the nails being driven into the hands and feet is inexpressible. Still less could anyone describe all that the Sacred Heart of Jesus endured in the midst of these torments. Jesus must doubtless have repeated the words He had said on entering into this world: Father, Thou wouldst no more holocausts of animals; they are insufficient to acknowledge Thy sanctity... "but a body Thou hast fitted to Me": *Corpus autem aptasti mihi*. "Behold I come."

Jesus unceasingly gazes into the face of His Father, and, with incommensurable love, He yields up His body to repair the insults offered to the Eternal Majesty: *Factus obediens usque ad mortem.* And what manner of death does He undergo? The death of the Cross: *Mortem autem crucis.* Why is this? Because it is written: "Cursed is everyone that hangeth on a tree." He willed to be "reputed with the wicked," in order to declare the sovereign rights of the Divine Sanctity.

He delivers Himself likewise for us. Jesus, being God, saw us all at that moment; He offered Himself to redeem us because it is to Him, High Priest and Mediator, that the Father has given us: *Quia tui sunt.* What a revelation of the love of Jesus for us! *Majorem hac dilectionem nemo habet, ut animam suam ponat quis pro amicis suis.* He could not have done more: *in finem dilexit.* And this love is likewise the love of the Father and the Holy Spirit, for these Three are but One....

O Jesus, Who "in obeying the will of the Father, and through the co-operation of the Holy Ghost did by Your death give life to the world; deliver me, by Your most sacred body and blood, from all my iniquities and from all evils; make me ever adhere to Your commandments and never suffer me to be separated from You."

Jesus Dies Upon the Cross

"And Jesus crying with a loud voice said: Father, into Thy hands I commend My spirit. And saying this, He gave up the ghost." After three hours of indescribable sufferings, Jesus dies. The only oblation worthy of God, the one sacrifice that redeems the world, and sanctifies souls is consummated: *Una enim oblatione consummavit in sempiternum sanctificatos.*

Christ Jesus had promised that when He should be lifted up from the earth, He would draw all things to Himself: *Et ego si exaltatus fuero a terra, omnia traham ad meipsum.* We belong to Him by a double title: as creatures drawn out of nothing by Him, for Him; as souls redeemed by His precious blood: *Redemisti nos, Domine, in sanguine tuo.* A single drop of the blood of Jesus, the God-Man, would have sufficed to save us, for everything in Him is of infinite value; but besides many other reasons, it was to manifest to us the extent of His love that He shed His blood to the last drop when His

Sacred Heart was pierced. And it was for all of us that He shed it. Each one can repeat in all truth the burning words of St. Paul: He "loved me, and delivered Himself for me."

Let us implore Him to draw us to His Sacred Heart by the virtue of His death upon the Cross; to grant that we may die to our self-love and our self-will, the sources of so many infidelities and sins, and that we may live for Him Who died for us. Since it is to His death that we owe the life of our souls, is it not just that we should live only for Him? *Ut et qui vivunt, jam non sibi vivant, sed ei qui pro ipsis mortuus est.*

O Father, glorify Thy Son hanging upon the gibbet. Since He humbled Himself even to the death of the Cross, exalt Him; may the name that Thou hast given Him be glorified, may every knee bow before Him, and every tongue confess that Thy Son Jesus lives henceforward in Thy eternal glory!

The Body of Jesus is Taken Down From the Cross and Given to His Mother

The mangled body of Jesus is restored to Mary. We cannot imagine the grief of the Blessed Virgin at this moment. Never did mother love her child as Mary loved Jesus; the Holy Spirit had fashioned within her a mother's heart to love a God-Man. Never did human heart beat with more tenderness for the Word Incarnate than did the heart of Mary; for she was full of grace, and her love met with no obstacle to its expansion.

Then she owed all to Jesus; her Immaculate Conception, the privileges that make of her a unique creature had been given to her in prevision of the death of her Son. What unutterable sorrow was hers when she received the bloodstained body of Jesus into her arms!

Let us throw ourselves down at her feet and ask her forgiveness for the sins that were the cause of so many sufferings.

O Mother, fount of love, make me understand the strength of your love, so that I may share your grief; make my heart glow with love for Christ, my God, so that I may think only of pleasing Him.

Christ's Work of Redemption

Jesus is Laid in the Sepulchre

Joseph of Arimathea, having taken the body of Jesus down from the Cross, "wrapped Him in fine linen, and laid Him in a sepulchre that was hewed in stone, wherein never yet any man had been laid."

St. Paul says that Christ was "in all things to be made like unto His brethren"; even in His burial, Jesus is one of us. They bound the body of Jesus, says St. John, "in linen cloths, with the spices, as the manner of the Jews is to bury." But the body of Jesus, united to the Word, was not "to suffer corruption." He was to remain scarcely three days in the tomb; by His own power, Jesus was to come forth victorious over death, resplendent with life and glory, and death was no more to "have dominion over Him."

The Apostle St. Paul tells us again that "we are buried together with Him by baptism" so that we may die to sin: *Consepulti enim sumus cum illo per baptismum in mortem.* The waters of baptism are like a sepulchre, where we have left sin behind, and whence we come forth, animated by a new life, the life of grace. The sacramental virtue of our baptism forever endures. In uniting ourselves by faith and love to Christ laid in the tomb, we renew this grace of dying to sin in order to live only for God.

Lord Jesus, may I bury in Your tomb all my sins, all my failings, all my infidelities; by the virtue of Your death and burial, give me grace to renounce more and more all that separates me from You; to renounce Satan, the world's maxims, my self-love. By the virtue of Your Resurrection grant that, like You, I may no longer live save for the glory of Your Father![6]

Christ in His Mysteries, Part II, chapter 14, section 2

---

6. This beautiful Way of the Cross has been published in pamphlet form by B. Herder Book Co., St. Louis, MO.

WITH CHRIST

Through His Death, Christ, Our Head, Sanctifies the Church, Which Has Become His Mystical Body

Now in Jesus Christ, human nature, perfect and integral in itself, is united to the Person of the Son of God. Many of Christ's actions could only be wrought in His human nature: if He works, walks, sleeps, eats, if He teaches, suffers, and dies, it is in His humanity, through His human nature; but all His actions belong to the Divine Person to Whom this humanity is united. It is a Divine Person *Who* acts and operates *by* human nature.

It results from this that all the actions accomplished by the humanity of Christ, however small, ordinary, simple or limited they may be in their physical reality and earthly duration, are attributed to the Divine Person to Whom this humanity is joined; they are the actions of a God. On this head, they possess transcendent beauty and splendour; they acquire, from a moral point of view, an inestimable price, infinite value, and inexhaustible efficacy. The moral value of Christ's human actions is measured by the infinite dignity of the Divine Person in Whom the human nature subsists and acts.

If this is true of the least action of Christ, how much truer yet is it of those that constitute, properly speaking, His mission here below, or are connected with it: namely, the voluntary substitution of Himself for us, as a stainless Victim to pay our debt and, by His expiation and the satisfaction He made, restore divine life to us.

For such is the mission He is to fulfil, the course He is to run. "God has laid on Him," a man like us, of Adam's race, yet just, innocent and stainless, "the iniquity of us all." *Posuit in eo iniquitatem omnium nostrum.* Because He has become, as it were, partaker of our nature, and has taken upon Himself our sin, Christ has merited to make us partakers of His justice and holiness. "God," according to the energetic expression of St. Paul, "sending His own Son, in the likeness of sinful flesh and of sin, hath condemned sin in the flesh." *Deus Filium suum mittens in similitudinem carnis peccati, et de peccato damnavit peccatum in carne*; and with yet more astounding energy: "Him, that knew no sin, for us He hath made sin." *Eum qui non noverat peccatum, pro nobis peccatum fecit.* What energy there is

Christ's Work of Redemption

in this expression: *peccatum fecit!* The Apostle does not say: *peccator*, "sinner," but even, *peccatum*, "sin."

Christ, on His side, accepted to take upon Himself all our sins, to the point of becoming in some manner, upon the Cross, universal sin, living sin; He has voluntarily put Himself in our place, and therefore death will strike Him. He has purchased us "with His own blood." Humanity is to be redeemed, "not with corruptible things as gold or silver . . . but with the precious blood of Christ, as of a lamb unspotted and undefiled, foreknown indeed before the foundation of the world."

Let us not forget that we have been "bought with a great price." Jesus Christ shed the last drop of His blood for us. It is true to say that a single drop of this divine blood would have sufficed to redeem us; the least suffering, the slightest humiliation of Christ, even a single desire of His Heart would have been enough to expiate every sin, all the crimes that could be committed; for each of Christ's actions, being the action of a Divine Person, constitutes a satisfaction of infinite price. But God willed to make the immense love His Son bears towards Him shine forth the more in the eyes of the world: *Ut cognoscat mundus quia diligo Patrem.* He willed to show the ineffable charity of this same Son towards us: *Majorem hac dilectionem nemo habet*; to bring home to us more vividly how infinite is the divine holiness, and how profound the malice of sin. For these and other reasons not revealed to us, the Eternal Father has required all the sufferings and the Passion and death of His Divine Son in expiation of the crimes of humanity. Indeed, the satisfaction was only complete, when, from the height of the Cross, Jesus, with His dying voice, pronounced the *Consummatum est.* "All is consummated." Then only, the personal mission of the Redeemer here below was fulfilled, and His work of salvation accomplished.

By these satisfactions, as, moreover, by all the acts of His life, Jesus Christ *merited* for us every grace of pardon, of salvation and sanctification.

What, exactly, is merit? It is a *right* to a recompense. When we say that the works of Christ are meritorious *for us,* we mean that by them, Christ has won the right that eternal life and all the graces leading to it or attached to it should be given to us. It is indeed what

St. Paul tells us: we are "justified freely by His grace, through the Redemption that is in Christ Jesus." Justified, that is to say, rendered just in the eyes of God, not by our own works, but by a gratuitous gift of God, namely, grace, which comes to us through the Redemption that is in Christ Jesus.

Christ, the Life of the Soul, Part I, chapter 3, sections 2–3

This immolation of a God, an immolation voluntary and full of love, has worked out the salvation of the human race. The death of Jesus redeems us, reconciles us with God, reestablishes the alliance whence all good flows for us, opens again the gates of heaven, and restores to us the inheritance of eternal life. This sacrifice henceforth suffices for all: that is why when Christ dies, the veil of the temple is rent in twain to show that the ancient sacrifices are forever abolished and replaced by the only sacrifice worthy of God. From this time forward salvation and righteousness are only to be had in the participation of the sacrifice of the Cross of which the fruits are inexhaustible. "By *one* oblation," says St. Paul, Christ "hath perfected *forever* them that are sanctified."

Christ, the Life of the Soul, Part II, chapter 7, section 2

Saint Paul never tires of enumerating the benefits purchased for us by the infinite merits which the God-Man acquired through His life and sufferings. When he speaks of them, he grows rhapsodic; and, to express his thought, he can find only words which indicate "abundance" and "superabundance," and "wealth" which he calls "unfathomable." The death of Christ "redeems us," "brings us near to God, reconciles us with Him," "justifies us" and "bestows on us the holiness and the new life of Christ." To sum up, the Apostle compares Christ to Adam, whose work He came to repair: Adam brought us sin, damnation, death; Christ, the second Adam, brings us holiness, grace, life. *Translati de morte ad vitam:* "We have passed from death to life" and "redemption has been plentiful"—*Copiosa apud eum redemptio.* "But not as the offence, so also the gift [of grace].... For if by one man's offence death reigned through one:

much more they who receive abundance of grace and of the gift and of justice shall reign in life through one, Jesus Christ. . . . And where sin abounded, grace did more abound." That is why "there is now . . . no condemnation to them that are in Christ Jesus, who walk not according to the flesh."

By offering infinite satisfaction to the Father in our name, our Lord destroyed the obstacle that existed between man and God. The Eternal Father looks upon the human race with love now that it has been redeemed by the blood of His Son; because of His Son, God showers down upon it all the graces which it needs in order to be united with Him, "to live unto Him" with the very life of God. *Ad serviendum Deo viventi.*

Every supernatural gift which is given to us, therefore, all the light which God grants us, all the care with which He surrounds our spiritual life—these are ours in virtue of the life, the Passion, and the death of Christ. All the graces of forgiveness and justification and perseverance which God gives and will always give to souls— these spring from the one source of all blessings: the Cross.

If, indeed, "God so loved the world as to give it His only-begotten Son"; if He "hath delivered us from the power of darkness and hath translated us into the kingdom of the Son of His love: in Whom we have redemption through His blood, the remission of sins"; if, as Saint Paul says again, Christ "hath loved each of us and delivered Himself for us" so as to prove what love He bore His brethren; if He delivered Himself up to redeem us from our iniquity and, "purifying us, to acquire a people unto Himself," why then should we still hesitate in our faith and confidence in Jesus Christ? He has atoned and paid for everything; He has merited everything. And His merits belong to us; we are made "rich with His goods" so that, if we but will it, "nothing is wanting to us in any grace"—*Divites facti estis in illo, ita ut* NIHIL *vobis desit in* ULLA *gratia.*

Nothing is more certain than is this union of Christ with His chosen ones in the divine thought; what makes Christ's mysteries ours is, above all, because the Eternal Father saw us with His Son in each of the mysteries lived by Christ and because Christ accomplished them as Chief of the Church. I might even say that, on account of this, the mysteries of Christ Jesus are more our mysteries than they are His. Christ, inasmuch as He is the Son of God, would not have undergone the abasements of the Incarnation, the sorrows and sufferings of the Passion; He would have had no need of the triumph of the Resurrection, which succeeded the ignominy of His death. He went through all this as Head of the Church; He took upon Himself *our* miseries and *our* infirmities: *vere languores* NOSTROS *ipse tulit*; He willed to pass through what we ourselves must pass through, and He merited for us the grace to follow after Him in each of His mysteries.

For neither does Christ Jesus separate us from Himself in anything that He does. He declares that He is the Vine and we are the branches. What closer union can there be than that, since it is the same sap, the same life which circulates in the root and in the shoots? Christ unites us so closely to Himself that all that is done to whomsoever it may be who believes in Him, it is to Himself that it is done: *Quamdiu fecistis uni ex his fratribus meis minimis, mihi fecistis*. He wills that the union which, by grace, attaches Him to His disciples, should be the same as that which, by nature, identifies Him with His Father: *Ut unum sint, sicut tu, Pater, in me, et ego in te*. This is the sublime end to which He wills to lead us through His mysteries.

Moreover, all the graces that He merited by each of His mysteries, He merited them in order to distribute them to us. He received the fulness of grace from His Father: *Vidimus eum plenum gratiae*; but He did not receive it for Himself alone; for St. John at once adds that it is of this fulness we have all received: *Et de plenitudine ejus nos omnes accepimus*; it is from Him that we receive it, because He is our Head and His Father has made all things subject to Him: *Omnia subjecit sub pedibus ejus; et ipsum caput supra omnem Ecclesiam*.

So His wisdom, His justice, His holiness, His strength have become *our* wisdom, *our* justice, *our* strength: [*Christus*] *factus est* NOBIS *sapientia a Deo, et justitia, et sanctificatio, et redemptio*. All that He has is ours; we are rich with His riches, holy with His holiness. "O man," says Ven. Louis de Blois, "if thou dost truly desire to love God, behold thyself rich in Christ, however poor and destitute thou art of thyself. For thou mayest humbly appropriate to thyself that which Christ did and suffered for thee."

Christ's Work of Redemption

Christ is truly our own, for we are His mystical body. His satisfactions, His merits, His joys, His glories are ours.... O ineffable condition of the Christian, associated so closely with Jesus and with His states! O surprising greatness of the soul to whom nothing is lacking of the grace merited by Christ in His mysteries! *Ita ut nihil nobis desit in ulla gratia!*

Christ in His Mysteries, first preliminary conference, section 4

The Continuance of the Sacrifice of Christ in Heaven

It is true that in their historical, material duration, the mysteries of Christ's terrestrial life are now past; but *their virtue remains,* and the grace which gives us a share therein is always operating.

In His glorious state, Christ no longer merits; He could merit only during His mortal life until the hour when He drew forth His last breath upon the Cross. But the merits that He had acquired, He never ceases to make ours. Christ was yesterday, He is today, He lives throughout the ages: *Christus heri, et hodie, ipse et in saecula.* Never let us forget that Christ Jesus *wills* the holiness of His mystical body: all His mysteries are to bring about this holiness: *Dilexit Ecclesiam et seipsum tradidit pro ea,* UT *illam sanctificaret.*

But what is the Church? The small number of those who had the privilege of seeing the God-Man living upon earth? Assuredly not. Our Saviour did not come only for the inhabitants of Palestine who lived in His time, but for men of all times: *Pro omnibus mortuus est Christus.* The gaze of Jesus, being divine, fell upon every soul; His love extended to each one of us; His sanctifying will remains as sovereign, as efficacious as on the day when He shed His blood for the salvation of the world.

If the time of meriting has ceased for Him, the time of communicating the fruit of His merits endures and will endure until the last of the elect is saved. Christ is ever living: *Semper vivens ad interpellandum pro nobis.*

Let us raise our thoughts up to heaven, up to the sanctuary whither Christ ascended forty days after His Resurrection; and there let us behold our Lord ever before the face of His Father: *Introivit in caelum, ut appareat* NUNC *vultui Deo pro nobis.*

Wherefore does Christ ever stand before the face of His Father? Because He is His Son, the only-begotten Son of God. "He thought it not robbery to be equal with God," since He is the true Son of God. The Eternal Father looks upon Him and says to Him: *Filius meus es tu, ego hodie genui te.* Now, at this very moment, Christ is there before His Father, and He says to Him: *Pater meus es tu*: "Thou art My Father," I am truly Thy Son. And inasmuch as He is the Son of God, He has the right of beholding His Father face to face, of treating with Him as equal with equal, as He has the right of reigning with Him forever and ever.

But St. Paul adds that it is *for us* that He uses this right; it is for us that He stands before His Father. What does this signify but that Christ stands before the face of His Father, not only by right of being His only-begotten Son, the object of the divine complacency, but as our Mediator. He is called Jesus, that is to say, Saviour; this name is divine, because it comes from God, it was given by God. Christ Jesus is in heaven, at the right hand of His Father as our Representative, our High Priest, and our Mediator. It was in this capacity that, here below, He did the Father's will unto the last iota and in all its details, and that He lived all His mysteries; it is in this capacity that He now lives at the right hand of God, presenting to Him His merits and unceasingly communicating the fruit of His mysteries to our souls, in order to sanctify them: *Semper vivens ad interpellandum pro nobis.*

Christ in His Mysteries, second preliminary conference, section 5

Thus there is in Heaven, and will be until the end of time, a sacrifice celebrated for us by Christ in an eminent and sublime manner, but it is in perpetual continuity with His immolation upon the Cross: *Per hostiam suam apparuit.*

Christ's Work of Redemption

After having shown us something of the greatness and power of this sacrifice, St. Paul gives us this exhortation: "Having therefore a great High Priest that hath passed into the heavens, Jesus, the Son of God, let us hold fast our confession." What confession? The confession of our faith in Jesus Christ, the supreme Mediator, faith in the infinite value of His merits, faith in the boundless extent of His divine power with the Father.

The Apostle continues: "Let us go therefore with confidence, *Adeamus ergo cum fiducia*, to the throne of grace, that we may obtain mercy, and find grace in seasonable aid."

Indeed what grace could be refused to us by this High Priest Who knows how to have compassion on our frailty, our infirmities, our sufferings, since, in order to be like unto us, He has experienced them all; this High Priest Who is so powerful, since, being the Son of God, He deals with His Father as with His equal: VOLO *Pater*; this High Priest Who wills to be united to us as, in the body, the head is united to the members? What graces of forgiveness, of perfection, of holiness may not be hoped for by a soul that truly seeks to remain united to Him by faith, confidence, and love?

Christ in His Mysteries, Part I, chapter 5, section 4

What a powerful motive of confidence it is to know that the Christ Whose life we read in the Gospels, Whose mysteries we celebrate, is ever living, ever interceding for us; that the virtue of His divinity is ever operating; that the power possessed by His sacred humanity (as the instrument united to the Word) of healing the sick, consoling the afflicted, and giving life to souls, is ever the same. As in the past, Christ is still the infallible Way that leads to God, the Truth that enlightens every man coming into this world, the Life that saves from death: *Christus heri, et* HODIE, *ipse et in saecula.*

I believe, Lord Jesus, but increase my faith! I have full confidence in the reality and plenitude of Your merits, but strengthen this confidence! I love You, O Jesus, You Who have manifested Your love in all Your mysteries, *in finem*, but make my love ever greater.

Christ in His Mysteries, second preliminary conference, section 5

WITH CHRIST

The Association of the Virgin Mary in the Redemptive Work of Her Son

If Jesus Christ is the Son of God by His ineffable and eternal birth "in the bosom of the Father," *Filius meus es tu, ego hodie genui te*, He is Son of man by His temporal birth in the bosom of a woman: *Misit Deus Filium suum, factum ex muliere.*

This woman is Mary, and she is a virgin. It is from her, and from her alone, that Christ takes His human nature; it is to her He owes it that He is Son of man; she is truly Mother of God. Mary, therefore, occupies a transcendent, essential and unique place in Christianity. In the same way as the quality of "Son of man" cannot be separated in Christ from that of "Son of God," so is Mary united to Jesus: indeed, the Virgin Mary enters into the mystery of the Incarnation by a title belonging to the very nature of the mystery.

By His temporal birth, He is truly the Son of Mary; the only Son of God is also the only Son of the Virgin.

Such is the ineffable union existing between Jesus and Mary: she is His Mother, He is her Son. This union is indissoluble; and as Jesus is at the same time the Son of God, come to save the world, Mary is indeed intimately associated with the vital mystery of all Christianity. All her greatness is founded on this special privilege of her divine motherhood.

Christ, the Life of the Soul, Part II, chapter 12, introductory remarks and section 1

In the divine plan, *Mary is inseparable from Jesus*, and our holiness consists in entering as far as we can into the divine economy. In God's eternal thoughts, Mary belongs indeed to the very essence of the mystery of Christ; Mother of Jesus, she is the Mother of Him in Whom we find everything. According to the divine plan, life is only given to mankind through Christ the Man-God: *Nemo venit ad Patrem nisi per me*, but Christ is only given to the world through Mary: *Propter nos homines et propter nostram salutem, descendit de caelis et incarnatus est . . . ex Maria Virgine.* This is the divine order and it is unchanging. For, notice that this order was not meant only for the day when the Incarnation took place; it still continues as regards the application of the fruits of the Incarnation to souls. Why is this? Because the source of grace is Christ, the Incarnate Word; but as Christ, as Mediator, He remains inseparable from the human nature which He took from the Virgin.

Christ, the Life of the Soul, Part II, chapter 12, section 4

Christ, having received human nature from Mary, has associated His Mother, as I have said, with all His mysteries from the offering in the Temple to the immolation on Calvary. Now what is the end of all Christ's mysteries? To make of Him the example of all our supernatural life, the ransom for our sanctification, and the source of all our holiness; to create for Him an eternal and glorious fellowship of brethren like unto Himself. That is why Mary, like a new Eve, is associated with the new Adam; but much more truly than Eve, Mary is "the Mother of all the living," the Mother of all who live by the grace of her Son.

This association was not only outward. Christ, being God, being the omnipotent Word, created in the soul of His Mother the feelings she was to have towards those whom, born of her and living by His mysteries, He willed to constitute His brethren. The Virgin, for her part, enlightened by the grace abounding in her, responded to this call of Jesus by a *Fiat* of entire submission and in union of spirit with her Divine Son. In giving her consent to the divine proposition of the Incarnation, she accepted to enter into the plan of the Redemption in a unique capacity; she accepted, not only to be the Mother of Jesus, but to be associated with all the mission of the Redeemer. To each of these mysteries of Jesus, she had to renew this *Fiat* full of love until the moment when she was able to say: "All is consummated," after having offered at Calvary, for the world's salvation, this Jesus, this Son, this body she had formed, this blood which was her own.

Christ, the Life of the Soul, Part II, chapter 12, section 4

Now the pre-eminent work of Jesus, the holy of holies of His mysteries, is His Passion; it is by His bloody sacrifice upon the Cross that He achieves the restoration of life to men, that He raises them up again to their dignity as children of God. Christ Jesus willed to make His Mother enter into this mystery by so special a title and Mary united herself so fully to the will of her Son, our Redeemer, that, while keeping her rank of simple creature, she truly shares with Him the glory of having at that moment brought us forth to the life of grace.

Let us go to Calvary at the moment when Christ Jesus is about to consummate the work that His Father has given Him to do here below. Our Lord has reached the end of His apostolic mission: He is about to reconcile all mankind with His Father. Whom do we find at the foot of the Cross at this supreme instant? Mary, the Mother of Jesus, with John, the beloved disciple, the Magdalen and several other women: *Stabat mater ejus*. Mary is standing there; she has just renewed the offering of her Son—that offering she made when she presented Him in the Temple; at this moment she offers the "blessed fruit of her womb" to the Eternal Father for the ransom of the world. Jesus has only a few minutes to live; then the sacrifice will be accomplished, and divine grace restored to men. He wills to give us Mary to be our Mother. This is one of the forms of the truth that the Word is united, in the Incarnation, to all humanity, and that the elect form the mystical body of Christ from Whom they cannot be separated. Christ will give us His Mother to be also ours in the spiritual order; Mary will not separate us from Jesus, her Son and our Head.

Then, before expiring and achieving, as St. Paul says, the conquest of the world of souls that He wishes to make His glorious kingdom, Jesus sees, at the foot of the Cross, His Mother, plunged in deep sorrow and the disciple He so much loved, the same who heard and has related to us the last words. Jesus says to His Mother: "Woman, behold thy son"; then He says to the disciple: "Behold thy mother." St. John here represents us all; it is to us that Jesus, when dying, bequeathed His Mother. Is He not our "Elder Brother"? Are we not predestined to be like to Him, so that He may be "the firstborn among many brethren"? Now if Christ has become our Elder Brother in taking from Mary a nature like ours, which makes Him one of our race, is it astonishing that, in dying, He should have given her to be our Mother in the order of grace who was His Mother according to human nature?

And as this word, being that of the Eternal Word, is omnipotent and of divine efficacy, it creates in the heart of St. John filial sentiments worthy of Mary, as it gives birth in the Blessed Virgin's heart to a special tenderness for those whom grace renders brothers of Jesus Christ. Can we doubt for a moment that, for her part, the Virgin responded as at Nazareth with a *Fiat,* a silent one this time, but equally full of love, humility and obedience, in which the plenitude of her will lost itself in that of Jesus, so as to bring about her Son's supreme wish.

St. Gertrude relates that hearing one day, in the chanting of the Divine Office, those words of the Gospel naming Christ: *Primogenitus Mariae Virginis,* "the Firstborn Son of the Virgin Mary," she said to herself: "The title of Only Son would seem to be more befitting for Jesus than that of Firstborn." While she was dwelling on this thought, the Virgin Mary appeared to her: "No," said she to the holy nun, "it is not 'Only Son' but 'Firstborn Son' which is most befitting; for, after Jesus, my sweetest Son, or more truly, in Him and by Him, I have given birth to you all in my heart and you have become my children, the brothers and sisters of Jesus."

Christ, the Life of the Soul, Part II, chapter 12, section 2

And because here below she is thus associated with all the mysteries of our Redemption, Jesus has crowned her not only with glory, but with power. He has placed His Mother at His right hand that she may dispose of the treasures of eternal life by a unique title—that of Mother of God: *Adstitit regina a dextris tuis.* This is what Christian piety means when it proclaims the Mother of Jesus: *Omnipotentia supplex.*

Full of confidence, let us then say to her with the Church: "Show thyself our Mother: Mother of Jesus by thy influence with Him; our Mother by mercy towards us. May Christ receive our prayers through thee, this Christ Who, born of thee to bring us life, willed to be thy Son."

WITH CHRIST

Monstra te esse Matrem
Sumat per te preces
Qui pro nobis natus
Tulit esse tuus.

Christ, the Life of the Soul, Part II, chapter 12, section 4

I understood today (Good Friday) that Mary was perfect in her sublime faith at the foot of the Cross. May she obtain for us the singular grace of perfect faith, even in the desolation and nakedness of trials!

Nothing so glorifies the Father as this unshakeable faith in Christ on Calvary.

Quoted in *Abbot Columba Marmion*

PART II

We Co-operate in Christ's Work of Redemption by Sharing in His Passion

The Christian is Called to Co-operate in the Redemptive Work of Christ

*"If anyone wishes to be My disciple,
let him take up his cross and follow Me."*

ACCORDING TO the divine plan which the Eternal Father has traced out for us, He wills that we should only go to Him by walking in the footsteps of His Son, Christ Jesus. Our Lord has given us the formula of this fundamental truth: "I am the Way.... No man cometh to the Father but by Me": *Nemo venit ad Patrem nisi per me.*

He also bequeathed this maxim to all His disciples: "If any man will come after Me, let him deny himself, and take up his cross, and follow Me": *Si quis vult post me venire, abneget semetipsum et tollat crucem suam et sequatur me.*

But if our Divine Saviour suffered that He might redeem us, it was also to give us the grace to unite our expiation to His own and thus render it meritorious. For, says St. Paul, "they that are Christ's, have crucified their flesh, with the vices and concupiscences": *Qui sunt Christi carnem suam crucifixerunt cum vitiis suis.* The expiation required by divine justice touches not only Christ Jesus; it extends to all the members of His mystical body. We share in the glory of our Head only after having shared in His sufferings; it is St. Paul again who tells us so: *Si tamen compatimur ut et conglorificemur.*

Having solidarity with Christ in suffering, we are however condemned to bear it for a quite different reason. He had but to expiate the sins of others: *Propter scelus populi mei percussi eum.* We, on the contrary, have first to bear the weight of our own iniquities: *Digna factis recipimus, hic vero nihil mali gessit.*

It is a lack of supernatural delicacy for souls who have offended God to wish to enter into union with Him before having done their share of expiation. How can the soul hope for intimate familiarity with God before having proved, by its deeds, that it is sincerely converted? Every personal sin, even after it has been forgiven, must be atoned for. By sin, we have contracted a debt towards God's justice; and, when the offence has been remitted, the debt still remains for us to pay. This is the role of satisfaction.

Christ, the Ideal of the Monk, Part II, chapter 9,
introductory remarks and section 1

We may associate ourselves with the Passion by bearing, for love of Christ, the sufferings and adversities which, in the designs of His providence, He permits us to undergo.

There is here an essential truth upon which we ought to meditate.

The Word Incarnate, Head of the Church, took His share, the greater share, of sorrows; but He chose to leave to His Church, which is His mystical body, a share of suffering. St. Paul demonstrates this by a profound and strange saying. "I... fill up those things that are wanting of the sufferings of Christ, in my flesh, for His body, which is the Church."

Christ in His Mysteries, Part II, chapter 13, section 4

What do these words mean? Is something then wanting to the sufferings of Christ? Certainly not. We know that in themselves they were, so to speak, measureless: measureless in their intensity, for they rushed like a mighty torrent upon Christ; measureless above all in their value, a value properly speaking infinite, since they are the sufferings of a God. Moreover, Christ, having died for all, has become by His Passion, the propitiation for the sins of the whole world. St. Augustine explains the meaning of this text of the Apostle: to understand the mystery of Christ, we must not separate Him from His mystical body. Christ is not the "Whole Christ," according to the expression of the great Doctor, unless He is taken as *united* to the Church. He is the Head of the Church which forms His mystical body. Hence, since Christ has brought His share of expiation, it remains for the mystical body to bring its share: *Adimpletae fuerunt passiones in capite, restabant adhuc passiones in corpore.*

Called to Co-operate in the Redemptive Work of Christ

In the same way as God had decreed that, to satisfy justice and crown His work of love, Christ was to undergo a sum of sufferings, so has He determined a share of sufferings for the Church to distribute among her members. Thereby each of them is to co-operate in the expiation of Jesus, whether in expiation of one's own faults, or in the expiation endured, after the example of the Divine Master, for the faults of others. A soul that truly loves our Lord desires to give Him this proof of love for His mystical body by means of these mortifications. Here is the secret of the "extravagances" of the saints, of that thirst for mortifications which characterises nearly all of them: "To fill up those things that are wanting" to the Passion of their Divine Master.

Christ, the Ideal of the Monk, Part II, chapter 9, section 2

Contemplate Christ Jesus on His way to Calvary, laden with His Cross; He falls under the weight of this burden. If He willed, His divinity would sustain His humanity; but He does not will it. Why? Because, in order to expiate sin, He wills to feel in His innocent flesh the burden of sin. But the Jews fear He will not live to reach the place of crucifixion; they therefore constrain Simon the Cyrenean to help to carry His Cross, and Jesus accepts his help.

Simon, in this, represents us all; as members of Christ's mystical body, we must help Jesus to bear His Cross. It is a sure sign we belong to Him, if, following Him, we deny ourselves and take up our cross: *Qui vult venire post me, abneget semetipsum et tollat crucem suam et sequatur me.*

Was it not this that St. Paul sought? Did he not write that he had suffered the loss of all things so that he might be admitted to the fellowship of Christ's sufferings and be made conformable to His death? *Ad cognoscendum illum et societatem passionum illius, configuratus morti ejus.*

Christ, the Life of the Soul, Part II, chapter 4, section 5

Christianity is a mystery of death and of life, but the object of this death is to safeguard the divine life in us. *Non est Deus mortuorum sed viventium.* "(Christ) by dying destroyed our death, and by rising again restored our life": *Mortem nostram moriendo destruxit et vitam resurgendo reparavit.* The essential work of Christianity, as well as the final end to which of its nature it tends, is a work of life; Christianity is the reproduction of the life of Christ in the soul.

Now, as I have said, Christ's life on earth can be summed up in this double aspect: "He was delivered up for our sins, and rose again for our justification": *Traditus est propter delicta nostra et resurrexit propter justificationem nostram.* The Christian dies to all that is sin, the better to live the life of God. Penance then serves primarily as the means of arriving at this aim.

That is what St. Paul so clearly expressed: "Always bearing about in our body the mortification of Jesus, that the life also of Jesus may be made manifest to our bodies." It must be our aim—there is no other—that the life of Christ which has its principle in grace and its perfection in love, may shine forth in us: that is the end; there is none other. To attain this end, mortification is necessary. St. Paul says: "They that are Christ's—and we belong to Christ by our baptism—"have crucified their flesh, with the vices and concupiscences," *Qui sunt Christi, crucifixerunt carnem suam cum vitiis et concupiscentiis suis.* And again he says still more explicitly: "If you live according to the flesh, you shall die; but if by the Spirit you modify the deeds of the flesh, you shall live," live the divine life.

Christ, the Life of the Soul, Part II, chapter 4, section 3

May our Lord take you *all* to Himself and give you courage to endure the trials so necessary for those who wish to be united to the Crucified. Here below our Lord presents Himself to us upon the Cross; the crucifix is His official image, and union with Him is impossible if we do not wish to feel the nails that pierce Him through.

You remember Jesus' words to the two disciples whom he walked with on the road to Emmaus. "Ought not Christ to have suffered these things, and so to enter into His glory?" We are His members and it is impossible for us to enter into His glory without having suffered with Him. The more one is united with Jesus Christ, the

Called to Co-operate in the Redemptive Work of Christ

more one lives by His life, and this life here below is a life of suffering. St. Paul says, "We have not a High Priest who cannot have compassion on our infirmities: but one tempted in all things like as we are, without sin." Look at His holy Mother, no one ever suffered as she did, for no one has ever been so united with Him as she was.

So, courage! you are on the right road, and one day you will understand this more clearly.

I rejoice that you have quite decided to refuse nothing to our Lord Who, certainly, is calling you to great union with Him. To arrive at this union, we must pass through many sorrows and trials and, above all, that of feeling how weak we are in ourselves.

It is impossible, dear child, to arrive at intimate union with a crucified Love, without feeling at times the thorns and nails. It is this which causes the union. You must not be discouraged if our Lord lets you see a *little* of your misery. He bears with it always... hides it from you, but you must see and feel it, before it comes out. This is painful and humiliating for a little Irish woman!

Union with God, chapter 3, section 2

The love of God is as incomprehensible and mysterious as God Himself. In truth, God is love: *Deus caritas est*. When we surrender ourselves to this God of love, when we rest on His fatherly bosom, we find ourselves in an infinite furnace. "Our God is a consuming fire," a fire which tends to consume everything that stands in the way of union. When, therefore, this fire comes into contact with imperfection, it produces suffering.

Weighted down with the sins of men ("Surely He hath borne our infirmities and carried our sorrows"), Jesus became "an accursed one" and "sin" itself for our sake: "Being made a curse for us, for it is written: Cursed is everyone that hangeth on a tree." From the first moment of the Incarnation, He flung Himself onto the bosom of the Father with love and perfect abandonment. And the Father loved Him with a perfect love: "The Father loved the Son and gave all things into His hand"—*Pater enim diligit Filium et omnia dedit ei in manu.* Christ is "the Son of His love." And yet, see how the God of love dealt with Him, delivering Him up to be spat upon, scourged, crowned with thorns, steeped in the anguish of Calvary.

Thus will it be with us if we surrender to Love. Jesus, however, has gone before us. He has carried the greater part of our crosses and has left us only the small part required by the wisdom and the justice of His Father in order that, by our sufferings, we might be able to fill up those things that are wanting to the Passion of Christ.

Our dependence upon the will of the Father is the homage which is due to Him as the First Principle of all things. God needs no one; He can raise up instruments to carry out His plans as He pleases. Still, our *utter dependence* upon Him—in everything He wills or *permits*—honours Him. That is the one thing He asks of us.

All who seek God sincerely sooner or later endure trials. That is necessary in order to be able to make progress of any kind. "He that abideth in Me, and I in him, the same beareth much fruit." "And every branch that beareth fruit My Father will cleanse, that it may bear more fruit." "Unless the grain of wheat falling into the ground die, itself remaineth alone; but if it die, it bringeth forth much fruit."

It is with us as with nature, which must die, in a sense, every year and remain in the icy grip of winter. It *seems* to die, but that death is necessary before spring can come. So it is with your soul because God has found pleasure in it. I shall pray every day that God may make you submissive and humbly abandoned into His hands and so be able to realise the designs which His love and His wisdom have over your soul.

Mélanges Marmion, pp. 83–84, 113

Basic Dispositions of the Soul Which Wants to Co-operate Worthily[1]

Silent Patience

OUR BLESSED SAVIOUR JESUS is in truth the most perfect Example of wonderful patience. He wishes us especially to learn that He is "meek of heart." The Evangelist applies to Him that beautiful text of Isaias—a text that the holy Legislator repeats in order to apply it in his turn to the Abbot—"The bruised reed He shall not break, and smoking flax He shall not quench."

Far from extinguishing the smoking flax, He awaits the hour of grace, the hour when it will burst forth in a magnificent flame of pure love. Thus it was with Magdalen and the Samaritan woman and so many others. What indulgent loving kindness He manifested to misery under every form, including that of sin which is most hideous in His divine sight! And what unwearied patience He shows with His disciples! He sees and hears them dispute among themselves, and express their ambitions; He sees the weakness of their faith; He witnesses their impatience: one day, they want to send little children away from Jesus; more than once, even after His Resurrection, He has to rebuke them for their hardness of heart, their slowness to believe in Him, despite so many miracles wrought under their eyes. He is the Model of admirable patience even so far as to endure having near Him the one He knows is to betray Him.

Such is our Model. Let us keep our eyes ever fixed upon Him.

Christ, the Ideal of the Monk, Part II, chapter 17, section 3

---

1. The basic dispositions which Dom Marmion requires of the soul in the face of suffering can be reduced to three: silent patience, generous love, filial abandonment—three qualities which blend into one and whose apex is holy abandonment, the supreme form of love.

If so admirable a patience appears very difficult for us to possess, let us turn our gaze upon our Divine Model during His Passion. He is God, the All-Powerful, and His soul is rich in all perfection. And behold, they spit in His face; He does not turn away: *Faciem meam non averti ab increpantibus et conspuentibus in Me.* He is silent before Herod who treats Him as a fool: *At ipse nihil illi respondebat;* He submits Himself to Pilate who condemns Him to an infamous death, He submits Himself because Pilate, being the legitimate governor of Judea, represented, pagan though he was, the authority that has its source in God: *Non haberes potestatem adversum me ullam nisi tibi datum esset desuper.* Why does Christ Jesus submit without complaint to all these outrages? From reverence and love for His Father Who has fixed the circumstances of His Passion: *Sicut mandatum dedit mihi Pater.*

Christ, the Ideal of the Monk, Part II, chapter 11, section 5

We must however remain firm and be patient till God's good time: *Viriliter age et sustine Dominum.*[2] God is never so near to us as when He places His Son's Cross upon our shoulders; never do we give our Father in heaven more of the glory that He receives from our patience than in these moments: *Afferunt fructum in patientia.*

Christ, the Ideal of the Monk, Part II, chapter 9, section 3

You are on the right road to God, a road which ever leads to Him despite our weakness. It is the road of duty accomplished through love despite obstacles. Jesus is our strength; *our weakness assumed by Him becomes divine weakness,* and it is stronger than all the strength of man. *Quod infirmum est Dei fortius est hominibus.* This is a great

---

2. Patience may appear as the virtue of passive, listless souls. But, following St. Thomas, Dom Marmion has demonstrated that fortitude is the principle not only of "aggression," *aggredi,* but also of "endurance," *sustinere*; and as this requires more steadfastness of soul than the former, it constitutes the principal act of the virtue of fortitude. Dom Marmion quotes the Scripture text: "The patient man is better than the valiant: and he that ruleth his spirit, than he that taketh cities." See *Christ, the Ideal of the Monk,* Part II, chapter 7, section 7.

but profound truth. Our dear Lord's Passion is nothing else than this triumph of divine weakness over all the strength and wickedness of men. But for this we require great patience and the loving acceptation of God's will at every moment, for *passionibus Christi per patientiam participamus.* "It is by patience that we share in His sufferings." Think well over this in prayer and you will make great progress.

Union with God, chapter 3, section 2

Let us also accept willingly the mortifications sent to us by Providence: hunger, cold, heat, small inconveniences of place or time, slight contradictions coming from those around us. You may again say that these things are trifles; yes, but trifles that form part of the divine plan for us. Is not that enough to make us accept them with love?

Finally, let us accept illness, if sent to us by God, or what is sometimes more painful, a state of habitual ill-health, an infirmity that never leaves us; adversities, spiritual aridity; to accept all these things can become very mortifying for nature. If we do so with loving submission, without ever relaxing in the service we owe to God, although heaven seems to be cold and deaf to us, our soul will open more and more to the divine action. For, according to the saying of St. Paul, "all things work together unto good" to those whom God calls to share His glory: OMNIA *cooperantur in bonum iis qui secundum propositum vocati sunt sancti.*

Christ, the Ideal of the Monk, Part II, chapter 9, section 4

When the Precursor announces to the world the coming of the Saviour, in what terms does he designate Him? "Behold the Lamb of God": *Ecce Agnus Dei.* Jeremias had already said: *Ego quasi agnus mansuetus qui ducitur ad victimam.* Isaias also: *Sicut ovis coram tondente se obmutescet.* Saint Peter tells us that we are "redeemed with . . . the precious blood of Christ, as of a lamb unspotted and undefiled." In the Apocalypse, Christ is represented like a lamb, as it were, slain. The lamb is then one of the scriptural figures of Christ as victim. And is it not the characteristic of the lamb to let one do with it as one will, to let itself be immolated without resistance? It was thus that the prophet Isaias symbolised the Messias.

How truly did Christ Jesus realize that figure! See Him, from the first instant of the Incarnation, giving Himself up to all the wishes and desires of the Father: "Behold! I come to do Thy will." That is the first movement of His Sacred Heart: not only a statement of obedience, but also an eager cry and an act of abandonment in view of all the humiliations and sufferings which awaited Him. He never withdrew His consent, and the exterior splendor of His submission was especially admirable during the Passion: "Father, if it be possible, let this chalice pass from Me. Nevertheless, not My will but Thine be done." What was His attitude when He gave Himself up to the executioners? "I did not turn My face away from them that struck Me and spat upon Me." They can insult Him, strike Him and cover Him with derision; but He does not seek to escape from the unheard-of treatment of which He, Eternal Wisdom and Sovereign Master of all things, is the object. He keeps silence: *Jesus autem tacebat*; He is "dumb as a lamb before his shearer": *Quasi agnus coram tondente se obmutescet*. But in the sanctuary of His blessed soul, what a prayer of abandonment to His Father! What an entire donation of Himself to justice and love! His last words are veritable hymns of abandonment: "It is consummated... Father, into Thy hands I commend My spirit."

Christ, the Ideal of the Monk, Part II, chapter 16, section 4; *Abbot Columba Marmion,* chapter 17

For spiritual direction I say this: I desire that you should try, with the grace of God, *to suffer in silence.* When Jesus, Eternal Wisdom, was treated like a fool and scoffed at by Herod's soldiers, He "remained silent." For it is by patience that we *possess our soul,* and it is a great thing and a great source of strength to possess it so.

Union with God, chapter 7

Basic Dispositions of the Soul

Let us recall our own experience. Is it not true that when we pour out our heart into that of men, to every comer, or turn over within ourselves our difficulties, especially those that arise from obedience, we are enervated, weakened, and each time feel our heart more empty? While if we address to God "those plaints full of reverence that a sorrow full of submission pours out before Him in order to make them die away at His feet," or if we confide our difficulties to the one who represents our Lord in our regard, we find light, strength, and peace. Evidently, we may also at times open our heart to a faithful and discreet friend; did not our Blessed Saviour, the Divine Model of every virtue do so Himself, in the Garden of Olives? Did He not confide to His Apostles the supreme anguish of His Sacred Heart? "My soul is sorrowful even unto death": *Tristis est anima mea usque ad mortem.* This is not forbidden; but to be ever craving from creatures what they are unable to give us, leaves us weak and restless; while there is no light and strength that we cannot find in Christ Jesus.

Christ, the Ideal of the Monk, Part II, chapter 16, section 4

However, we must distinguish the difference between complaining and murmuring. Complaining is in nowise an imperfection, it may even be a prayer. Look at our Lord Jesus, the Model of all holiness. Upon the Cross, did He not complain to His Father of being forsaken? But what is it that makes the difference between these two attitudes? Murmuring evidently implies opposition, malevolence (at least transitory) in the will; however, it proceeds more formally from the mind; it is a sin of the mind derived from the spirit of resistance. It is a contentious manifestation. Complaint on the contrary, if we suppose it to be pure, comes only from the heart; it is the cry of a heart that is crushed, that feels suffering, but however accepts it entirely, and lovingly. We can feel the difficulties of obedience, experience even movements of repugnance: that may happen to the most perfect soul; there is no imperfection in this as long as the will does not adhere to these movements of revolt which sometimes get the better of the sensitive nature. Did not our Lord Himself feel such inward trouble? *Coepit taedere et pavere et maestus esse.*

And what did He Who is our Ideal say in these terrible moments? *Pater, si possibile est, transeat a me calix iste.* "My Father, if it be possible, let this chalice pass from Me." What a plaint wrung from God's innermost Heart in the face of the most terrible obedience ever proposed here below! But likewise how this cry from the depths of crushed sensitive nature is covered by the cry, far deeper still, of entire abandonment to the divine will: *Verumtamen fiat voluntas tua, non mea!*

From murmuring, on the contrary, love is absent: therefore murmuring separates from God; it destroys precisely what our holy Patriarch wishes to establish in us: that "amen" of every instant, that loving "fiat" coming more from the heart than the lips: in a word, that perpetual and incessant submission of our whole being to the divine will for love of Christ.

Christ, the Ideal of the Monk, Part II, chapter 12, section 10

I have received a useful light during these days on the words of Scripture: *Revela Domino viam tuam et spera in eo, et ipse faciet.* Why "reveal" anything to God? Because He wills that we should act towards Him like good children who go in all confidence to recount all their difficulties to their father. Saint Paul says the same: *In omni oratione et obsecratione cum gratiarum actione petitiones vestrae* INNOTESCANT *apud Deum.* The Psalmist reveals all *his way*, that is to say, all his troubles, the persecutions he has to endure, and his temptations (cf. Ps. xxxvii). When we have troubles we are inclined to reveal them, to recount them to ourselves or to others: which serves for nothing, except to vex us or to wound charity. Whilst when we recount them to God *it is a prayer* which opens the heart and fills us with light and courage—above all if, leaning upon Jesus Christ, we go to God *in the spirit of adoption*, and that notwithstanding our sins, after the example of the prodigal son.

Abbot Columba Marmion, chapter 16

It is a *great* perfection to unite ourselves to the Lamb in this offering and to accept, with Him, without murmuring, all the sufferings and all the trials that our Heavenly Father permits, saying: *Dominus est.* "It is the Lord."³

Abbot Columba Marmion, chapter 17

I have been meditating during these days on these words from the Office of the Passion: *Faciem meam non averti ab increpantibus et conspuentibus in me. Domine Deus auxiliator meus,* IDEO NON SUM CONFUSUS. That is the secret of the silence, of the peace of Jesus's soul in His Passion: *the beholding of His Father.* I try to imitate Him by finding in this *beholding* all my strength.

Enter more and more into the *great silence.* Silence: (*a*) of the tongue; (*b*) of the movements of the passions; (*c*) of reasons and reflections on the manner in which others act. Leave that to our Heavenly Father. I am finding great peace of soul now that I do not allow myself to be concerned with the doings of others, as far as my duty as abbot permits. *I speak of these things to the Heavenly Father,* as the Psalmist constantly does. Then that becomes a prayer which makes peace and silence only the more profound.

Abbot Columba Marmion, chapter 17

In hours of trial and suffering, look at Christ Jesus in His agony or hung upon the Cross, and let us say to Him from the depths of our heart: *Diligam te et tradam meipsum pro te:* "Because I love Thee

---

3. On a visit to Rome, in 1912, Dom Marmion was received in audience by the Sovereign Pontiff Pius X. These two great hearts, both so supernatural, were well made to understand one another. At the end of the interview Dom Columba begged the Holy Father to deign to give him, as he said, "a text for *his own* soul." Pius X reflected an instant, took a holy picture and wrote on the back these lines: *In cunctis rerum angustiis, hoc cogita: Dominus est. Et Dominus tibi erit adjutor fortis.* "In all difficult circumstances think of this: it is the Lord. And the Lord will be to you a strong helper." These lines from Christ's Vicar were too much in accordance with Dom Columba's own thoughts and feelings to fail to strike him particularly. He saw in them, as it were, a confirmation of the way of self-abandonment which he had made his own. He often meditated on these words. We find the direct echo of them in his spiritual letters, as well as in the quotation just given. See *Dom Columba Marmion,* chapter 16 and 17.

I accept Thy will." Then divine peace—that peace which passes all understanding—will descend into our soul with the sweetness of heavenly grace. This alone will give us the strength and patience to endure all things in silence of heart and lips: *Tacita conscientia patientiam amplectatur*.

Christ, the Ideal of the Monk, Part II, chapter 12, section 9

Generous Love

Let us again look at our Divine Saviour in His Passion. We know that He accepted it out of love for His Father, and that this love was immense: "That the world may know that I love the Father": *Ut cognoscat mundus quia diligo Patrem*. But did He not suffer despite this love? Certainly He did: what suffering has ever equalled His suffering which He accepted on coming into this world? Hear the cry which escapes from His Heart crushed beneath the burden: "My Father, if it be possible, let this chalice pass from Me. Nevertheless not as I will, but as Thou wilt." Love for His Father lifted Him above the shrinking of His sensitive nature. And yet His agony was terrible, His sorrows indescribable. His Heart, says the Psalmist, became like wax, melting beneath the intensity of suffering. But because He remained fastened to the Cross by love, He gave His Father infinite glory, worthy of the divine perfections.

Love will solve all the difficulties which may crop up in our lives likewise. Wherever we may be on earth, we shall always encounter difficulties, vexations, and contradictions. It is all the more impossible to escape them as they stem less from circumstances than from our very condition as human beings.

If we truly love Christ Jesus, we shall not try to avoid the difficulties and sufferings that occur in the faithful practice of the duties of our state of life; we shall embrace them as our Divine Lord embraced His Cross when it was offered to Him. Some have a heavier cross than others; however heavy it may be, love gives them the strength to bear it; the unction of divine grace makes them cling to it instead of seeking how to cast it away, and in the end they come to feel affection for it as a means of continually testifying to their love: *Aquae multae non potuerunt exstinguere caritatem.*

Christ, the Ideal of the Monk, Part II, chapter 9, section 3

Let us not fear trials: we may pass through great difficulties, undergo serious contradictions, endure deep sufferings, but from the moment we begin to serve God through love, these difficulties, these contradictions and sufferings serve to nourish love. When we love God, we may still feel the cross; God even makes us feel it the more in the measure we advance, because the cross establishes in us a greater likeness to Christ; but we then love, if not the cross itself, at least the hand of Jesus Who lays it on our shoulders; for this hand gives us also the unction of grace wherewith to bear this burden; love is a powerful arm against temptations and an invincible strength in adversities.

Christ, the Life of the Soul, Part II, chapter 6, section 9

When Jesus was ascending the road to Calvary, bowed down under His heavy Cross, He fell beneath the weight. We see Him humbled, weak, prostrate upon the ground. He Whom Scripture calls "the strength of God," *Virtus Dei,* is incapable of carrying His Cross. It is a homage that His humanity renders to the power of God. If He so willed, Jesus could, despite His weakness, bear His Cross as far as Calvary: but, at this moment, the divinity wills, for our salvation, that the humanity should feel its weakness, in order that it should merit for us the strength to bear our sufferings.

God gives us, too, a cross to carry, and each one thinks that his own is the heaviest. We ought to accept the one given to us without reasoning, without saying: "God might have changed such or such a circumstance in my life." Our Lord tells us: "If any man will come after Me, let him . . . take up *his* cross and follow Me."

In this generous acceptation of *our* cross, we shall find union with Christ. For in bearing our cross, we truly bear our share in that of Jesus. Consider what is related in the Gospel. The Jews, seeing how faint and weary their Victim was becoming, and fearing that

He would not arrive as far as Calvary, stop Simon the Cyrenean upon the way, and force him to come to the Saviour's aid. As I have just said, Christ could, had He so willed, have derived the necessary strength from His divinity, but He consented to be helped. He wishes to show us thereby that each of us ought to help Him to bear His Cross. Our Lord says to us: "Accept this share of My sufferings which, in My divine foreknowledge, on the day of My Passion, I reserved for you."

How shall we refuse to accept, from Christ's hands, this sorrow, this trial, this contradiction, this adversity? To drink some drops from the chalice which He Himself offers to us and from which He drank the first? Let us then say: "Yes, Divine Master, I accept this share, with all my heart, because it comes from You." Let us take it, as Christ took His Cross, out of love for Him and in union with Him. We shall sometimes feel ready to sink beneath the burden. St. Paul confesses that certain hours of his life were so full of weariness and disappointment that he was "weary even of life": *Ut taederet nos etiam vivere*. But, like the great Apostle, let us look upon Him Who loved us so much as to deliver Himself up for us; let us unite ourselves to Christ with yet more love at those hours when the body is tortured, or the soul is crushed, or the mind is in darkness, or the deep action of the Spirit in His purifying operations is making itself felt. Then the virtue and unction of His Cross will be communicated to us, and we shall find peace in it as well as strength, and that innermost joy which knows how to smile in the midst of suffering: *Superabundo gaudio in omni tribulatione nostra*.

These are the graces which our Lord has merited for us. Indeed when He went up Mount Calvary, helped by the Cyrenean, Christ Jesus, the God-Man, thought of all those who, in the course of the centuries, would help Him to carry His Cross in accepting their own; He merited for them, at that moment, inexhaustible graces of strength, resignation, and self-surrender which would cause them to say like Him: "Father, not My will, but Thine be done."

Christ in His Mysteries, Part II, chapter 13, section 4

Basic Dispositions of the Soul

Loving souls follow Jesus everywhere, as well and even more willingly to Golgotha as to the Mount of the Transfiguration. Who remained at the foot of the Cross with Jesus? His Virgin-Mother, who loved Him with a love into which not the least self-seeking entered; Magdalen, whom Jesus had forgiven much because she loved much; St. John, who possessed the secrets of the Divine Heart. These three stayed there near to Jesus.

Christ, the Ideal of the Monk, Part II, chapter 13, section 6

God often makes use of suffering in the spiritual life to develop our love, because, in such moments, the soul has to overcome itself, and that is a mark of the strength of its charity.[4] Look at our Lord; He made no act of love more intense than when in His agony He accepted the bitter chalice offered to Him, and when, abandoned by His Father, He achieved His sacrifice upon the Cross.

Christ, the Life of the Soul, Part II, chapter 11, section 2

I want you to apply yourself with order and attention to act *solely* out of love for God in all that you do. Each action done out of pure love is an act of pure love of God, and the more this act costs you, the greater and more meritorious is the love. Thus it was upon the Cross that our Lord showed most love. What costs nothing is worth nothing.

Union with God, chapter 2, section 4

---

4. In this paragraph, as in the two following ones, Dom Marmion sets forth an important doctrine. The merit of an act is measured by the degree of charity which the soul possesses at the moment it accomplishes the act. In general, the *sign* of this charity is the goodness, the excellence, of the work to be done—which goodness results primarily from the conformity existing between the work and the divine will. As to the difficulty experienced in performing the deed, if the difficulty is *inherent to the deed itself*, both are considered to be one and the same. Furthermore, if the difficulty is *overcome*, it evinces a more intense *actual* charity (love of God). In other words, a difficulty overcome is a *sign of the charity* which overcame it, but the charity alone is the immediate source of merit, whereas the difficulty is only the indirect source, in the sense that it moves charity to act or is the occasion of charity's manifesting itself more resplendently. If the difficulty experienced arises from

The value of our whole life depends on the motive by which we act.[5] Now it is certain that the highest motive is that of love. St. Paul said, *Dilexit me et tradidit semetipsum pro me.* This conviction of the love of Christ constrained the Apostle to give himself all to Christ. His answer was, *Impendam et superimpendar.* "I most gladly will spend and be spent myself." Once a soul has thus given herself out of love, nothing stays her, neither sufferings, nor difficulties, nor all

---

unfavorable subjective dispositions in the agent (cowardice in the face of duty, negligence, self-love, headstrongness, susceptibility, etc.), not only is it not a source of merit, but it only too often indicates a lukewarm love of God. What is said concerning difficulties may be applied to trials and suffering. We see also that Dom Marmion, in line with the doctrine of Saint Paul and of Saint Thomas Aquinas as well as with the whole of theological and ascetical tradition, makes the supernatural value of our actions (including the acceptance of suffering) depend on charity (love of God). Suffering is meritorious for heaven only insofar as it is accepted by a soul which is in the state of grace and which is motivated by the love of God. "If I should deliver my body to be burned, and have not charity, I am nothing." Echoing this thought of Saint Paul's, Dom Marmion writes, in *Christ, the Ideal of the Monk* (chapter 9): "One truth upon which it is important to insist here, in relation to exterior mortification, is that, although renunciation is an indispensable means, afflictive practices have no value *in themselves* in the plan of Christianity. Their value comes to them from their union through faith and love with the sufferings and expiation of Christ Jesus."

It would be impossible to exaggerate the importance of this principle of the supernatural life, for, as Father Lemonnyer, O.P., writes in *Notre vie divine*: "To make holiness rest on suffering as on its foundation is, I say without hesitation, to orient it on a false and dangerous road." In *Christ, the Life of the Soul* read the conferences entitled "Truth in Charity" and "Our Supernatural Growth in Christ," in which Dom Marmion masterfully establishes the true hierarchy of values in the spiritual domain. The following pages complete the presentation of his thought.

5. It is hardly necessary to say that for Dom Marmion as for all moralists the first source of morality is the goodness of the action itself. That goodness is two-fold: there is the goodness of the deed considered in itself, absolutely; and the goodness of the deed considered from the viewpoint of its *actual* conformity with the will of God. The latter is of prime importance. In itself, assisting at Mass is excellent; but it would not be—far from it—if, to go to weekday Mass, the mother of a family had to neglect her duties. Read the chapter "Truth in Charity" in *Christ, the Life of the Soul.* —In the passages quoted here, Dom Marmion was writing to souls who were seeking God and whose actions regularly possessed this basic goodness; he therefore had reason to insist on purity of motive and on the primacy of love over all other motives.

Basic Dispositions of the Soul

that troubles us, for *Ubi amatur non laboratur*. Try then to give yourself to Christ in this way without reserve, "for good" and out of love; then all will go on well; your life will be extremely pleasing to God and very meritorious.

Union with God, chapter 2, section 1

Do all things solely for love of our Lord and, for love of Him, accept all that He permits; give yourself up to love without looking either to the right or the left. Accept, without troubling yourself about them, the annoyances and difficulties through which you are passing at present; what you have to do by obedience, do as well as ever you can, but without being anxious whether others are pleased with you or blame you, whether they love you or don't love you. It ought to be enough for you to be loved by our Lord.

Have but one thing in view, namely, to love our Lord and to please Him in everything. God will draw near to you, He will abide in you, you will live in the fellowship of the Father, the Son and the Holy Spirit.

And say often to God, "My God, You indeed merit that I love You solely and that I seek but You."

Union with God, chapter 2, section 1

God repays this joyful generosity of the soul with a further increase of joy. "God loveth a cheerful giver": *Hilarem datorem diligit Deus*, says St. Benedict, repeating the expression of the Apostle. And as God is the source of all beatitude and we have left all things in order to cleave to Him alone, He says to us: "It is I Myself Who will be thy reward, a reward exceedingly great: *Ego merces tua magna nimis.* EGO: Myself! I will not leave the care of crowning thee to any other." God says to the soul: "Because thou art My victim, because thou art wholly Mine, I will be all thine, thy inheritance, thy possession, and thou shalt find in Me thy beatitude: *Ego merces tua!*"

Yes, Lord, it is thus indeed: "For what have I in heaven? And besides Thee what do I desire upon earth? ... Thou art the God of my heart, and the God that is my portion for ever": *Quid enim mihi est in caelo, et a te quid volui super terram? Deus cordis mei et pars mea Deus in aeternum.*

Christ, the Ideal of the Monk, Part II, chapter 6, section 4

In making my Way of the Cross this morning I saw that Jesus has done for us *all* that His Father's justice and holiness demand, but that He invites us, like Simon the Cyrenean, to take our little share. That is why I carry my cross with joy.

Abbot Columba Marmion, chapter 17

As interior practice, I feel more and more urged to *lose myself in Jesus Christ.* May He think and will in me and bear me towards His Father. In the *Pater,* the only petition that He teaches us to make to God for our souls is *Fiat voluntas tua* SICUT IN CAELO. I TRY *to love* His holy will in the thousand little vexations and interruptions of each day.

Abbot Columba Marmion, chapter 8

I try to meet all vexations with a smile.

Abbot Columba Marmion, chapter 17

Basic Dispositions of the Soul

Filial Abandonment[6]

The Will of God, the Foundation of Abandonment

The objective basis of holy abandonment is the divine will. All that God decides, all that He decrees, is absolutely perfect: *Judicia Domini vera, justificata in semetipsa.* Now God *wills* our holiness and our beatitude, but this holiness and this beatitude are not of some indefinite kind. There are two divine utterances—and these two utterances are the completing of one another—which make known to us the ways of Providence as regards ourselves, and in the light of which we may comprehend the wherefore of the spirit of abandonment.

Christ Jesus pronounced the first of these utterances: "Without Me, you can do nothing": *Sine me, nihil potestis facere.* We have often meditated upon these words, but it is sovereignly useful to penetrate into them anew. All the united efforts of nature cannot produce one supernatural act, one act which has any proportion with our end, which is the beatifying vision of the adorable Trinity.

God, Who accomplishes all His works with infinite wisdom, has given us, in grace, the means of realising within ourselves His divine designs. Without grace, which comes from God only, we are incapable of doing anything whatsoever in order to reach our supernatural end; St. Paul tells us that without grace we cannot have a good thought to be counted worthy of eternal beatitude: *Non quod sufficientes simus cogitare aliquid a nobis* QUASI EX NOBIS. This is the echo of Christ's words: "Without Me you can do nothing," you cannot attain the supreme end; you cannot become saints. Christ Jesus Himself has commented upon this truth: He has told us that He is the Vine and we are the branches; to bring forth fruit, we must abide

---

6. Dom Marmion was familiar with the doctrine of holy abandonment. On this grave subject, which he treated with rare sureness and precision, see chapter 16, "The Spirit of Abandonment to God's Will"—one of the most beautiful conferences in *Christ, the Ideal of the Monk*; and also the section "The Self-Surrender of Love" in *Union with God*. These two sources furnish the excerpts which follow. We have quoted them at great length because of the intrinsic importance of the doctrine of abandonment for the spiritual life and because they reveal one of the characteristics of Dom Marmion's spirituality.

united to Him through grace, in order that, drawing supernatural sap from Him, we may bring to His Father fruit pleasing to Him.

You hence see the necessity for the soul of not separating itself from God, the Fount of grace, without Whom we can do nothing. But, much more than this, we ought to give ourselves to Him without reserve, for with this grace we can "do all things": this is the second of the two utterances that show the reason of holy abandonment: *Omnia possum in eo qui me confortat*. There is no honest deed, however commonplace it be, that, done under the inspiration of grace, cannot contribute to make us reach that supreme exaltation which is the beatific vision, for all things work together unto good, to such as God calls to live in union with Himself: *Omnia cooperantur in bonum iis qui secundum propositum vocati sunt sancti*.

Christ, the Ideal of the Monk, Part II, chapter 16, section 1

The Will of God is Love

God's will towards souls is full of love: "God is Love": *Deus caritas est*. Not only does He possess love: He *is* Love, boundless, unfailing, indefectible Love. It has not entered into the heart of man to understand what is infinite love. Now the weight of this infinite love draws God to give Himself: *Bonum est diffusivum sui*. All that God does for us has love as its motive power, and as God is not only Love, but Eternal Wisdom and Almighty Power, the works that Love causes this Wisdom and this Power to accomplish are ineffable. Love is at the foundation of the creation and of all the mysteries of the Redemption.

This love bears moreover a particular character: that of being the love of a father for his children: *Videte qualem caritatem . . . ut filii Dei nominermur et simus*. God loves us as His children. He is the Father essentially: all paternity is derived from His: *Ex quo* OMNIS *paternitas in caelis et in terra nominatur*. This is not a meaningless word. And as, in God, all is active, this paternity in relation to us is all that is most great, most solicitous, most constant: God *acts* with us as with His children, and leads us during our whole life in the light of His incomparable fatherly love.

Christ, the Ideal of the Monk, Part II, chapter 16, section 1

Basic Dispositions of the Soul

God Loves Us in His Son

The marvels and manifestations of God's love for us are inexhaustible. Divine Love shines out not only in the *fact* of our adoption, but in the admirable *way* chosen by God of realising it in us.

God loves us with an infinite love, a fatherly love; but He loves us *in His Son*. To make us His children, God gives us His Son Christ Jesus: that is love's supreme gift. "God so loved the world, as to give His only-begotten Son": sic Deus dilexit *mundum ut Filium suum unigenitum* daret. And why does He give Him to us? That He may be our Wisdom, Sanctification, Redemption, and Justice; our Light and our Way; our Food and our Life: in a word, that He may be the Mediator between Him and us. Christ Jesus, the Word Incarnate, fills that chasm separating man from God.

It is "in His Son" and through His Son, that God pours down from Heaven upon our souls all divine blessings of grace that make us live as children worthy of this Heavenly Father: *Qui benedixit nos* in omni *benedictione spirituali in caelestibus* in Christo. All graces come to us through Jesus, and God loves us in the measure in which we love His Son Jesus and believe in Him. Our Lord Himself tells us these consoling words: "The Father Himself loveth you, because you have loved Me, and have believed that I came out from God": *Ipse enim Pater amat vos, quia vos me amastis et credidistis quia ego a Deo exivi*. When the Father sees a soul full of love for His Son, He showers His most abundant blessings upon it.

That is the order, the plan established from all eternity: Jesus has been constituted Head and King over all God's heritage because it is He Who, through His blood, has restored to us the rights of this heritage: "The Father... hath given all things into His hand": Omnia *dedit Pater in manu ejus*. We abide in Him by faith and love; He abides in us by His grace and merits; He offers us to His Father, and His Father finds us in Him.

Shall we not, therefore, abandon ourselves in all confidence to this all-powerful will, which is love itself and has not only fixed the laws of our perfection but is the principle and source of it? Grace goes before, aids, and crowns all the acts that we do. For, says St. Paul, "I can do *all* things in Him Who strengtheneth me": omnia *possum in eo qui me confortat*. This *qui me confortat* shows us that holy abandonment does not consist in doing nothing; let us guard ourselves against that false quietude, that *"farniente"* falsely esteemed as mystical passivity. "By the grace of God, I am what I am," says the Apostle again, "and His grace in me hath not been void." Grace acts sovereignly, it leads to a high degree of holiness, but only where it meets with no obstacles to its action; the Spirit of God acts powerfully but only where it is not opposed, "grieved"—speaking still in the language of St. Paul—and where the created powers are surrendered to Him.

Christ, the Ideal of the Monk, Part II, chapter 16, section 1

The Manifested Will of God

Abandonment is first of all the consecration of one's self, in faith and love, to God's will. The will of God is not distinct from Himself; it is God intimating to us His wishes; it is as holy, as powerful, as adorable, as immutable as God Himself.

In relation to us, this will is in part manifested, and in part hidden. God's will is revealed, is manifested to us by Christ. "Hear ye Him": *Ipsum audite*; this is what the Father said in sending us His Son. On His side, our Lord tells us that He has made known to us all that His Father has given Him to reveal: *Omnia quaecumque audivi a Patre meo nota feci vobis*. The Church, the Bride of Christ, has received the deposit of these revelations and these precepts, whereto are joined the voice of Superiors for persons in the religious life, the precepts of the Rule: these are so many manifestations of the divine will. [In addition, there are the duties of our state of life.]

What ought to be the attitude of the loving soul with regard to this will? The soul ought to feel itself fire and flame to fulfil it. Every energy of our being should be employed, with fidelity and constancy, to carry out this will. The more intimate we are with anyone, the more careful we are not to displease him; in regard to God, our fidelity ought to be absolute: "I do always the things that please Him": *Quae placita sunt ei facio* SEMPER. Such ought to be the passion of a soul that seeks God solely; his eyes, as the Psalmist says, should be "ever towards the Lord": *Oculi mei* SEMPER *ad Dominum*, thereby to learn His will and to do it.

Basic Dispositions of the Soul

Love serves as the measure of this self-surrender, and the deeper love is, and the more intense and active, the more complete and absolute it renders self-surrender.

Christ, the Ideal of the Monk, Part II, chapter 16, section 3

The Hidden Will of God

The loving soul does not only adhere to the will of God manifested; it yields itself also, and especially, to the hidden will of God; this enwraps our natural existence and our supernatural life, in the whole as in detail. The state of health or sickness, the events in which we are involved, the success or failure of our undertakings, the hour and circumstances of our death, the degree of our holiness, the particular means which God wills to employ to lead us to this degree, these are so many things whereof we are ignorant, that God wills to keep hidden from us.

In face of God's designs, our attitude will be one of abandonment; to give ourselves to God, to place within His hands our personality, our own views, in order to accept His, in all humility: such will be the order we follow. In this matter, true wisdom is not to have any wisdom of our own but to trust entirely in the infallible word, the eternal wisdom and ineffable tenderness of a God Who loves us.

At present God hides from me certain of His designs over me; I ought to find it well that He hides them from me, without troubling myself as to wherefore. I do not know if I shall live a long time, or if I shall die soon; if I shall remain in good health, or if sickness will weigh me down; if I shall keep my faculties, or if I shall lose them long before my death; I do not know whether God will lead me by one particular path or by another. In this domain God keeps the sovereign right of disposing everything both as concerns my natural existence and my supernatural perfection; for He is the Alpha and Omega of all things.

And what am I to do? To lose myself in adoration. To adore God as Principle, as Wisdom, as Justice, as Infinite Goodness; to throw myself into His arms, like a child in the arms of its mother, letting itself be swayed with her every movement. Are you afraid of throwing yourself into your mother's arms? Certainly not, for what mother, unless a monster, has ever betrayed the confidence of her child? And where has a mother derived her tenderness, her goodness, her love? From God. Or rather, these virtues of a mother are but the pale reflection of the perfections of goodness, love, and tenderness, that are in God. Has He not compared Himself to a mother? "Can a mother forget her infant... and if she should forget, yet will I not forget thee." Therefore whether this divine will leads me by wide paths strewn with roses, or draws me along rugged ways bristling with thorns, it is still the adorable and loving will of God, of my God.

But I *know* that this will wills my holiness, that, guided by love, it works ever and mightily to this end; beyond the means that God has officially established to lead me to perfection, such as the sacraments, prayer, the practice of virtue, He possesses a thousand particular means for realising in me, little by little, the special form of holiness that He wills to see in my soul. The whole thing for me, in this hidden domain, is to surrender myself entirely to His action, with faith, confidence, and love. All is salutary for me that comes from God: joys and sorrows, light and darkness, consolations and aridities, for "all things work together unto good" for those whom God calls to holiness. This is what our Lord said to His faithful servant, St. Gertrude: "Make an act of abandonment to My good pleasure, leaving Me the full disposal of all that concerns thee, in the spirit of obedience which dictated to Me this prayer: 'Father, not My will, but Thine be done.' Be resolved to receive adversity or prosperity from My hand, for My love it is that sends them to thee for thy salvation. In all things, unite thy thoughts and desires to those of My Heart. My love it is that gives thee days of dilatation and of joy, out of indulgence to thy weakness, and in order to raise thine eyes and hopes towards heaven; welcome these joys with gratitude and unite this gratitude to My love. Again it is My love that sends thee days of weariness and sadness that they may gain for thee everlasting treasures; accept them, uniting thy resignation to My love."

Christ, the Ideal of the Monk, Part II, chapter 16, section 3

Basic Dispositions of the Soul

When a soul yields herself *entirely*, out of love, with closed eyes, to the guidance of Wisdom, of Omnipotence and Love, that is to say, to God, "all things work together unto good" for her. *His qui diligunt Deum omnia cooperantur in bonum.* Jesus assures us that the Father's love is so tender, so vigilant that not even a hair of our head falls without His permission. That is the way for you; keep in it in spite of all the devil may do to get you out of it.

When one gives oneself over entirely to the divine direction all events work together for good. St. Catherine of Siena, if she had followed her inclination, would have stayed all her life alone in her cell, but our Lord wanted her in the midst of the multitude, of armies, and in relation with Popes; and as in all this, she only obeyed the divine call, our Lord kept her always near Him.

God will care for you just insofar as you cast yourself and all your cares on the bosom of His paternal love and providence.

Abandon yourself blindly into the hands of this Heavenly Father Who loves you *better* and *more* than you love yourself.

Abandon yourself blindly to Love; He will take care of you despite every difficulty. Nothing honours God so much as this surrender of oneself into His Hands.
Union with God, chapter 4, section 3

The best form of mortification is to accept with all our heart, in spite of our repugnance, all that God sends or permits, good and evil, joy and suffering. I try to do this. Let us try to do it together and to help one another to reach that absolute abandonment into the hands of God.
Abbot Columba Marmion, chapter 17

I find absolute submission to God's will a sovereign remedy in every trouble, and when I consider that in reality God's will is God Himself, I see that this submission is but the supreme adoration due to God, due to Him in whatever manner He may manifest Himself.

Abbot Columba Marmion, chapter 6

Once it is thoroughly understood that the will of God is the same thing as God Himself, we see that we ought to prefer His adorable will to all besides, and take it, in what it does, in what it ordains, in what it *permits,* as the one *norm* of ours. Let us keep our eyes fixed upon this holy will, and not upon the things that cause us pain and trouble.

Abbot Columba Marmion, chapter 8

Holy Abandonment, an Act of Faith

To put our confidence in God, is it not indeed to believe in His word? to be assured that in listening to Him we shall attain to holiness, that in abandoning ourselves to Him, He will bring us to beatitude? This faith is easy when we meet with no difficulty, and walk in a way of light and consolation: it is a little like the case of those who read the account of expeditions to the North Pole while comfortably sitting by the fireside. But when we are struggling with temptation, with suffering and trial, when we are in dryness of heart and spiritual darkness, then it needs a strong faith to abandon ourselves to God and remain entirely united to His holy will. The more difficult the exercise of this faith is for us, the more pleasing to God is the homage that flows from it.

Christ, the Ideal of the Monk, Part II, chapter 16, section 5

If only we knew how to listen to our Lord saying to us: "I, Who know the divine secrets; I, Who see all that My Father does, say to you that not a hair of your head falls without the permission of your Heavenly Father. Solomon, in all his glory, was not arrayed in splendour to be compared to that of the lilies of the field. The birds of heaven sow not neither do they spin, and your Father does not leave them without food. And you, with your immortal souls, who have been purchased with My blood, you think that God does not concern Himself about you? *Modicae fidei,* men of little faith, what do you fear? All the sufferings, all the humiliations and annoyances that may come upon you, come from the hand of your Father Who knows what is most expedient for you. He knows by what road, by

Basic Dispositions of the Soul

what winding paths, He will bring you to beatitude; He knows the form and the measure of your predestination. Give yourself up to Him, for He is a Father full of goodness and wisdom Who wills to lead you to closest union with Himself."

Do not then let us be afraid of the sufferings, humiliations, temptations, and desolations that come upon us; let us try to "support God," *Sustine Dominum*, that is to say, to accept everything, absolutely everything, that He would have us accept. The Father is the Vinedresser Who purges the branch, says Christ Himself, "that it may bring forth more fruit." He wishes to enlarge our capacity; He wishes to make us sound the depth of our weakness, our insufficiency, so that, convinced of our powerlessness to pray, to work, to advance, we may place all our trust in Him. Only let us remain docile, generous, faithful: *Viriliter age;*[7] the hour will come when having emptied us of ourselves, God will fill us with His own fulness: *Ut impleamini in omnem plenitudinem Dei.*

Christ, the Ideal of the Monk, Part II, chapter 16, section 4

We are members of Jesus Christ and so united to Him, having such *solidarity* with Him, that all our sorrows, all our weariness, our heaviness, our trials of body and soul are assumed by Him and unceasingly cry for mercy to the Father. It is His Son, His beloved Son, Whom He sees in us, and His mercy unceasingly inundates us with graces for ourselves and for others. Say from the bottom of your heart: *Nos credidimus caritati Dei*. I believe in the love of Jesus for me, a love so great that His sufferings and His merits become mine. Oh! how rich we are in Him.

Union with God, chapter 4, section 2

The Good God sustains me. Despite great temptations and inward trials, I keep very united to His holy will. He seems sometimes to reject me, and I well deserve this, but I persist in hoping in Him....

---

7. The remarks made previously concerning patience as an act of the virtue of strength apply even more to holy abandonment.

I see that the true way to go to God is often to bow down before Him in a deep sense of our unworthiness, and then, *believing* in His goodness: *nos credidimus caritati Dei*, to throw oneself into His arms, upon His paternal Heart.

Abbot Columba Marmion, chapter 16

Holy Abandonment, an Act of Hope

Sometimes, it seems to us as if God does not keep His promises, that we are mistaken in confiding ourselves to Him. Let us however learn how to wait patiently. Let us say to Him: "My God, I know not where Thou art leading me, but I am sure that if I do not separate myself from Thee, if I remain generously faithful to all that Thou askest of me, Thou wilt be solicitous for my soul and for my perfection. Therefore, though I should walk in the midst of the shadow of death, even if all should seem to be lost, I will fear nothing for Thou art with me, and Thou art faithful." This is an admirable, heroic act of confidence in God, suggested by the spirit of abandonment; an act which glorifies God's almighty power, and forces from Him, as it were, the most precious favours.

Christ, the Ideal of the Monk, Part II, chapter 16, section 5

When our Lord wishes to unite a soul very closely to Him, He makes her pass through many trials. But if this soul remits herself without reserve into His hands, He arranges *everything* for her greatest good, according to St. Paul's words, "All things work together for good to them that love God." God's glory demands that we hope in Him in difficult circumstances. To hope in God, to rest upon His bosom when things go well is not a lofty virtue and gives little glory to Him Who wishes to be served by faith and *against all human hope*. But always to remain convinced that God will never forsake us, in spite of the difficulties which seem to us to be insurmountable, that His wisdom, His love and His power will know how to find a way, that is true virtue.

Union with God, chapter 4, section 3

Basic Dispositions of the Soul

When God discovers to us the abyss of our misery, it needs all the strength of the Holy Spirit, all our confidence in the love of our Heavenly Father, all our faith in the blood of Jesus Christ in order not to be crushed by the weight of our weakness, and yet what glorifies God is when, in the full knowledge of our misery, we persist in hoping in His love.

Union with God, chapter 4, section 2

There will never be any peace for you except in the *complete abandonment* of yourself in the hands of your Heavenly Father. It is always necessary to come back to this point, for our Lord requires of you this testimony of your confidence and love. Each time then that you feel troubled and distrustful, you should try *quietly* by prayer and through union with Jesus, to bring your will to this *absolute submission,* to this complete abandonment of yourself, of your future and of everything, into God's hands.

Having left all for God, you ought to expect neither happiness nor satisfaction until you are with Him forever. The Good God gives you *so many* tokens of fatherly tenderness and solicitude, that you ought to respond by complete abandonment. Nothing honours God so much as this surrender of oneself into His Hands.

Union with God, chapter 4, section 3

When we have given ourselves entirely to Jesus, we greatly insult Him by being preoccupied with anything whatsoever.

Abbot Columba Marmion, chapter 8

Holy Abandonment, an Act of Love

The love which abandonment supposes is so great that it honours God perfectly. Is it not equivalent to this declaration: "I love Thee so much, O my God, that I want none but Thee; I only want to know and do Thy will; I lay down my will before Thine, I wish to be directed only by Thee. I leave to Thee all that is to befall me. Even if

Thou shouldst leave me the choice of Thy graces, the liberty of arranging all things according to my will, I would say: No, Lord, I prefer to commend myself wholly to Thee; dispose of me entirely, both in the vicissitudes of my natural life, and in the stages of my pilgrimage towards Thee; dispose of everything according to Thy good pleasure, for Thy glory. I desire one thing alone: that all within me may be fully subject to Thy good pleasure, to Thyself and to those who hold Thy place; and this, whatever be Thy will, whether it leads me by a flower-bordered path, or makes me pass by the way of suffering and darkness"? Such language is the translation of perfect love; the spirit of self-surrender which is nourished with such dispositions of love and complacency and makes us find in them the rule of all our conduct is likewise the source of a continual homage to the wisdom and power of God.

Christ, the Ideal of the Monk, Part II, chapter 16, section 5

Indeed holy abandonment is one of the purest and most absolute forms of love; it is the height of love; it is love giving to God, unreservedly, our whole being, with all its energies and activities in order that we may be a veritable holocaust to God: when the spirit of abandonment to God animates a monk's whole life, that monk has attained holiness. What in fact is holiness? It is substantially the conformity of all our being to God; it is the *amen* said by the whole being and its faculties to all the rights of God; it is the *fiat* full of love, whereby the whole creature responds, unceasingly and unfalteringly, to all the divine will: and that which causes us to say this *amen,* to utter this *fiat,* that which surrenders, in a perfect donation, the whole being to God is the spirit of abandonment, a spirit which is the sum total of faith, confidence, and love.

Christ, the Ideal of the Monk, Part II,
chapter 16, introductory remarks

Complete and Sincere Abandonment

What gives simplicity and peace to our lives is the sincere and complete abandon of oneself to God for His glory. To abandon ourselves

Basic Dispositions of the Soul

is to give to God all that we are and all that we have in order to be *His thing* of which He can dispose at will.

Jesus says, "Father, all My things are Thine," and the Father took Him at His word and delivered Him to unheard-of torments. Many people speak of abandon, but very few keep their word with God. They give themselves to God to be His property, and as soon as ever God begins to dispose of this property for His glory and according to the designs of His wisdom, they cry out, they murmur, and let it be seen that their abandon was not serious, it was only a meaningless word.

I see more and more that what Jesus Christ wants of you is that you abandon yourself without reserve to His will and His love. Place no reservation, no condition to doing this, for He only gives Himself entirely to those who give themselves to Him without counting the cost.

But, my dear daughter, don't be under any illusion, it is much easier to *say* to our Lord, "I give myself to You without reserve" than to do so in reality. There are very few, even among His spouses, who love Him *for Himself*. The greater number love themselves more than they love Jesus, for it suffices for Him to impose something upon them that upsets their customary plans or goes against their inclinations for them to want no more of Him. The generosity with which a Carmelite makes her novitiate is of *great* value. Consider it as a great evil, a great fault[8] to say to our Lord, "Lord, I know that You desire this from me; I know that it would be more pleasing to You for me to do this, but I do not consent to do it." For when one allows oneself to say "No" to our Lord, to bargain with Him, that perfect understanding, that mutual abandon which constitutes real union between the Bridegroom and the bride becomes impossible.

Union with God, chapter 4, section 3; chapter 3, section 2

---

8. Evidently, Dom Marmion does not mean that the "evil," the "fault" is mortal (unless, of course, there is question of a grave precept); what he means, as the context shows, is that a *fully deliberate refusal*, even in light matter, constitutes an act which destroys the "*perfect* understanding" which would result in "*true* union."

Those whom God destines to intimate union with Himself ought to put no reserve to their *abandon*. You must throw yourself into His arms with your eyes shut. You must make an act of complete abandonment to God; give yourself to Him, once and for all, without reserve. This condition must be regarded as essential. I understand such or such a thing makes you suffer, but all that is accidental. What is essential is that you belong altogether to God. Consider yourself as God's "thing" and never take yourself back. When you have communicated, tell our Lord that you accept, like Him, all the Father's will; tell the Father that you wish to belong to Him like this Word that you possess.

The more I gaze at God through the eyes of Jesus living in my heart, the more clearly I see that nothing can be so high, so divine as to remit oneself totally to God. Surely the Creator has a right to dispose of the creature whom He has drawn from nothing; surely He in His infinite wisdom knows what we are best suited to accomplish in His plan; surely His infinite love is the most secure resting place for our blindness and weakness.

Union with God, chapter 4, section 3

Abandonment in Times of Trial

It is above all on days of weariness, sickness, impatience, temptation, spiritual dryness, and trials, during hours of sometimes terrible anguish which press upon a soul, that holy abandonment is pleasing to God.

More than once we have considered this truth, namely, that there is a sum total of sufferings, of humiliations and sorrows, which God has foreseen for the members of Christ's mystical body in order to "fill up those things that are wanting of the sufferings of Christ." We cannot reach perfect union with Christ Jesus unless we accept that portion of the chalice which our Lord wills to give us to drink with Him and after Him.

Our Lord knew all about the terrible way along which His Father had ordained that He should travel; did He refuse to accept the divine will or refuse to fulfil it? No, He embraced it. "Behold I come,

Basic Dispositions of the Soul

O Father; I have placed this law of suffering in My Heart, and I accept it for love of Thee." The Word of God, Eternal Wisdom, Christ likewise foresaw the part that we should have in His Passion. What is there better than to surrender ourselves, with Him, to our Father and accept this participation in the sufferings and humiliations of His Son Jesus? "O Father, I accept all the sorrows, all the humiliations, all the sufferings that it shall please Thee to send me, all the misunderstandings to which it shall please Thee to subject me, all the painful obediences that it shall please Thee to impose upon me; and all this for love of Thee, in union with Thy beloved Son."

If we could always keep ourselves in these inward dispositions, never stopping at secondary causes, never asking, murmuringly, when annoyed and contradicted: "Why has this happened? Why do they treat me in this manner?" If we could lift ourselves up to that supreme will which permits everything, and without the permission of which nothing happens; if we could always look up above creatures with hearts uplifted, *sursum corda*, to see only God, to abandon ourselves to Him, we should constantly abide in peace.

A great nun, the Blessed Bonomo, wrote to her father, at a time when she was exposed to sharp persecution through an unenlightened confessor: "I say to the Lord, 'All is for Thee, I will not be troubled: *Fiat voluntas tua in aeternum*.' I let everything pass, as the water passes returning to the sea; if things come from God, I at once return them to God; and I live in my state of peace; if I am tempted, I commend myself to God and await His help and light; and thus all goes well. Let your Lordship then have no trouble on my account, even when you hear that I am sick and in anguish; for I know not what trouble is, because all is love, and I fear but one thing: to die without suffering."

Christ, the Ideal of the Monk, Part II, chapter 16, section 4

There is nothing more perfect or more agreeable to God than to abandon ourselves unreservedly to His good pleasure, even, and especially, when that good pleasure places the cross upon our shoulders. To realise His works God loves to choose what is weak and small, in order that *everything* may be *divine*.

Let us ever keep our gaze fixed upon the face (i. e., the good pleasure) of the Father through the eyes of Jesus Christ: *Quaerite faciem ejus semper.*

Union with God, chapter 2, section 4

How to Produce These Interior Dispositions Within Ourselves

Contemplation of the Suffering Christ

OUR LORD possesses every virtue within His soul, but the occasions of manifesting them especially arise in His Passion. His immense love for His Father, His charity for mankind, hatred of sin, forgiveness of injuries, patience, meekness, fortitude, obedience to lawful authority, compassion, all these virtues shine out in a heroic manner in these days of sorrow.

When we contemplate Jesus in His Passion, we see the Exemplar of our life, the Model—admirable and accessible at the same time—of those virtues of compunction, abnegation, patience, resignation, abandonment to God's will, charity, meekness, which we ought to practice so as to become like unto our Divine Head: *Si quis vult post me venire, abneget semetipsum et tollat crucem suam et sequatur me.*

Moreover, when we contemplate the sufferings of Jesus, He grants us, according to the measure of our faith, grace to practise the virtues which He revealed during those holy hours. How is this?

When Christ dwelt upon earth, an all-powerful virtue went out from His Divine Person, healing bodily infirmities, enlightening the mind, and quickening the soul: *Virtus de illo exibat, et sanabat omnes.*

Something analogous comes to pass when we place ourselves in contact with Jesus by faith. To those who lovingly followed Him along the road to Golgotha or were present at His immolation, Christ surely granted special graces. This virtue which then went out from Him still does so; and when, in a spirit of faith, in order to compassionate His sufferings, and to imitate Him, we follow Him from the pretorium to Calvary and take our stand at the foot of the

Cross, He gives us the same graces, He makes us partakers of the same favours.

Christ in His Mysteries, Part II, chapter 14, section 1

I can never repeat often enough how eminently useful it is for our souls to remain united to our Lord by the contact of faith. You know that from the beginning of their journeying in the desert, the Israelites murmured against Moses. To punish them, God sent serpents whose bite caused them great suffering. Then, touched by their repentance, God commanded Moses to lift up a brazen serpent of which the sight alone sufficed to heal the wounds of the children of Israel. Now, according to our Lord's own words, this brazen serpent was the figure of Christ lifted up on the Cross. And our Lord said: "And I, if I be lifted up from the earth, will draw all things to Myself." Because He has merited all grace for us by the sacrifice of the Cross, Jesus Christ has become for us the source of all light and strength. And that is why the humble and loving glance of the soul upon the holy humanity of Jesus is so fruitful and so efficacious.

We do not think enough of the power of sanctification that Christ's humanity possesses, even outside of the sacraments.

The means of placing ourselves in contact with Christ is faith in His divinity, in His almighty power, in the infinite value of His satisfactions, in the inexhaustible efficacy of His merits. In one of his sermons to the people of Hippo, St. Augustine asks how we can "touch Christ," now that He has ascended into Heaven. *In caelo sedentem quis mortalium potest tangere?* He answers: By faith; he touches Christ who believes in Him. *Sed ille tactus fidem significat; tangit Christum qui credit in Christum.* And the holy Doctor recalls the faith of that woman who touched Jesus to obtain her cure: *Fide tetigit et sanitas subsecuta est.* There are, he says, many carnal men who have only seen Jesus Christ as man, and have not understood the divinity which was veiled by His humanity. They did not know how to touch Him because their faith was not what it ought to have been. Would you touch Jesus Christ with profit? Believe in the divinity which, as the Word, He shares from all eternity with the Father. *Vis bene tangere? Intellige Christum ubi est Patri coaeternus—et tetigisti.*

How to Produce These Interior Dispositions Within Ourselves

How, then, can we doubt that when we approach Him, even outside the sacraments, with humility and confidence, divine power comes forth from Him to enlighten, strengthen, and help us? No one has ever approached Jesus Christ with faith without being touched by the beneficent rays that ever escape from this furnace of light and heat: *Virtus de illo exibat.*

Jesus Christ, Who is always living, *semper vivens*, and Whose humanity remains indissolubly united to the Divine Word, thus becomes for us—and that in the measure of our faith, and the ardour of our desire to imitate Him—a light and a source of life; and little by little, if we are faithful in contemplating Him in this manner, He will imprint His likeness in us, by revealing Himself more intimately to us, by making us share the sentiments of His Divine Heart and by giving us the strength to live according to these sentiments.

Christ, the Life of the Soul, Part I, chapter 4, section 4

If you contemplate with faith and devotion the sufferings of Jesus Christ you will have a revelation of God's love and justice; you will know, better than with any amount of reasoning, the malice of sin. This contemplation is like a sacramental causing the soul to share in that divine sadness which invaded the soul of Jesus in the Garden of Olives, to share in His sentiments of religion and zeal and abandonment to the will of His Father.

On the night of the Passion, Peter, the Prince of the Apostles to whom Christ had revealed His glory upon Tabor, who had just received Holy Communion from Jesus' own hands, Peter, at the voice of a servant-maid, denies His Master. Soon afterwards, the gaze of Jesus, abandoned to the caprices of His mortal enemies, meets that of Peter. The Apostle understands; he goes out, and bitter tears flow from his eyes: *Flevit amare.*

A like effect is produced in the soul that contemplates the sufferings of Jesus with faith: it, too, has followed Jesus, with Peter, on the night of the Passion; it, too, meets the gaze of the Divine Crucified, and that is for it a true grace. Let us often keep close in the footsteps of the suffering Christ, by making the Way of the Cross. Jesus will say to us: "See what I have suffered for thee; I have endured a three hours' agony, endured the desertion of My disciples, and having My face spat upon, the false witnesses, the cowardice of Pilate, the derision of Herod, the weight of the Cross beneath which I fell, the nakedness of the gibbet, the bitter sarcasms of My most deadly enemies, the thirst which they would have quenched with gall and vinegar, and, above all, the being forsaken by My Father. It was for thee, out of love for thee, to expiate thy sins that I endured all; with My blood I have paid thy debts; I underwent the terrible exigencies of justice that mercy might be shown to thee!" Could we remain insensible to such a plea? The gaze of Jesus upon the Cross penetrates to the depths of our soul and touches it with repentance, because we are made to understand that sin is the cause of all these sufferings. Our heart then deplores having really contributed to the divine Passion. When God thus touches a soul with His light, in prayer, He grants it one of the most precious graces that can be.

It is a repentance, moreover, full of love and confidence. For the soul does not sink down in despair beneath the weight of its sins: compunction is accompanied with consolation and comfort; the thought of the Redemption prevents shame and regret from degenerating into discouragement. Has not Jesus purchased our pardon superabundantly: *Et copiosa apud eum redemptio?* The sight of His sufferings, at the same time as it gives birth to contrition, quickens within us hope in the infinite value of the sufferings by which Christ satisfied for us, and this brings us ineffable peace: *Ecce in pace amaritudo mea amarissima.*

Christ, the Ideal of the Monk, Part II, chapter 8, section 6

When we consider the sufferings of Jesus, which of His perfections do we see especially shine out? It is love.

Love brought about the Incarnation: *Propter nos ... descendit de caelis et incarnatus est;* love caused Christ to be born in passible and weak flesh, inspired the obscurity of the hidden life, nourished the zeal of the public life. If Jesus delivers Himself up to death for us, it is because He yields to the excess of a measureless love; if He rises

How to Produce These Interior Dispositions Within Ourselves

again, it is "for our justification"; if He ascends into heaven, it is to prepare a place for us in that abode of blessedness.

It is necessary that our faith in this love of Christ Jesus should be living and constant. And why? Because it is one of the most powerful supports of our fidelity.

Look at St. Paul. Never did man labour and spend himself as he did for Christ. One day when his enemies attack the lawfulness of his mission, he is led, in self-defence, to give a brief outline of his works, his toils and sufferings. However well we know this sketch drawn from the life, it is always a joy to the soul to read again this page, unique in the annals of the apostolate. Often, says the great Apostle, was he brought nigh to death: "Of the Jews five times did I receive forty stripes, save one. Thrice was I beaten with rods, once I was stoned, thrice I suffered shipwreck, a night and a day I was in the depth of the sea. In journeying often, in perils of waters, in perils of robbers, in perils from my own nation, in perils in the city, in perils in the wilderness, in perils in the sea, in perils from false brethren. In labour and painfulness, in much watchings, in hunger and thirst, in fastings often, in cold and nakedness. Besides those things which are without: my daily instance, the solicitude for all the churches." Elsewhere, he applies to himself the words of the Psalmist: "For Thy sake, we are put to death all the day long, we are accounted as sheep for the slaughter...." And yet he immediately adds: "But in all these things we overcome, because of Him that hath loved us": *Sed in his omnibus superamus*. And where does he find the secret of this victory? Ask of him how he endures everything, though "weary even of life"; how, in all his trials, he remains united to Christ with such an unshaken firmness that neither "tribulation, or distress, or famine, or nakedness, or the sword" can separate him from Jesus. He will reply: *Propter eum qui dilexit nos:* "Because of Him Who hath loved us." What sustains, strengthens, animates, and stimulates him is the deep conviction of the love that Christ bears towards him: *Dilexit me et tradidit semetipsum pro me.*

And, indeed, that which makes this ardent conviction strong within him is the sense that he no longer lives for himself—he who blasphemed the name of God and persecuted the Christians—but for Him Who loved him to the point of giving His life for him:

Caritas Christi urget nos.... "The charity of Christ presseth us," he exclaims. Therefore, I will give myself up for Him, I will spend myself willingly, without reserve, without counting the cost; I will consume myself for the souls won by Him: *Libentissime impendam et superimpendar!*

This conviction that Christ loves him truly gives the key to all the work of the great Apostle.

Nothing urges one to love like knowing and feeling oneself to be loved. "Every time that we think of Jesus Christ," says St. Teresa, "let us remember the love with which He has heaped His benefits upon us.... Love calls forth love."

Christ in His Mysteries, Part II, chapter 19, introductory remarks

During His mortal life, Jesus said to the Jews, and now repeats to us: *Ego si exaltatus fuero a terra, omnia traham ad meipsum.* When once I have been lifted up on the Cross, My power will be such that I shall be able to lift up to Myself all those who have faith in Me. Those who, of old, in the desert, looked at the brazen serpent lifted up by Moses, were healed of the wounds with which they had been stricken on account of their sins; thus all those who look upon Me with faith and love merit to be drawn to Me. I, Who am God, consented, through love of you, to be hung upon the Cross as one who was cursed; in return for this humiliation, I have the power of drawing you to Myself, of purifying you, of adorning you with My grace, of lifting you up as high as heaven where I now am. I came down from heaven; I have ascended thither, after having offered My sacrifice; I have power to make you enter there with Me, for in this I am your Forerunner. I have power to unite you to Myself, in so close a manner that "no man shall pluck... out of My hand that which the Father hath given Me," and that I have redeemed by My precious blood. *Et ego vitam aeternam do eis; et non peribunt in aeternum, et non rapiet eas quisquam de manu mea.*

"And I, if I be lifted up from the earth, will draw all things to Myself." Let us think on this infallible promise of our supreme High Priest when we gaze on the crucifix: it is the source of most absolute confidence. If Christ died for us while we were His enemies, what

How to Produce These Interior Dispositions Within Ourselves

graces of forgiveness, of sanctification can He refuse us, now that we detest sin, and strive to detach ourselves from the creature and from ourselves, so as to please Him alone?

O Father, draw me to the Son! . . . O Christ Jesus, Son of God, draw me entirely to Thee. . . .

Christ in His Mysteries, Part II, chapter 13, section 3

Prayer

If, when faced with suffering, our nature feels some repulsion, let us ask our Lord to give us the strength to imitate Him by following Him even to Calvary.

According to the beautiful thought of St. Augustine, the innocent Christ, like a compassionate physician, reserved for Himself the dregs of the chalice of suffering and renunciation of which we have only to drink a few drops: *Sanari non potes nisi amarum calicem biberis; prior bibit medicus sanus, ut bibere non dubitaret aegrotus.* For, says St. Paul, Christ knows, by experience, what sacrifice is. "We have not a high priest Who cannot have compassion on our infirmities, but one tempted in all things like as we are, yet without sin."

I have said to what an extent our Lord has shared our sufferings, but never let us forget that in thus sharing our sorrows and such of our miseries as were compatible with His divinity, Christ has sanctified our sufferings, our infirmities, our expiations. He has merited for us that we may have the strength to bear them in our turn and that they may be accepted by His Father. But for this to be effected, we must unite ourselves to our Lord by faith and love, and consent to carry our cross after Him. It is from this union that our sufferings and sacrifices derive their value; of themselves they have no value for heaven, but, when joined to those of Christ, they become extremely pleasing to God and salutary for our souls.

This union of our will with our Lord in suffering also becomes for us a source of solace.

When we suffer, when we are in pain, in sadness, in weariness, in adversity or difficulties, and we come to Jesus we are not delivered from our cross, for "the disciple is not above his master," but we are comforted. Christ Himself has told us that He wills us to take up our cross; it is the indispensable condition for becoming His true disciple—but He promises too that He will refresh those who come to find in Him a balm for their sufferings. And He Himself invites us: "Come to Me, all you that labour, and are burdened, and I will refresh you." His words are infallible. If you go to Him with confidence, be assured He will turn tenderly towards you because, according to the words the Gospel applied to Him, He will be touched with compassion: *Misericordia motus*. Was He not crushed under suffering to the point of crying out: "Father, let this chalice of bitterness pass from Me"? St. Paul expressly tells us that one of the reasons Christ wished to endure sorrow was that He might succour those who would come to Him. He is the Good Samaritan Who bends over suffering humanity and brings to it, with salvation, the consolation of the Spirit of Love. It is from Him all true consolation is born for our souls. St. Paul repeats to us: "As the sufferings of Christ abound in us, so also *by Christ* doth our comfort abound." You see how he identifies his tribulations with those of Jesus, since he is a member of Christ's mystical body, and how also it is from Christ he receives consolation.

Christ, the Life of the Soul, Part II, chapter 4, section 5

It is recounted of St. Mechtilde that, in her sorrows, she had the custom of taking refuge with our Lord and of abandoning herself to Him in all submission. Christ Jesus Himself had taught her to do this: "If a person wishes to make Me an acceptable offering, let him seek refuge in none beside Me in tribulation, and not complain of his griefs to anyone, but entrust to Me all the anxieties with which his heart is burdened. I will never forsake one who acts thus." We ought to accustom ourselves to tell everything to our Lord, to entrust to Him all that concerns us. "Commit thy way to the Lord," that is, reveal to Him thy thoughts, thy cares, thy anguish, and He Himself will guide thee: *Revela Domino viam tuam, et spera in eo, et ipse faciet*. How do most men act? They talk over their troubles either within themselves, or to others; few go to pour out their souls at the feet of Christ Jesus. And yet that is a prayer so pleasing to

How to Produce These Interior Dispositions Within Ourselves

God, and so fruitful a practice for the soul! Look at the Psalmist, the singer inspired by the Holy Ghost. He discloses to God all that happens to him; he shows Him all the difficulties that beset him, the afflictions that come to him through men, the anguish that fills his soul. "Look upon my weariness, my miseries, my sufferings! Why, O Lord, are they multiplied that afflict me? *Domine quid multiplicati sunt qui tribulant me* . . . ? Look upon me, and have mercy on me, for I am alone and poor. The troubles of my heart are multiplied: deliver me from my necessities . . . ! Bow down Thy ear to me: make haste to deliver me. Be Thou unto me . . . a house of refuge to save me. . . . I am afflicted and humbled exceedingly . . . my groaning is not hidden from Thee. . . . Withhold not Thou, O Lord, Thy tender mercies from me . . . for evils without number have surrounded me. . . . I am a beggar and poor, but the Lord is careful for me. . . ."

Christ, the Ideal of the Monk, Part II, chapter 16, section 4

When the soul is in trouble, in distress, when beset by temptation, when sadness overpowers it, when discouragement takes possession of it, it has but to open the inspired Book: "O God, come to my assistance; O Lord, make haste to help me. Why, O Lord, are they multiplied that afflict me? Many are they who rise up against me. Many say to my soul: There is no salvation for him in his God. But Thou, O Lord, art my protector, my glory, and the lifter up of my head. . . . Arise, O Lord, save me. Why art thou sad, O my soul? and why dost thou disquiet me? Hope in God, for I will still give praise to Him: the salvation of my countenance, and my God. And let all them be glad that hope in Thee. . . . O Lord, Thou hast crowned us, as with a shield of Thy good will": *Et laetentur omnes qui sperant in te. . . . Scuto bonae voluntatis tuae coronasti nos.* "In the Lord I put my trust, how then do you say to my soul: Get thee away from hence to the mountain? Hear, O Lord, the voice of my supplication, when I pray to Thee; when I lift up my hands to Thy holy temple. . . . Save, O Lord, Thy people, and bless Thy inheritance: and rule them and exalt them forever."

Does the soul need light? strength? courage? Words wherewith to invoke God flow endlessly to our lips: "My soul is as earth without water unto Thee. Send forth Thy light and Thy truth, they have conducted me, and brought me unto Thy holy hill, and into Thy tabernacles. And I will go to the altar of God: to God Who giveth joy to my youth. To Thee, O God my God, I will give praise upon the harp": *Confitebor tibi in cithara Deus, Deus meus.*

Whether our troubles come from men, from the devil, or arise from our fallen nature or from circumstances, we ought to confide everything to God.

Christ, the Ideal of the Monk, Part II, chapter 14, section 1

There is no light and strength that we cannot find in Christ Jesus: He is the surest Friend; He is, as He Himself said again to St. Mechtilde, "essential fidelity." Let us then say to Him: "Lord Jesus, behold I come to Thee, with such or such a sorrow, difficulty, suffering, or affliction; I unite it to those which Thou didst endure here below, when Thou wast in Gethsemane; I abandon myself to Thee, assured that Thou wilt accept this sacrifice in expiation of my sins: *Vide humilitatem meam et laborem meum, et dimitte universa delicta mea.* In return Thou wilt give me strength, constancy, and joy." This confidence will not be deceived; a virtue goes out from Christ Jesus which heals all the wounds of those who unite themselves to Him in this way: *Virtus de illo exibat et sanabat omnes.* Indeed, says St. Teresa, "this Divine Master will behold you with those eyes, so beauteous and compassionate, big with tears; He will forget His own sorrows to comfort yours, and that only because you went to seek consolation from Him and turned to look upon Him."

Christ, the Ideal of the Monk, Part II, chapter 16, section 4

It would be like blasphemy to believe that God is indifferent to our needs and sufferings. *God always looks upon us with an infinite look,* one that is infinitely intense, penetrating to the very depths of our soul and knowing all its griefs and its needs.

Let us tell ourselves that every day, every hour, every instant of suffering borne with Jesus and for love of Him will be a new heaven for all eternity, and a new glory given God for ever.

How to Produce These Interior Dispositions Within Ourselves

Let us never forget it: God *alone* is necessary. All else could be wanting; but He will never be wanting, and He alone is sufficient for us.

In all circumstances we should have recourse to Jesus by prayer; He is our peace, our strength, our joy—and He belongs entirely to us.

Unpublished text

When the soul withdraws into its own depths there to find God in prayer, she finds Him, the adorable Trinity, Christ Jesus Who dwells in us by faith. Christ unites us to Himself; we live with Him *in sinu Patris*; and there we are united to the Divine Persons; our life becomes a communing with the Father, Son, and Holy Spirit; and in this union we find the well-spring of joy. We meet sometimes with sorely tried souls who yet by a life of prayer make within themselves a sanctuary where the peace of Christ reigns. It is enough to ask them: "Would you not like to have some diversion in your life?" to hear them at once reply: "Oh, no, I wish to dwell alone with God." Happy state of a soul living the life of prayer! It everywhere finds God—and God suffices for it, because it is filled with God, the Infinite Good.

Christ, the Ideal of the Monk, Part II, chapter 15, section 8

For love, work, suffer, bear up despite monotony, just as Jesus on the Cross.

If He asks for anything, never refuse, but if it seems too hard to nature, pray, pray till He gives you the grace.

May God bless and love you, and make you a holocaust of love united with your Crucified Spouse.

Union with God, chapter 2, section 1

During my prayer, I love to cast myself at the feet of Jesus Christ and to say to Him: I am very miserable, I am nothing, but You can do all: You are my wisdom, my sanctity. You behold Your Father, You adore Him, You say to Him ineffable things. O my Jesus! that which You say to Him I would say to Him also; say it to Him in my place.

You behold in Your Father all that He wills of me, all that He wills for me; You see in Him if I shall have sickness or health, consolation or suffering; You see when and how I am to die. You accept all for me. As for me, I will it with You, because You will it.

Abbot Columba Marmion, chapter 8

Offering Ourselves to the Father in Union with Christ Immolated on the Altar

The Passion of Jesus holds such a large place in His life, it is so much His work, He attaches such a price to it that He has willed that the remembrance of it should be recalled amongst us, not only once a year, during the solemnities of Holy Week, but every day. He has instituted a sacrifice whereby the memory and the fruits of His oblation on Calvary should be perpetuated: this is the Sacrifice of the Mass: *Hoc facite in meam commemorationem.*

To assist at this Holy Sacrifice, or to offer it with Christ, constitutes an intimate and very efficacious participation in the Passion of Jesus.

Indeed, upon the altar the same sacrifice as that of Calvary is reproduced; it is the same High Priest, Jesus Christ, Who offers Himself to His Father by the hands of the priest; it is the same Victim; the only difference is the manner in which He is offered. We sometimes say: Oh! if I could have been at Golgotha with the Blessed Virgin, St. John, and Magdalen! But faith brings us face to face with Jesus immolated upon the altar; He there renews His sacrifice, in a mystical manner, in order to give us a share in His merits and satisfactions. We do not see Him with our bodily eyes; but faith tells us that He is there, for the same ends for which He offered Himself upon the Cross. If we have a living faith, it will make us cast ourselves down at the feet of Jesus Who immolates Himself: it will unite us to Him in His love for His Father and for mankind and in His hatred of sin: it will make us say with Him: Father, behold I come to do Thy will: *Ecce venio, ut faciam, Deus, voluntatem tuam.*

Christ in His Mysteries, Part II, chapter 13, section 4

How to Produce These Interior Dispositions Within Ourselves

We must be united to Christ in His immolation and offer ourselves with Him; then lie takes us with Him, He immolates us with Him, He bears us before His Father, *in odorem suavitatis*. It is ourselves we must offer with Jesus Christ. If the faithful share, through baptism, in the priesthood of Christ, it is, says St. Peter, that they may "offer up spiritual sacrifices, acceptable to God by Jesus Christ": *Sacerdotium sanctum, offerre spirituales hostias acceptabiles Deo per Jesum Christum*. This is so true that in more than one prayer following the offering about to be made to God, the Church, while awaiting the moment of the consecration, lays stress on this union of our sacrifice with that of her Bridegroom. "Vouchsafe, O Lord," she says, "to sanctify these gifts, and receiving the oblation of this spiritual victim, make *us* an eternal sacrifice to Thyself": *Propitius, Domine, quaesumus, haec dona sanctifica, et hostiae spiritualis oblatione suscepta,* NOSMETIPSOS *tibi perfice munus aeternum*.

But in order for us to be thus accepted by God, the offering of ourselves must be united to the offering Christ made of Himself upon the Cross and renews upon the altar. Our Lord substituted Himself for us in His immolation, He took the place of us all, and that is why when He died we, in principle, died with Him: *Si unus pro omnibus mortuus est, ergo omnes mortui sunt*. For this mystical death to take place effectually in each one of us, we must unite ourselves to His sacrifice on the altar. And how are we to unite ourselves to Christ Jesus in this character of victim? By yielding ourselves, like Him, to the entire accomplishment of the divine good pleasure.

It is for God to fully dispose of the victim offered to Him; we must be in this essential attitude of giving *all* to God, of making our acts of self-renunciation and mortification, of accepting the sufferings and trials of each day for love of Him, so that we may be able to say, like Jesus Christ at the moment of His Passion: *Ut cognoscat mundus quia diligo Patrem, sic facio*. That is to offer ourselves with Jesus. Let us offer the Divine Son to His Eternal Father and offer ourselves with this "holy Host" in the same dispositions that animated the Sacred Heart of Christ upon the Cross: intense love of His Father and of our brethren, ardent desire for the salvation of souls, and full abandonment to all that is willed from on high, above all, if it contains what is painful and vexatious for our nature.

When we do this, we offer God the most acceptable homage He can receive from us.

Christ, the Life of the Soul, Part II, chapter 7, section 5

"It is then only," as St. Gregory so well says, "that Christ is our Victim, when we offer ourselves, in order to share, by our generosity and sacrifice, in His life of immolation": *Tunc ergo vere pro nobis hostia erit Deo, cum nos ipsos hostiam fecerimus.*

Christ in His Mysteries, Part II, chapter 18, section 4

Our Lord has willed that the immolation of the altar shall renew the immolation of the Cross, by reproducing it in order to apply its fruit to every soul. It is the same Christ Who offers Himself to His Father "in the odour of sweetness": *cum odore suavitatis*; this unbloody oblation is as acceptable to God as the sacrifice of Calvary: here Jesus is the Victim, as He was when upon the Cross, and as He was when He came upon earth. Upon the altar, Christ Jesus comes again into this world every day as Victim; every day He repeats his oblation and His immolation for us. Doubtless He wishes us to offer Him to the Father; but neither does He ever weary of urging us to offer ourselves to His Father, in union with Him, that we too may thus be accepted, and, having shared in His sacrifice here below, may likewise share in His eternal glory.

In this, as in all things, Christ Jesus is our Model, the Model of all those who follow Him, of all those who are His members.

Our condition as creatures already obliges us to offer ourselves to God, for His dominion over us is sovereign: "The earth is the Lord's and the fulness thereof: the world and all they that dwell therein": *Domini est terra et plenitudo ejus, orbis terrarum et universi qui habitant in eo.* We ought to confess, by our adoration and the sacrifice of our submission to God's will, His supreme perfection and our absolute dependence.

But our condition as members of Jesus Christ also obliges us to imitate our Divine Head. St. Paul addresses these words to Christians: "I beseech you, therefore, brethren, by the mercy of God"—

How to Produce These Interior Dispositions Within Ourselves

that is to say, because of God's infinite bounty towards you—"that you present your bodies a living sacrifice, holy, pleasing unto God, your reasonable service": *Obsecro vos, fratres, per misericordiam Dei, ut exhibeatis corpora vestra hostiam viventem, sanctam, Deo placentem, rationabile obsequium vestrum.*

O God, Infinite Being, Who art very Beatitude, what an immense and inestimable grace Thou dost give to Thy poor creatures in calling them to be, with the Son of Thy love, acceptable sacrifices, wholly consecrated to the glory of Thy Majesty!

Christ, the Ideal of the Monk, Part II, chapter 6, section 2

Let us unite the sacrifice of ourselves with that of Christ Jesus. Let us offer ourselves with Him "in the spirit of humility, and with a contrite heart that our sacrifice may be pleasing in the eyes of the Lord": *In spiritu humilitatis et in animo contrito suscipiamur a te, Domine, et sic fiat sacrificium nostrum in conspectu tuo hodie, ut placeat tibi, Domine Deus.* O Eternal Father, receive not only Thy Divine Son, but ourselves with Him of Whom we say that He is "a pure Host, a holy Host, an immaculate Host": *Hostiam puram, hostiam sanctam, hostiam immaculatam.* Of ourselves, we are only poor creatures, but, miserable as we are, Thou wilt not reject us, for the sake of Thy Son Jesus Who is our Propitiation, and to Whom we would be united, so that through Him, and with Him, and in Him, all honour and glory be to Thee, O Father Almighty, in the unity of the Holy Ghost: *Per ipsum, et cum ipso, et in ipso est tibi Deo Patri omnipotenti, in unitate Spiritus Sancti, omnis honor et gloria.*

Christ, the Ideal of the Monk, Part II, chapter 6, section 5

Each morning, let us join ourselves to Jesus in His obedience, in the entire submission that He made of Himself at the moment of the Incarnation: "Behold me, O my God, I give myself to Thee, to Thy good pleasure. Because I love Thee, I will give Thee the homage that consists in submitting my whole being to Thy will, whatever it may be."

Christ, the Ideal of the Monk, Part II, chapter 12, section 11

Lord Jesus, in union with that intention and that love with which You became obedient unto death, and the death of the Cross, and ever did that which was pleasing to our Father, I wish to do all things today in Your name and in the spirit of humility, obedience, and submission.

Abbot Columba Marmion, chapter 8

Eternal Father, even as Your Divine Son, Our Lord Jesus Christ, offers Himself to Your Majesty as holocaust and victim for the human race, even so do I offer myself body and soul to You; do with me what You will; to this end I accept all the troubles, mortifications, afflictions, which it shall please You to send me this day. I accept all from Your divine will; O my God, may my will ever be conformed to Yours!

Abbot Columba Marmion, chapter 17

During the day let us think of our morning Mass. We were then united to the immolation of Jesus and placed upon the altar with the Divine Victim; let us therefore accept generously the sufferings, the vexations, the burden of the day and the heat thereof, the difficulties and self-denial inherent to the common life. Thus we shall practically live our Mass. Indeed, is not our heart an altar whence the incense of our sacrifice and our submission to His adorable will unceasingly rises up to God? What altar could be more pleasing to Him than a heart full of love constantly offered up to Him? For we can always sacrifice upon this altar, and offer ourselves with the Son of His love, for His glory and the welfare of souls.

This is the teaching that our Lord Himself gave to St. Mechtilde. One day whilst she was thinking that her illness made her useless and that her sufferings were unavailing, the Lord said to her: "Place all thy pains in My Heart and I will give them the most absolute perfection that suffering can possess. As My divinity drew to itself the sufferings of My humanity and made them its own, so will I transport thy pains into My divinity, I will unite them to My Passion and make thee share in that glory which God the Father has bestowed on My sacred humanity in return for all its sufferings. Confide, therefore, each of thy pains to Love in saying: 'O Love, I give them to Thee with

How to Produce These Interior Dispositions Within Ourselves

the same intention that Thou hadst when Thou didst bring them to me from the Heart of God, and I beseech Thee to offer them to Him again, made perfect by intensest gratitude...." "My Passion," added Christ Jesus, "bore infinite fruit in heaven and upon earth; thus thy pains, thy tribulations offered to Me and united to My Passion will be so fruitful that they will procure more glory for the elect, new merit for the just, forgiveness for sinners, and an alleviation of their pains for the souls in purgatory. What is there indeed that My Heart cannot change for the better, since it is from the goodness of My Heart that all good flows both in heaven and on earth?"

Christ, the Ideal of the Monk, Part II, chapter 9, section 5

Jesus is ever in your heart; lay down your *whole* being at His feet a hundred times a day, leaving to Him the full disposal of everything. And then, when He takes you at your word, when He cuts into the living flesh, shudder, yes, but kiss the hand of God Who is preparing you for divine union with the Crucified.

Union with God, chapter 3, section 2

This sacrifice of Jesus Christ never ceases, for He is ever immolated on an altar, and He ever remains Victim in the tabernacle. Our life ought always to be united to this life of Jesus Christ as Priest and Victim.[9] *Abbot Columba Marmion*, chapter 8

Uniting Ourselves to Christ in Holy Communion

The Eucharist is not only a sacrifice, the sacrifice of the Cross recalled and renewed, it is also a sacrament, the sacrament of union, as the word "communion" indicates; it is in order to unite Himself to us that our Lord comes to us. To unite is to make of two things

---

9. Many sick persons cannot assist at Mass physically, but, as Dom Marmion suggests here, they can always, at any time of the day or night, unite themselves in spirit to the sacrifice of Christ unto the glory of the Father and the salvation of their fellow men.

only one thing. But we unite ourselves to Christ as He is. Now every Communion presupposes the Sacrifice of the Altar, and consequently, the immolation of the Cross. In the offering of the Holy Mass, Christ associates us to His state of High Priest, and in Communion He causes us to participate in His condition of Victim. The Holy Sacrifice supposes, as I have said, that inward and entire oblation that our Lord made to the will of His Father when entering into the world, an oblation that He often renewed during His life and completed by His death on Calvary. All this, says St. Paul, is recalled to our minds by Communion: "*As often* as you shall eat this bread and drink the chalice, you shall show forth the death of the Lord." QUOTIESCUMQUE *enim manducabitis panem hunc et calicem bibetis, mortem Domini annuntiabitis donec veniat.* Jesus Christ gives Himself to us as Food, but after having been first offered as Victim; Victim and Food are, in the Eucharist, sacrifice and sacrament—two inseparable characters. And that is why this habitual disposition of giving oneself totally is so important. Christ gives Himself to us in the measure we give ourselves to Him, to His Father, to our brethren who are the members of His mystical body; this essential disposition makes us one with Christ, but with Christ as victim; it establishes sympathy between the two terms of the union.

Christ, the Life of the Soul, Part II, chapter 8, section 5

But Communion itself supposes sacrifice. That is why we already associate ourselves with the mystery of the altar in assisting at the Sacrifice of the Mass.

We would have given anything to have been at the foot of the Cross with the Blessed Virgin, St. John, and Magdalen. Now the oblation of the altar reproduces and renews the immolation of Calvary in order to perpetuate its remembrance, and apply its fruits.

During Holy Mass, we ought to unite ourselves to Christ, but to Christ immolated. He is, upon the altar, *Agnus tamquam occisus,* the Lamb offered as a victim, and it is with His sacrifice that Jesus wills to associate us. After the consecration, the priest with his hands joined together upon the altar—a gesture which signifies the union of the priest and all the faithful with Christ's sacrifice—says this prayer:

How to Produce These Interior Dispositions Within Ourselves

"We beseech Thee, almighty God, command that these things be carried to Thy sublime altar, in the sight of the Divine Majesty."

The Church here places in relation two altars: that of the earth and that of heaven—not that there is a material altar in the sanctuary of heaven, but the Church wishes to point out there is but one sacrifice: the immolation which is accomplished mystically upon earth is one with the offering that Christ, our High Priest, makes of Himself in the bosom of the Father, to Whom he offers for us the satisfactions of His Passion.

"These things," of which the Church speaks, says Bossuet, are truly the body and blood of Jesus, but they are this body and this blood together with us all and with our desires and prayers, and all these compose one same oblation.

Thus in this solemn moment, we are introduced *ad interiora velaminis*, in the sanctuary of the Divinity, but we are brought there by Jesus and with Him; and there, before the Infinite Majesty, in presence of all the heavenly court, we are presented with Christ to the Father in order that the Father may fill us "with all heavenly benediction and grace": *Omni benedictione caelesti et gratia repleamur*.

It is only by being united to the victim that one perfectly participates in the sacrifice—but on condition that we participate in this sacrifice by the reception of the body and blood of Jesus: *Quotquot ex hac altaris participtione sacrosanctum Filii tui corpus et sanguinem sumpserimus*.

It is then only by Communion that we perfectly enter into the thoughts of Jesus, that we fully respond to the desires of His Heart on the day on which He instituted the Eucharist: "Take ye and eat"; "Except you eat the flesh of the Son of man . . . you shall not have life in you."

Christ in His Mysteries, Part II, chapter 18, section 4

The life that Christ gives us by Communion is His *whole life* that passes into our souls to be the exemplar and the form of ours, to produce within us the divers affections of the Heart of Jesus, to make us imitate all the virtues He practised in His states, and to shed within us the special grace which He merited for us when living His mysteries.

Doubtless we must never forget that under the Eucharistic species is found only the substance of the *glorious* body of Jesus, such as it is at present in heaven, and not such as it was, for example, in the crib of Bethlehem.

But when the Father looks upon His Son Jesus in the heavenly splendours, what does He behold in Him? He sees the One Who lived thirty-three years upon earth for us, He beholds all the mysteries that this mortal life contained, the satisfactions and the merits whereof these mysteries were the source; He beholds the glory that this Son gave Him in living each of them. In each of them too He beholds ever the same Son in Whom He was well pleased, although now Christ Jesus sits at His right hand only in His glorious state.

In the same way, it is Jesus born of Mary Whom we receive, Jesus, Who dwelt at Nazareth, Who preached to the Jews of Palestine; it is the Good Samaritan; it is He Who healed the sick, delivered Magdalen from the devil, and raised Lazarus from the dead; it is He Who, wearied, slept in the ship; it is He Who was crushed by anguish; it is He Who was crucified upon Calvary; it is the glorious Jesus risen from the sepulchre, it is the mysterious Pilgrim of Emmaus, Who made Himself known "in the breaking of bread"; it is He Who ascended to heaven to the Father's right hand; it is the eternal High Priest, ever living, Who never ceases to pray for us.

All these states of the life of Jesus are, in substance, given to us in Communion, with their properties, their spirit, their merits, and their virtue: under the diversity of states, and the variety of mysteries, is perpetuated the identity of the Person Who lived them and now lives eternally in heaven.

When, therefore, we receive Christ at the Holy Table, we may contemplate Him and converse with Him in any of His mysteries; although He is now in His glorious state, we find in Him the One Who has lived for us and merited for us the grace that these mysteries contain; dwelling in us, Christ communicates this grace to us in order to effect little by little that transformation of our life into Him, which is the effect proper to the sacrament.

Jesus is in us, really present, He Who was present in the crib, at Nazareth, upon the mountains of Judaea, in the supper-room, upon the Cross. It is this same Jesus Who said to the Samaritan woman:

How to Produce These Interior Dispositions Within Ourselves

"If thou didst know the gift of God!" Thou who art athirst for light, peace, joy, happiness, if thou didst know Who I am, thou wouldst ask of Me living water . . . that water of divine grace which becomes "a fountain of water springing up into life everlasting."

He is in us, really present, He Who said: "I am the Way, the Truth and the Life . . . He that followeth Me, walketh not in darkness. . . . No man cometh to the Father but by Me. . . . I am the Vine, you are the branches; he that abideth in Me, and I in him, the same beareth much fruit: for without Me you can do nothing. . . . Him that cometh to Me, I will not cast out. . . . Come to Me all you that labour and are burdened, and I will refresh you . . . and you shall find rest to your souls."

He is in us, the same Christ Who healed the lepers, stilled the tempest and promised to the good thief a place in His kingdom. We find there our Saviour, our Friend, our Elder Brother, in the fulness of His almighty power, in the ever fruitful virtue of His mysteries, the infinite superabundance of His merits, and the ineffable mercy of His love.

He is in our hearts, not only in order to receive our homage, but to communicate His grace to us. If our faith in His work is not a mere sentiment, we shall go to Him, we shall put our soul in contact, by faith, with His sacred humanity. Be assured that "virtue goes out from Him," as of old, to fill us with light, peace, and joy.

Christ in His Mysteries, Part II, chapter 18, sections 3 and 4

When we receive our Lord in Holy Communion, we possess within us that Divine Heart which is a furnace of love. Let us ask Him earnestly that He will Himself grant us to understand this love, for, in this, one ray from on high is more efficacious than all human reasoning; let us ask Him to enkindle within us the love of His Person. "If, by our Lord's grace," says St. Teresa, "His love is imprinted one day in our heart, all will become easy to us; very rapidly and without trouble we shall come by this means to the works of love."

If this love for the Person of Jesus is in our heart, our activity will spring forth from it. We may meet with difficulties, be subject to great trials, undergo violent temptations; if we love Christ Jesus, these difficulties, these trials, these temptations will find us steadfast: *Aquae multae non potuerunt exstinguere caritatem.* For when the love of Christ urges us we shall not wish any longer to live for ourselves, but for Him Who loved us and delivered Himself up for us: *Ut et qui vivunt, jam non sibi vivant sed ei qui pro ipsis mortuus est.*

Christ in His Mysteries, Part II, chapter 19, section 5

I have the custom of going every day at noon to make a short visit to the Blessed Sacrament, and there, putting everything else out of my mind, I say to our Lord: "My Jesus, tomorrow I am to receive You into my heart, and I wish to receive You perfectly. But I am altogether incapable of this. You have Yourself said: 'Without Me you can do nothing.' O Eternal Wisdom, do You Yourself prepare my soul to become Your temple. I offer You, with this intention, my actions and sufferings of this day, in order that You may render them pleasing in Your divine eyes and that You may verify Your words: *Sanctificavit tabernaculum suum Altissimus.*"

Such a prayer is excellent; the day is thus directed towards union with Christ; love, principle of union, envelops our actions; far from murmuring at anything disagreeable or troublesome that happens to us, we offer it to Jesus with a feeling of love, and the soul thus finds itself, as it were quite naturally, prepared when the moment comes to receive its God.

Abbott Columba Marmion, chapter 18

We are infinitely rich in Jesus if we are united to Him by sanctifying grace and if we rely upon Him. Try, then, to become a saint by recognizing the extent of your wretchedness and, at the same time, relying with absolute confidence upon the merits of Jesus. "Through Him, with Him, and in Him," as we say at daily Mass, "is all glory given to the Trinity." Even the praise of the angels ascends to God only through Jesus Christ, for, as we say in the Preface of the Mass each day, "... through Whom the angels praise Thy majesty." That is why acts of praise, offering, adoration, and acceptance of humiliation and scorn, when performed in union with Jesus (especially after Holy Communion), are infinitely agreeable to the Most Holy Trinity.

How to Produce These Interior Dispositions Within Ourselves

Every day, in Holy Communion, Christ gives Himself entirely to us; He takes us and gives us to the Word. If our whole day could flow from our Communion of the morning, little by little, Christ would transform us and raise us to sublime holiness. What we cannot do, Jesus does for us. In the world, the bridegroom is the strength of his bride who is weak, and the more powerless she is, the more he acts for her. You are, by your religious profession, the bride of Christ. The more weak, miserable, powerless you are, the more Christ becomes your strength, the more He supplies for you.... When you cannot say the prayers that you would wish, Jesus says them for you.

As for me, if you asked me in what the spiritual life consists, I should say, "It is very simple, it is resumed in one word: Christ." In his Epistle to the Galatians (6:16), St. Paul, after having said all that Christ is for us, sums up his thought in this beautiful text: *Et quicumque hanc regulam secuti fuerint pax super illos et misericordia.* Yes, those who seek Christ have peace and mercy.

God has poured forth all "the treasures of His wisdom and of His science" on the sacred humanity of Jesus Christ because of its union with the Word, and *the measure of His gifts to us is the degree of our union with this same Word.* Now this union with the Word is effected by the power and *efficacy of the sacred humanity, especially in Holy Communion.* What we have to do is to maintain ourselves, through the sacred humanity in an habitual state of absolute adoration and submission to the Word, Who resides within us. Our life must be an *Amen* ever echoing the wishes and designs of that Word on us.[10] A soul once arrived at that state becomes the object of God's best gifts.

Union with God, chapter 2, section 4

---

10. In these last lines Dom Marmion shows how—in default of sacramental Communion, which is often impossible for many of the sick to receive—spiritual Communion can, without having the same effects, produce precious benefits in the soul; all the more so, he suggests, as spiritual Communion can be frequently repeated. No formula is needed—a movement of the heart is enough.

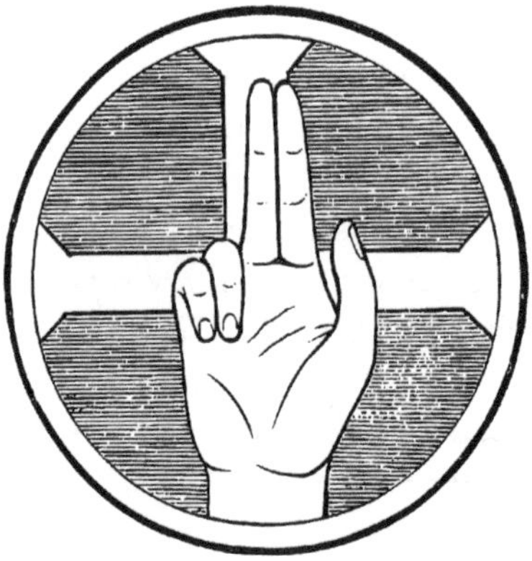

PART III

On Human Misery and
Some Forms of Trial and Suffering

Seeing the Mercy of God in Our Trials

Human Misery and Divine Mercy[1]

WE CANNOT KNOW all the ways of God; it is impossible for us to understand them perfectly. "My thoughts," says the Lord, "infinitely surpass any created intellect, and My ways of acting are far removed from yours; for, just as the heavens are exalted above the earth, so do My ways differ from your ways." *Sicut exaltantur coeli a terra, sic exaltatae sunt viae meae a viis vestris.*

Nevertheless, our faith should wish to become enlightened and our soul should desire to know God's ways of acting in regard to us. His is the thought of Infinite Wisdom. If we accept it fully, setting aside our small human concepts, our acceptance will enable us to receive grace more abundantly, to glorify God as He wills to be glorified, and to better raise our souls towards eternal life; because our efforts and our life work will have been in full accord with the plan of Divine Wisdom.

---

1. This theme of divine mercy bending over human misery was particularly dear to Dom Marmion. His vital faith made him see—in his original, one might even say daring, and penetrating way—the divine plan from the angle of mercy. This appeared as early as 1888, when he was a novice; and thirty-five years later (fifteen days before his death, in January, 1923), when he made it the subject of his last conference to the Carmelites of Louvain. These facts appear in *Abbot Columba Marmion*; a beautiful development of this thought runs throughout *Union with God*. Numerous persons have testified that Dom Marmion's teaching on this point is consoling and immensely inspiring. Among others, a priest well-known for his learning and his long experience of human misery wrote apropos *Paroles en marge du missel:* "I see there just how much Dom Marmion insisted on the mercy of God. It is an inexhaustible theme and, for many souls in these times, an extremely important one.... I have learned from experience that drawing attention to that excellent tonic, the mercy of God, means for many souls the beginning of a new life."

That plan is to shower upon men the treasures of mercy; the special glory which God wants is the praise of that merciful goodness whereby, in hovering over human misery, He wills to relieve it, to sublimate and unite it to Himself.

In heaven we shall see that God, in eternal splendour, wanted to erect an admirable monument of mercy: *in aeternum misericordia aedificabitur in coelis*. We humans, formerly weighed down with infirmities of both body and soul, we will be the living stones of that monument unceasingly witnessing to the infinite goodness of God.

What, then, is mercy?

Mercy is goodness or love which, in the presence of wretchedness, is moved with compassion. In God, therefore, mercy is nothing but the limitless love of His infinite goodness which, at the sight of the creature's miseries, stoops down to relieve and help him, to forgive and make him happy.

All God's ways in dealing with us are ways of mercy. Without our wretchedness to ease, God could never have revealed the unfathomable riches of His condescending love.

When He created the first man, God had established him in the grace of supernatural adoption which made him the child of God and the heir of eternal glory. Sin thwarted that divine plan. Abusing of his freedom, Adam, made head of the human race, transgressed the law. At that moment he lost, both for himself and for all his descendants, any right to the divine life and inheritance. All his children share in his disgrace. As soon as a man enters into this world, he is as it were destined for all sorts of woe: we are all born sinners, deprived of original justice, exposed to the attacks of concupiscence and illness, filled with all manner of shortcomings and weaknesses, both physical and moral. That is how we look in the sight of God.

God's attitude in regard to us is wholly one of merciful compassion. *Quomodo miseretur pater filiorum, misertus est Dominus.* "He has pity on us just as a father has compassion on his children, because He knows the dust from which we were formed." God makes His glory consist in manifesting His mercy to us; our infirmities—our very sins, provided we repent of them—give Him

Seeing the Mercy of God in Our Trials

an occasion to exercise that divine perfection, even while He is correcting us. See how the inspired author of the Epistle to the Hebrews makes us understand this great truth: "And you have forgotten the consolation which speaketh to you, as unto children, saying: 'My son, neglect not the discipline of the Lord: neither be thou wearied whilst thou art rebuked by Him. For whom the Lord loveth, He chastiseth: and He scourgeth every son whom He receiveth. Persevere under discipline. God dealeth with you as with His sons. For what son is there, whom the father doth not correct? [God corrects us] for our profit, that we might receive His sanctification.'" And, in what follows that text, see how well the Holy Spirit Himself, the creating and comforting Spirit, understands the human heart: "Now all chastisement for the present indeed seemeth not to bring with it joy but sorrow: but afterwards it will yield to them that are exercised by it the most peaceable fruit of justice."

I said at the beginning that God's thoughts—He Himself tells us so—infinitely surpass ours. Elsewhere He says so just as clearly: "I know what thoughts I have for you: thoughts of peace and not of affliction; for I want to give an end to your ills and patience."

When God looks upon the world, He is touched by the misery which He sees there—not only by misery in the moral order, but by all the sufferings of His creatures. We know well that passage in the Gospels: *Nonne duo passeres asse veneunt: et unus ex illis non cadet super terram sine Patre vestro.* "Consider these little birds: they are worth almost nothing, and yet," says Jesus, "not a single one of them falls without My Father's permission." We could add: or without His compassion. God's goodness extends to every one of His creatures: *Nihil odisti eorum quae fecisti.* After the creation, He saw that everything that had come out from His hands "was excellent"—*valde bona.* And now that woe has descended upon creation in the wake of sin, none of His creatures can suffer without moving the heart of God to compassion.

But even that is not mercy: it is only the pity which the Author of nature has for all that He has created. God is also the Author of grace; and mercy is His goodness, which—at the sight of our moral miseries, of which sin is the deepest—delights in relieving and forgiving us.

This divine mercy enfolds our entire life. Each time God grants us His pardon, each time He bestows some grace upon us, it is an effect of His merciful love. In heaven we shall see clearly that we are beholden to Him for every benefit lavished on us and for the blessedness which we shall enjoy eternally. With the elect in the Apocalypse, we shall cast our crowns before the throne of God to acknowledge that we have them through His goodness, and we shall praise His mercy for ever: *Misericordias Domini in aeternum cantabo.*

Let us love to repeat the words of the Psalmist: *Deus meus, misericordia mea.*[2] "Yes, Lord," Thou art not only merciful, but "Thou art *my* mercy." Thou art "compassionate and full of goodness; Thy mercy extends to each one of Thy creatures." *Miserator et misericors Dominus.... Et miserationes ejus super omnia opera ejus.* Graciously hear us; "for the glory of Thy name" forgive our sins, "for which we are justly afflicted"; assist our weakness; relieve our wretchedness: *Ut qui juste pro peccatis nostris affligimur, pro tui nominis gloria misericorditer liberemur.* We know that our misery is vast, but we also know that Thy mercy surpasses it infinitely. We have no fear of exhausting it, for "Thy goodness is a treasure without limits"—*Deus cujus misericordiae non est numerus et bonitatis infinitus est thesaurus.* We want to establish that conviction firmly in the depths of our soul; we want to live by it so that the constant avowal of our indignity and misery may both open our soul to the action of Thy grace and glorify Thee, O Lord, rising up to Thee as an undying hymn to Thine infinitely merciful ways.

Mélanges Marmion, pp. 2–6, 15

---

2. Dom Marmion himself loved to repeat this invocation. As he lay dying, he was reminded by his encouraging confessor of the good he had done through his writings and the conversions he had effected. But he immediately protested, indicated dissent, and murmured: *Deus meus, misericordia mea.*

Seeing the Mercy of God in Our Trials

Taking Our Miseries Upon Himself, Christ Became the Most Miserable of Men

The plan of God appears admirable especially in the way in which He has realized His merciful designs.

We have spoken of the eternal monument of mercy which God is building in heaven. What is the foundation stone of that edifice? It is Christ Jesus.

We are all creatures filled with misery and we can all apply to ourselves the words of the psalm: "I am poor and needy"—*Egenus et pauper sum.*

Still, let us not be afraid to say it, the Poor One, the Man most weighed down with wretchedness, is our Divine Saviour. How so? Without doubt, His all-holy soul—*Tu solus sanctus, Jesu Christe*—has never known sin or imperfection; and His humanity, hypostatically united to the Word, enjoyed uninterruptedly, even in the midst of His sufferings, the infinite delights of the vision of God.

But having become our Elder Brother and our Head through the Incarnation, He wished to take upon Himself all the miseries and sufferings of His members. He espoused our human nature together with all the weaknesses which accompany it. Spotless, He took on the iniquities of all men, who had become His brethren: *Posuit Dominus in eo iniquitatem omnium nostrum.*

Let us contemplate Christ during His existence here below. Is He not truly one who knows sorrow and infirmity—*Vir dolorum et sciens infirmitatem?* He is born in the most abject poverty; He spends thirty years in a lowly carpenter's workshop, subject to the hard law of labor. Then in His public life He knows weariness and journeys, strife with the Pharisees, and the implacable hatred of His enemies. At last, He experiences the unspeakable tortures of His Passion and death. Let us look at Jesus enduring His terrible agony in the Garden of Olives. Saint Paul tells us that Jesus prayed "with tears and groanings," that He begged mercy "with mighty cries," *cum clamore valido et lacrymis,* both for Himself and for those whom He had come to save.

Thrice does this Man of sorrows Who has become such for our sake, ask His Father to let the bitter chalice pass. He will merit the salvation of humanity, but only on condition that He die, and die the death of the Cross.

When Jesus is nailed to the Cross, a prey to excruciating torments, deserted by His friends, abandoned by His Father, He lets this cry of anguish escape from His dying lips: "My God, My God, why hast Thou forsaken Me?" Is that not the cry of a poor wretch overwhelmed with woe? Was ever anyone more worthy of compassion?

In order to save the world, God exacted that excess of suffering and the death of His Son on Calvary; and the Son, through love for the Father, accepted it all. We know, in fact, that love for His Father is the prime motive which made Jesus undergo the Passion: *Ut cognoscat mundus quia diligo Patrem... sic facio.* In a transport of supreme love and sovereign freedom our Lord accomplished all that the Father wanted of Him and, in return, asked Him to have pity on us: "Father, My members have need of Thy mercy; what Thou dost for them is done unto Me; their miseries have become Mine, and I have paid all their debts." Then God is filled with mercy for the members of His Son and He compassionates their miseries when presented thus; He forgives us, opens His paternal Heart and floods us with graces. That is how He repays His Son for all the love which the Son showed for Him in the sacrifice on Calvary.

All the mercies of God in our behalf are answers to the prayers of His Son. When the members of Christ beg for God's mercy, it is His Son Jesus Who asks for it through them. His prayers and groanings alone give worth to ours. Let us remember that though the entire human race raised a cry of distress towards God and delivered itself up to the most frightful macerations for centuries on end, all that, without Jesus, would not reach God. Christ knew that, without Him, our sins could not be forgiven; He made Himself our ransom, and now all the mercies of God must pass through Him in order to reach us.

If, therefore, we wish to experience the blessings of the Redemption, let us remain closely united to our Lord. We are the objects of God's merciful love insofar as He sees us in His Son. Those who wilfully and deliberately place themselves outside of Jesus Christ stray from the orbit of divine mercy.

Seeing the Mercy of God in Our Trials

Calvary is the luminous center of mercy upon which God looks. Before the Incarnation, God's mercies flowed upon the world in view of the divine sacrifice which would be offered on that hill; since the death of Christ, it is that same hill to which the Heavenly Father unceasingly looks. If He grants us pardon and grace, He does so solely in virtue of that sacrifice which, while it obtained salvation for us, procured eternal glory for God.

The drama of Golgotha is reproduced and renewed each day on the altar; the Holy Sacrifice of the Mass is essentially the same as that on the Cross, only the manner of oblation being different: *sola offerendi ratione diversa*. The same Christ Who, on the Cross, offered Himself in a bloody manner, is now offered, through the ministry of the priest, in an unbloody manner. God receives the same glory; we obtain the same graces. All the sufferings of Christ are represented to the Eternal Father at that moment (*mortem Domini annuntiabitis*), and Christ sends up the same appeal for mercy. And then, because we are members of His Son, God forgives us and becomes clement to us, whose miseries are without number.

Yes, God is truly admirable in all His works. How rightly could the Psalmist cry out: *Quam magnificata sunt opera tua, Domine! Omnia in sapientia fecisti*—"O Lord, Thou hast stamped all Thy works with magnificence and wisdom!" In His adorable wisdom and goodness, God has combined things so perfectly that He derives glory from our very wretchedness. Not only is it an occasion for His exercising His mercy; but—since Jesus Christ has taken upon Himself our sins and weaknesses and has expiated them in His own Person—each time God has mercy on us, He glorifies His Son and acknowledges the worth of His precious blood.

From the satisfactions of Christ there constantly rises up toward "the Father of mercies" the incense of adoration and of infinite glory.

Mélanges Marmion, pp. 7–10

Vere languores nostros ipse tulit et dolores nostros ipse portavit: "Truly hath He borne our infirmities," etc., has a very deep meaning.

It means that He took all actual deliberate sin on Himself and expiated it in His Person. *Posuit in eo Dominus iniquitatem omnium nostrum*: The Lord hath placed on Him the iniquity of us all.

It also means that as Head of the Church, He accepted in our name (His members) all our miseries, our meanness, our infidelities, our sufferings, and suffered from them in our name, and sanctified and deified them in His Person. No pain or suffering or weakness of His members was hidden from Him. He took them *willingly* on Himself.

It also means that by thus taking them on Him, He took the sting out of them, and helped us to bear them.

Union with God, chapter 4, section 2

St. John tells us that at the outset of our Divine Saviour's public life, when He was passing through Samaria, He came to a city called Sichar, near Jacob's well. Among the details of this scene carefully noted by the Evangelist, there is one that especially moves our hearts: *Jesus ergo fatigatus ex itinere, sedebat sic supra fontem*: "Jesus therefore being wearied with His journey, sat thus on the well." What a touching revelation of the reality of the humanity of Jesus!

We ought to read the wonderful commentary which St. Augustine has given of these details, with that opposition of ideas and terms of which he has the secret, especially when he wants to place in relief the union and the contrast of the divine and the human in Jesus. "He is weary, He Who refreshes those who are weary; He Whose absence fills us with weariness, He Whose presence strengthens us": *Fatigatur per quem fatigati recreantur; quo deserente fatigamur, quo praesente firmamur.* "It is for you that Jesus is wearied on His journey. We find Jesus full of strength and of weakness. Why full of strength? Because He is the Eternal Word and all things were created by His wisdom and power. Why full of weakness? Because this Word was made flesh and dwelt amongst us. The strength of Christ created you; the weakness of Christ re-created you." *Fortitudo Christi te creavit; infirmitas Christi te recreavit.*

And the Saint concludes: *Infirmus in carne Jesus; sed noli tu infirmari; in infirmitate illius tu fortis esto!* "Jesus is weak in His Humanity; but as for you, take care not to remain in your weakness; go

Seeing the Mercy of God in Our Trials

rather to draw strength from Him Who, being by nature almighty, willed to become weak for love of you."

Christ in His Mysteries, Part I, chapter 4, section 4

"... In Order That the Strength of Christ Might Dwell in Me"

If we could only have a deep conviction that we are powerless without Christ, and that we have all in Him! *Quomodo non etiam cum illo omnia nos donavit?* Of ourselves we are weak, very weak; in the world of souls there are weaknesses of all kinds, but that is not a reason for being discouraged; these miseries, when they are not wilful,[3] rather entitle us to Christ's mercy. See the unfortunate who wish to excite the pity of those from whom they ask alms; far from hiding their poverty, they make a display of their rags, they show their sores; that is what entitles them to the charity and compassion of the passers-by. For us also, as for the sick who were brought to Christ when He lived in Judea, it is our misery confessed and displayed in His sight that draws down His mercy. St. Paul tells us that Christ willed to experience our infirmities—excepting sin—that He might have compassion on us; and in fact, we read several times in the Gospel that Jesus was moved with compassion at the sight of the sufferings He witnessed: *Misericordia motus.* St. Paul expressly adds that Jesus keeps this sentiment of compassion in glory, and he immediately concludes: "Let us go therefore with confidence, *cum fiducia,* to the throne" of Him Who is the source "of grace"; for if we do so in these dispositions, we shall "obtain mercy."

Christ, the Life of the Soul, Part I, chapter 3, section 4

---

3. Needless to say, Dom Marmion was always careful to distinguish between infirmities and infidelities. And just as he had compassion on weaknesses and infirmities, so did he take pains to warn souls against the smallest shortcomings springing from negligence and against willful infidelities even in the smallest details. This point is borne out again and again in *Union with God, Sponsa Verbi,* and *Christ, the Ideal of the Monk.*

Let us turn to Christ Jesus and lean upon Him, not only in prayer, but in all that we do. And we shall be strong. If without Him we can do nothing: *Sine me, nihil potestis facere*; with Him, we can do all things: *Omnia possum in eo qui me confortat*. We have in Him, Who is the source of our confidence, the most efficacious motive for fidelity and patience in the midst of the sadness, the disappointments, the trials, and the sufferings that we must undergo here below until the end of our exile.

When the mortal life of Jesus was drawing to its close, He made a touching prayer to His Father for the disciples whom He was about to leave: "Holy Father, when I was with them, I kept them in Thy name.... And now I come to Thee.... I pray not that Thou shouldst take them out of the world, but that Thou shouldst keep them from evil": *Cum essem cum eis, ego servabam eos; nunc autem ad te venio; non rogo ut tollas eos de mundo, sed ut serves eos a malo.*

What wholly divine solicitude is revealed in this prayer! Our Lord says it for us all.

Christ in His Mysteries, Part II, chapter 16, section 6

A thought which ought to aid and encourage you is that all that God does for us proceeds from His mercy. *In aeternum misericordia aedificabitur in caelis.* God builds an eternal monument to His mercy in Heaven. The stones of this monument are *the miserable* who draw down mercy by their misery. For mercy is goodness in face of misery. The foundation stone of this monument is Christ Who has espoused all our miseries. *Vere languores nostros ipse tulit et dolores nostros ipse portavit.* He deifies them and gives them an immense merit and value in His Father's sight. If every morning you unite your fatigues, your weariness, your sufferings of every kind with those of Jesus Christ, He *will take them upon Himself* and make them His own. As our Blessed Father St. Benedict says: *Per* PATIENTIAM *passionibus Christi* PARTICIPAMUS. In patiently suffering the sorrows and fatigues of life we share in the Passion of Jesus Christ. Then, His strength, His virtue, reign in us. *Libenter gloriabor in infirmitatibus meis ut inhabitet in me virtus Christi.*

Oh! my dear child, it is a *great grace* to understand this and to fol-

Seeing the Mercy of God in Our Trials

low Jesus in His faintness and weariness. Nothing can draw down divine favours and mercies more than this *patient* union of our sufferings and weaknesses with those of Jesus.

As subject of examen, take the *patient and loving acceptation* of the trials and sufferings of your life. In this way your life will become a continual *crying out* to the Heart of the Heavenly Father.

Union with God, chapter 3, section 2

Jesus living in you is your *All*: *Factus est nobis sapientia a Deo et justitia et sanctificatio et redemptio.* He is your Supplement, so much so that when we act in His name, the Father beholds in us only a member of His Son, and our weaknesses are the weaknesses of His Son. From time to time, as it was for Him in the Garden of Olives, He makes us feel all the weight of our burden and of our weaknesses. Then go ahead perfectly abandoning yourself to Jesus Christ.

Union with God, chapter 4, section 2

There is no heavier cross here below than that state of exhaustion and lassitude produced by the climate and by the life you have to lead. But, believe me, there is nothing that brings about the true divine life within us like *union with the weakness of Jesus*.

In espousing our nature in the Incarnation, He took upon Himself all our weaknesses, all our powerlessness, all our sufferings; He made them His own: *Vere languores nostros ipse tulit et dolores nostros ipse portavit.* At the time of the Incarnation the Word did not assume a glorious body, like that of Tabor, not an impassible body like that of the Resurrection, but *in similitudinem carnis peccati*, a body made in the likeness of sinful flesh, like to ours in all things, save personal sin. In taking our sins, He uplifted and rendered our weaknesses *divine*, and thenceforth they cry out in us to the Father, like those of Jesus Christ Himself.

It is by *pure* faith, by love without any feeling that this is brought about; and, in place of our weaknesses, we receive *the strength of Christ in an immense degree*.

I want so much to teach you this great truth and to help you to put it into practice. To do so, you must give yourself up unconditionally to Jesus Christ by accepting in *pure faith* all that He sends or permits. Know, my daughter, that in a soul like yours, which has left all for Him, which in reality seeks only Him, there is an *unconscious* prayer, unfelt but very real, which rises up to God in the midst of your sense of failure, for our desires are true prayers for Him "Who searcheth the reins and hearts." *Desiderium pauperum exaudivit auris tua.* But, for this, the great virtue for you must be *patience*. *Patientia vobis* NECESSARIA *est.* It is by patience, the absence of any, even inward, murmuring, by meeting every trouble with a smile, that Jesus makes you share in His Passion.

Christ divinises our sufferings and gives them an immense merit and value in His Father's sight. If every morning you unite your fatigues, your weariness, your sufferings of every kind with those of Jesus, He *will take them upon Himself* and make them His own.

Union with God, chapter 3, section 2

For the moment, I will only give you two or three principles which should be the tenor of *your* spiritual life:

1.—God does all things for the glory of His Son Jesus. Now, Jesus is specially glorified by those who, convinced of their extreme incapacity, lean upon Him, and look to Him for light, help, everything.

2.—You should try to realise more vividly that, being a member of Jesus by your baptism and more and more by each Communion, your needs, your infirmities, your faults are, in a true sense, the needs, the infirmities, the faults of Jesus. *Vere languores nostros ipse tulit et dolores nostros ipse portavit. Posuit in eo Dominus iniquitatem omnium nostrum. Factus est pro nobis peccatum.*

3.—When you feel your weakness and misery, present yourself fearlessly before the eyes of your Heavenly Father in the name and in the Person of His Divine Son. *Libenter gloriabor in infirmitatibus meis ut inhabitet in me virtus Christi.*

Seeing the Mercy of God in Our Trials

You are rich in infirmities and were you to lean on Christ alone, doing all, suffering all in His name, united with Him, He would render you more and more agreeable to His Father. He would bring you with Him into that sanctuary which He calls *Sinus Patris*, His Father's bosom, and there, under God's eye, you would constantly try to please Him by doing what you feel is *most* pleasing to Him. Those alone dwell in God's bosom who have an immense confidence in His fatherly goodness and mercy which are infinite, and who try their best to please Him in all things.

Now there is your programme for the present.... I feel Our Lord has given you to me as my child whom I am to present to Him as one of the triumphs of His mercy, for St. Paul says, "He hath chosen the weak, and the feeble and the things of nothing that no flesh might glory in His sight."

I have been thinking about your soul. Despite your very real defects and misery which are doubtless much greater than what we see, God loves you dearly, and wishes to substitute His greatness to your littleness; His generosity to your meanness; His truth and wisdom to your insufficiency. He can do all that if you only let Him. *Confiteor tibi, Pater, Domine caeli et terrae, quia abscondisti haec a sapientibus et revelasti ea* PARVULIS. You are one of these very little people whom God deigns to look upon.

Try to look much more at God than at yourself; to *glory* in your miseries; to love virtue more than you fear vice; to glorify the *infinite* merits and virtues of Jesus by drawing from them lovingly to supply your need.

Now, my child, there's a programme for a whole year, yea, for a life.

Your last letter almost pained me, for I see that you allow the sight of your miseries—which are very *limited*—to hide the riches which are yours in Jesus Christ, and these are *infinite*. It is a great grace to see our miseries and littleness, which, in reality, are much more extensive than we imagine. But this knowledge is a real poison unless completed by *immense* faith and confidence in the "all-sufficiency" of our dear Lord's merits, riches, and virtues which are all ours. *Vos estis corpus Christi et membra de membro.* You are His body and the very members of His members. The members really possess as *their own* all the dignity and merit of the person whose members they are. And this is what glorifies Jesus, namely, to have such a high appreciation of His merits and such a great conviction of *His love in giving them to us* (*Et nos credidimus caritati Dei*) that our misery and unworthiness do not discourage us.

There are two categories of people who give little glory to Jesus Christ:

1.—Those who neither see their misery nor realize their unworthiness, and consequently *don't feel their need of Jesus Christ*;

2.—Those who see their misery, but have not that strong faith in the divinity of Jesus Christ which makes them, as it were, happy to be thus weak in order that Jesus may be gloried in them. How far you are from glorying in your infirmities!

Strive to have a *very pure intention* in all that you do. Unite your intentions to those of your Divine Spouse and do not trouble about the result. God does not give a premium to success.

Despite our miseries, or rather because of our miseries, we ought to lean fearlessly upon Him. *Libenter gloriabor in infirmitatibus meis.* I see more and more that when we come before the Heavenly Father as the members of His beloved Son—*vos estis corpus Christi et membra de membro*—the sight of our miseries does but draw down His look of mercy. *Abyssus abyssum invocat.* The abyss of our miseries calls upon the abyss of His mercy.

Union with God, chapter 4, section 2

Even upon the Cross, whilst all the inferior powers of the soul of Jesus were submerged in a sea of sorrow and darkness, this fine point (of His spirit) ever beheld the face of the Father.

I will ask for you that in the midst of your trials the fine point of your soul may remain always attached to the face (i.e., good pleasure) of the Heavenly Father. Do not be astonished at your weaknesses. It is in weakness that virtue is perfected. The more you feel

Seeing the Mercy of God in Our Trials

your incapacity, your weakness, the more you lean upon *Him*—the more your virtue is supernatural and pleasing to God.

Abbot Columba Marmion, chapter 16

Before going to Him, the soul must *see* and *feel* and *know* that all comes to her from Him, and that it is our misery, poverty, and imperfection which, having been *assumed* by His sacred humanity, are raised to a divine value in Him. This is a great secret which few understand. St. Paul expresses it in these words: "Willingly do I glory in my infirmities, in order that it be Christ's virtue and strength which dwells in me. This is why I take pleasure in my infirmities."

Abbot Columba Marmion, chapter 19

I have suffered much during my stay in.... The trials that our Lord has sent me are beyond counting. The conviction I have drawn from them is that God wills to be glorified by the union of our weakness with the infinite strength of Christ. Christ is the *Virtus Dei*; but He has deigned to take upon Himself our human weakness, and the whole earthly life of Jesus is the revelation of this weakness. This union of human weakness with the divine strength gives glory to God. Hence St. Paul's great cry, *Libenter gloriabor in infirmitatibus meis ut inhabitet in me virtus Christi*: "Gladly therefore will I glory in my infirmities, that the power of Christ may dwell in me." This thought has always followed and sustained me in all contrarieties and difficulties, but now it is so engraven in my soul that it, as it were, makes part of myself. I am convinced that I am nothing and can do nothing, but that, on the other hand, I must have unbounded confidence in the strength of Christ, and that in Him I can do all things.

Abbot Columba Marmion, chapter 9

The whole history of Jesus is the triumph of the *virtus Verbi* supporting the weakness of His humanity.

Jesus is ever before God's face, *facies*, and hidden in Him. His prayer as He gazes in His Father's face becomes ours. I understand so well St. Paul's *libenter gloriabor in infirmitatibus meis* UT *inhabitet in me virtus Christi.*

The poorer we are, the more Christ's ineffable riches find their place in us. Our misery, known and avowed, draws down His liberality.

Union with God, chapter 4, section 2

Sickness

You must not be surprised if in your present state of languor you do not always feel that fervour and ardour in your prayers that you would like to have. The poor soul depends so much on the body that when the latter is suffering or languishing it cannot do much. Even the great Saint Teresa, despite her ardour and generosity, bitterly complained that her physical weakness hindered her soul from rising to God in prayer. When we bear this state patiently we are much more pleasing to God and nearer His Heart than when we are full of fervour and consolation, for then we have the merit of sacrifice and we prove that our love is pure and disinterested.

I was very grieved on hearing you were so weak and suffering, or as you yourself say, so like a little flower drooping upon its stalk. I beg our Lord daily to give you the courage to suffer, to bear this painful state, for His love and in union with His faintness and weariness and sufferings during His Passion. Yes, indeed, my child, to suffer with Jesus is true happiness, if we could only understand this—for one who suffers is so near His Sacred Heart! But you must often lovingly unite yourself with Him and accept *with Him* and *for Him* all that the Good God wills to lay upon you.

Your good letter was a real joy to me, because I saw that you had the true happiness which can be had here below: surrendering to the divine will and finding one's joy in the performance of one's everyday duties. Yes, life is serious, because it reaches even into eternity; and very sad is the spectacle of those who seem to live only for pleasure.

Seeing the Mercy of God in Our Trials

There is no unalloyed joy here below. If your health sometimes tries you, it is because God does not want you to become too attached to this world, since our true home is in heaven with our Heavenly Father.

Union with God, chapter 3, section 2

I do not like to leave you without a word, especially as you are suffering. When one gives oneself to God unreservedly and in *all confidence* one falls into the hands of Infinite Wisdom and Love. From that moment, not a hair of our head falls without His knowledge, without His permission. He ordains *everything* to this great end: our union with Him. This is why I can only desire what His Love disposes. We must love in Him, and with Him, and like Him. I pray for you with all my heart that this trial may lead you to perfect union.

I suffer, my dear daughter, with you in what you suffer, but I would not take you down from this cross on which you find your Spouse; He is for you a *Sponsus sanguinis*. Be sure that in prayer I do not leave you, and often every day I place you in His Sacred Heart.

I learnt yesterday that you have been suffering very much. I asked the Sacred Heart of Jesus to take upon Himself your sufferings and to make them His own. He has said: "As long as you did it to one of these My least brethren, you did it to Me." For we are the members of Jesus, and you are a suffering member. The Father looking upon you sees His crucified Son in you. Your *state* is a continual prayer. I am going to ask Jesus to unite as closely *as possible* your weariness and suffering to His.

I feel great compassion for you according to nature, but when I look at you *in God*, in Whom alone I desire to find you, I cannot separate myself from His adorable will for you.

May Christ be your strength. I want you to be weak, so that your weakness, in drawing down His compassion, may fill you with His strength: *Ut inhabitet in me virtus Christi.*

United to Jesus, we enter by right into the *sanctuarium exauditio-*

nis[4] where all petitions are heard. My daughter, when you are weak and suffering, you are like Jesus *in sinu Patris*, but upon the Cross. Jesus on the Cross, in agony, in weakness, forsaken by His Father, was ever *in sinu Patris* and never dearer to the Father, never nearer to the Father. I leave you there: it is the tabernacle of the Carmelite here on earth. In heaven she will sing: *Secundum multitudinem dolorum meorum in corde meo, consolationes tuae laetificaverunt animam meam.*

Since you cannot pray much, I will do so in your place; at Holy Mass, in the Divine Office, I am the mouth of our two hearts to sing the praises of the Blessed Trinity and to plead in your favour.

Take courage! *His qui diligunt Deum,* OMNIA *cooperantur in bonum.*

Abbot Columba Marmion, chapter 11

When I make my Stations daily and contemplate *God* the *Infinite, All-powerful,* crushed by weakness and trembling in Gethsemane, I see that instead of taking on Himself a glorified body, He has assumed a body like unto that of us sinners *in order to render our weakness divine in Him.*

Abbot Columba Marmion, chapter 19

Jesus has made me understand that when He said: *Corpus autem aptasti mihi,* His Father had not given Him a glorious body or one exempt from weakness. He had, says Saint John Damascene, all the infirmities that were not unworthy of His Divine Person: *Vere languores nostros ipse tulit.* This is why He asks us to share them. He *assumes* them, *divinises* them, and they become the fount of that *virtus Christi* of which Saint Paul speaks.

It is an excellent thing to accept uncomplainingly from our Lord's

---

4. "The sanctuary where requests are granted" and which is "the bosom of the Father." Though the term itself is not found in Scripture, the idea—so dear to Dom Marmion—is borrowed from St. Paul's Epistle to the Hebrews: 5:6–7; 6:19–20; 7:25; and 9:11–12.

hands the body we have received with its weaknesses, its heaviness, its sufferings, and to say as Christ did: *Corpus autem aptasti mihi*: "O Father, I will to have this body such as You have willed it for me, with all the trouble it may bring me."

Abbot Columba Marmion, chapter 17

To endure your sufferings, your state of languor, peacefully and gently, in union with the sufferings of Jesus, is *to do* much.

Union with God, chapter 3, section 2

Temptation

Why Does God Permit Temptations and Trials?

We come across people who imagine that the interior life is but a pleasant, easy ascent, along a flower-bordered path.

You know it is not generally so, although God, the Sovereign Master of His gifts, can lead us by such a path if He pleases. Long ago God said in Holy Writ: "Son, when thou comest to the service of God"—and it is for that we have come to the monastery, which is a school where we learn how to serve the Lord: *Schola dominici servitii*—"prepare thy soul for temptation": *Fili, accedens ad servitutem Dei, praepara animam tuam ad tentationem.* In fact, it is impossible under the conditions of our present humanity, to find God fully without being beset by temptation. And the devil is most often infuriated against those who seek God sincerely and in whom he sees the most living image of Christ Jesus.

But is not temptation a danger for the soul? Would it not be highly preferable not to be tempted? We are spontaneously inclined to envy those who we may imagine are never tried by temptation. "Happy the man," we would willingly say, "who has not to undergo its assaults."

That is what our human wisdom might suggest, but God, Who is the infallible Truth, the source of our holiness and beatitude, says quite the contrary: "Blessed is the man that endureth temptation": Beatus vir *qui suffert tentationem.…* Why does the Holy Spirit proclaim this man "blessed" when we should have been inclined to think quite otherwise? Why does the Angel say to Tobias: "*Because thou* wast acceptable to God, it was *necessary* that temptation should prove thee": QUIA *acceptus eras Deo,* NECESSE FUIT *ut tentatio probaret te?* Is it for the sake of the temptation itself? Evidently not, because God uses it in order to obtain a proof of our fidelity, which, upheld by grace, is strengthened and manifested in the conflict and wins at last a crown of life. *Cum probatus fuerit, accipiet coronam vitae.*

Temptation patiently borne is a source of merit for the soul and is glorious for God. By its constancy in trial, the soul is the living testimony of the might of grace: "My grace is sufficient for thee: for power is made perfect in infirmity": *Sufficit tibi gratia mea, nam virtus in infirmitate perficitur.* God awaits this homage and glory from us.

Look at the holy man Job. Scripture lends God a kind of pride in the perfection of this great just man. One day—the sacred writer has dramatised the scene—when Satan stands before Him, God says to him: "Whence comest thou?" And Satan replies: "I have gone round about the earth, and walked through it." The Lord says again: "Hast thou considered My servant Job, that there is none like him in the earth, a man simple and upright, and fearing God, and avoiding evil?" Satan sneers and asks what merit Job has in showing himself perfect when all prospers with him and smiles upon him. "But," he adds, "put forth Thy hand, and touch his bone and his flesh and then Thou shalt see that he will bless (or rather curse) Thee to Thy face." God gives Satan leave to strike His servant in his possessions, in his family, even in his person. And now see Job, despoiled little by little of all his goods, covered with ulcers, seated upon his dunghill, and obliged over and above this to undergo the sarcasms of his wife and friends who would excite him to blaspheme. But he remains unshaken in his fidelity to God. No feeling of revolt rises from his heart, not a murmur passes his lips, only words of wonderful submission: "The Lord gave and the Lord hath taken away ... blessed be the name of the Lord! ... If we have received good things at the hand of God, why should we not receive evil?" What heroic constancy! And what glory is given to God by this man who, overwhelmed with such woes, blesses the divine hand! And we know how God, after having tried him, renders testimony to him, and restores all his possessions while multiplying them. Temptation had served to show the extent of Job's fidelity.

In many a soul, temptation does another work which nothing else could do. Souls there are, upright but proud, who cannot attain divine union unless they are first humbled down to the ground. They have, as it were, to fathom the abyss of their frailty, and learn by experience how absolutely dependent they are on God, so that they may no longer trust in themselves. It is by temptation alone that they can measure their powerlessness. When these souls are buffeted by temptation, and feel themselves at the edge of the abyss, they realise the necessity of humbling themselves. At that moment a great cry escapes them and rises up to God. And then comes the hour of grace. Temptation keeps them in a state of vigilance over their weaknesses, and in a constant spirit of dependence upon God. For them, temptation is the best school of humility.

Trial profits others by preserving them from lukewarmness. Without temptation, they would fall into spiritual sloth. Temptation is for them a stimulus, for, in combating it, love is quickened while fidelity finds an opportunity of manifesting itself. Look at the Apostles in the Garden of Olives. In spite of the warning given them by their Divine Master to watch and pray, they sleep; all unconscious of danger, they let themselves be surprised by the enemies of Jesus, they take to flight, forsaking their Master, despite all their previous protestations. How different was their conduct from what it had been when they were struggling against the tempest on the lake. Then in face of the imminent peril of which they are fully aware, they awake Jesus from His sleep with cries of distress: "Lord, save us, we perish": *Domine, salva nos, perimus!*

Again, temptation gives us the great formation of experience. This is a precious fruit because we become skilled in helping souls when they come to us seeking light and help. How can anyone instruct or effectually help another who is tempted, if he himself does not know what temptation is? St. Paul says of Jesus Christ that He willed to be tempted as we are, though without sin, that He might have compassion on our infirmities: *Tentatum per omnia absque peccato; in eo enim in quo passus est ipse et tentatus, potens est et eis qui tentantur, auxiliari.*

Let us then not be afraid of the fact of temptation, nor of its frequency or violence. It is only a trial; God never permits it save in view of our greater good. However much it besets us, it is not a sin, provided that we do not expose ourselves wilfully to its attacks and never *consent* to it. We may *feel* its sting or its seductions; but as long as that fine point of the soul which is the will remains steadfast against it, we ought to be tranquil. Christ Jesus is with us, in us; and who is stronger than He?

Christ, the Ideal of the Monk, Part II, chapter 8, section 4

Relying on Christ in Temptation

For us, the acceptation of trial and resistance to temptation go on through our whole life here below. Daily we have to struggle against corrupting seductions, and to be patient in the contradictions willed or permitted by Providence: *Militia est vita hominis super terram.*

The first man was subjected to trial. He faltered, he fell away, he preferred the creature and his own satisfaction to God. He drew all his race into his rebellion, his fall, and his chastisement.

That is why it was necessary that the second Adam, Who represented all the predestined, should act in a directly contrary manner. In His adorable wisdom, God the Father willed that Christ Jesus, our Head and our Model, should be placed in the face of temptation, and, by His free choice, come forth victorious in order to teach us to do the same.

If the Christ, the Incarnate Word, the Son of God, willed to enter into combat with the evil spirit, shall we be astonished if the members of His mystical body must follow the same path?

Christ, our Model in all things, was tempted before us, and not only tempted, but touched by the spirit of darkness; He permitted the devil to lay a hand upon His most holy humanity.

Seeing the Mercy of God in Our Trials

Above all, do not let us forget that it was not only as the Son of God that Jesus overcame the devil, but likewise as Head of the Church; in Him and by Him, we have triumphed and we triumph still over the suggestions of the rebel spirit.

This is in fact the grace that the Saviour won for us by this mystery; herein is to be found the source of our confidence in trials and temptations.

Christ in His Mysteries, Part II, chapter 10, sections 3 and 4

Moreover, St. Paul tells us, "God will not suffer you to be tempted above that which you are able; but will make also with temptation issue, that you may be able to bear it." The great Apostle is himself an example of this. He tells us that lest he should exalt himself on account of his revelations, God placed what he called a thorn in his flesh, a figure of temptation; "there was given me... an angel of Satan, to buffet me." "Thrice," he says, "I besought the Lord, that it might depart from me. And He said to me: My grace is sufficient for thee: for power is made perfect in infirmity"—that is to say, in making it triumph by God's grace.

It is indeed divine grace that helps us to surmount temptation, but we have to ask for it: *Et orate.* In the prayer Christ taught us, He makes us beseech our Father in heaven "lead us not into temptation, but deliver us from evil." Since Jesus has willed to place this prayer upon our lips, let us often repeat it whilst relying on the merits of our Saviour's Passion.

Nothing is more efficacious against temptation than the remembrance of the Cross of Jesus. What did Christ come to do here below if not to "destroy the works of the devil"? And how has He destroyed them, how has He "cast out" the devil, as He Himself says, if not by His death upon the Cross? During His mortal life, our Lord cast out devils from the bodies of the possessed; He cast them out also from souls, when He forgave the sins of Magdalen, of the paralytic man and of so many others; but it is above all, as you know, by His blessed Passion that He overthrew the dominion of the devil. At the precise moment when, in bringing about the death of Jesus at the hands of the Jews, the devil hoped to triumph forever, he himself received the death-blow. For Christ's death destroyed sin, and gave as a right to all who are baptised, the grace of dying to sin.

Let us then lean by faith upon the Cross of Christ Jesus: its virtue is not exhausted and, as children of God, our baptism gives us the right to do so. In baptism we were marked with the seal of the Cross, we became members of Christ, enlightened by His light, and partakers of His life and of the salvation He brings to us. Hence, united to Him, whom shall we fear? *Dominus illuminatio mea et salus mea; quem timebo?*

Christ, the Life of the Soul, Part II, chapter 3, section 4

Recourse to Christ Jesus is indeed the most certain means of overcoming temptation; the devil fears Christ and trembles at the Cross. Are we tempted against faith? Let us at once say: "All that Jesus has revealed to us He receives from His Father. Jesus is the only-begotten Son Who from the bosom of the Father has come to manifest to us the divine secrets which He alone can know. He is the Truth. Yes, Lord Jesus, I believe in Thee, but increase my faith!" If we are tempted against hope, let us look at Christ upon the Cross: has He not become the Propitiation for the sins of the whole world? Is He not the holy High Priest Who has entered for us into heaven and ever intercedes with the Father on our behalf? *Semper vivens ad interpellandum* PRO NOBIS. And He has said: "Him that cometh to Me, I will not cast out": *Et eum qui venit ad me non ejiciam foras.* Does want of confidence in God seek to insinuate itself into our heart? But who has loved us more than God, more than Christ: *Dilexit me et tradidit semetipsum pro me?* When the devil whispers thoughts of pride, let us again look on Christ Jesus; He was God and He humbled Himself even to the ignominious death on Calvary. Can the disciple be above the Master? ... When wounded self-love suggests that we should return the injuries done to us, let us again look at Jesus, our Model, during His Passion: He did not turn away His face from them that spat upon and struck Him: *Faciem meam non averti ab increpantibus et conspuentibus in me.* If the world, the devil's accomplice, holds before our eyes the reflection of senseless,

Seeing the Mercy of God in Our Trials

transitory joys, let us take refuge with Christ to Whom Satan promised the kingdoms of the world and the glory of them if He would adore him: "Lord Jesus, it was for Thee that I left all things, that I might follow Thee more closely, Thee alone; never suffer me to be separated from Thee!" *A te nunquam separari permittas.*

Christ, the Ideal of the Monk, Part II, chapter 8, section 5

Temptations Against Faith and Hope

You are passing through one of those terrible trials through which every soul called to close union with Jesus must pass. "Because you were pleasing to God," said the Angel to Tobias, "it was necessary that temptation should try you." My child, we cannot go to God but through union with Jesus. "I am the way—*no one* goeth to the Father but through Me." Now Jesus went to His Father by passing through Gethsemane and Calvary, and every soul united to Him must pass by the same way.

These temptations against faith are a real crucifixion, and yet you really *do* believe, but unconsciously, and that is why your love subsists and seems to go ahead of your faith. The devil is doing his best to cast you into despair, for he sees that you will one day be very closely united with Him Whom he hates, hence he casts darkness and trouble into your soul, and revolt perhaps in your senses, but this is the path by which all interior souls must pass, if they are to reach perfect union. Blessed is the man who suffers temptation, says St. James, for when he has been tried, he will receive the crown of life.

The Holy Ghost says, "Blessed is the man who is tempted," and St. James adds, "Beloved, be filled with great joy when you pass through various temptations."

Those against faith and hope are the most distressing, and a real agony, but *most* salutary. The secret subconscious longing for God is a sure sign of the presence of the Holy Ghost in your soul, it is a vision of God's beauty in the darkness of faith; but just as the beatific vision which the soul of Jesus *always* enjoyed did not diminish His agony, nor prevent His soul being sad even unto death, so with yours. It is your purgatory, and our Lord is holding your soul in those flames until all selfishness and self-seeking are burned out, then you will enter into the ineffable grandeur of God.

The *very nature* of the trial through which you are passing is the terrible uncertainty it leaves in the soul as to her state. She seems to herself to have lost faith and love, for she *feels* nothing. It is pure naked faith. This longing for God is a most powerful and constant prayer, for God reads the inmost thoughts of our hearts, and this thirst for Him is a way to His Father's Heart. "Thy ear hath heard the desire of the poor," and no one is poorer than those who are serving God in the trials of pure faith.

So now courage! You are on the right road and all you require is *great* patience and absolute confidence in our Lord's loving care. You are very dear to Him though you may imagine the contrary. He wants you to see for yourself how really miserable and unworthy you are, and that it is His sheer mercy which thus clasps you to His Heart. During all eternity God will give Himself to you in the full and unremitting blaze of His beauty. Here below His glory requires that He be served *in faith*. Let us try to serve Him in faith, just as if we gazed on Him in vision.

In practice adore God profoundly, then tell Him you accept *all* He has revealed *on His Word alone*, and as the Church speaks in His name you accept her voice and teaching as His. Make these acts through love, even though you feel nothing.

You are passing through a winter, but it is that you may reach a greater union. For the moment remain *united* (with Jesus) by *faith*: *Sponsabo te mihi in fide,* says the Spouse: "I will espouse thee in faith." But faith has its darkness as well as its light, and God is as good when He presents Himself in the darkness of faith as when He appears upon the Tabor of consolation.

Union with God, chapter 4, section 1

Adoring God's Designs in Disconcerting Events

More than ever, amid the painful events of the war, let us seek support in the words of Holy Scripture, in communing alone with God.

Seeing the Mercy of God in Our Trials

Sometimes, when we are living united in this way to Him, He raises our soul above earthly contingencies, and one feels strengthened afresh. Assuredly you cannot be disinterested in the grave events passing beneath your eyes nor be absorbed in a kind of contemplation which would make you forget everything else. No. Look at Christ Jesus. He shed tears over Jerusalem, His native country. And why? Because He foresaw for it evils identical to those now overwhelming us. Stoicism is not piety, it is a pose. As Moses prayed upon the mountain that the victory might be won by the people of Israel contending against the Amalekites, so pray fervently for those who are fighting. Keep united to God and in adoration of the designs of His Providence: Providence has its views and will bring them about. And remember that all our support, all our confidence rests on God: *Hi in curribus et hi in equs; nos autem in nomine Dei nostri invocabimus*: "Let our enemies trust in their chariots and their horses; as for us, we will call upon the name of the Lord our God... may He save the king and hear us in the day that we call upon Him."

Abbot Columba Marmion, chapter 9

Temptations to Discouragement

The only real danger for you at present would be to yield to the temptation to discouragement. Every cloud has a silver lining and after a storm comes a calm. And I am sure that when this trial has done its work in your soul, it will cease and you will enjoy such peace and union with God as you have never known. One of the principal results that God intends for you by sending you this cross is an ABSOLUTE *resignation and submission* to His holy will. Try to place yourself in this disposition and that will hasten the end of the trial.

Union with God, chapter 3, section 2

We are conscious of our infirmities; we know how deep-seated they are, how overwhelming at times. But is that a reason to be discouraged? Quite the contrary. The Lord likes to choose what is weakest: *Infirma mundi elegit Deus*. Why? *Ut non glorietur omnis caro in conspectu ejus*: "So that no being may glory in himself before God."

If our bemoaning of our misery leads to immense trust in God, then our cries are salutary and God listens to them favourably.

But if our sorrow brings us to discouragement, it is rather an injury to God since we forget His goodness; it shows that we have understood nothing of God's ways. We are then like the Jews, who, despite the favours God had always showered on them, "forgot the multitude of His mercies": *Non fuerunt memores multitudinis misericordiae tuae.* May this reproach never be levelled at you!

Mélanges Marmion, pp. 11 and 14

Discouragement cannot penetrate into a soul wholly yielded to God, nor trouble it; it knows something of "the unsearchable riches of Christ": *Investigabiles divitias Christi.* Doubtless, of itself, it can do nothing, nor even have a good thought, but it submits to the order willed by God, the Author of the supernatural life, and it knows that in this order is likewise contained the power the soul has of appropriating to itself the riches of Jesus: "I can do all things in Him Who strengtheneth me": *Omnia possum in eo qui me confortat.* It knows that, with Him, through Him, in Him, it is rich with the very riches of Christ, "so that nothing is wanting to [it] of any grace": *Divites facti estis . . . ita ut nihil vobis desit in ulla gratia.* Its confidence cannot be shaken, because the soul belongs to Him Who is for it the Way, the Light, and the Life; He Who is the Master above all others, the Good Shepherd, the charitable Samaritan, the faithful Friend. Our Lord revealed to a soul that one of the reasons of His bounteous gifts to St. Gertrude was the absolute confidence that this great nun had in His goodness and His treasures.

Christ, the Ideal of the Monk, Part II, chapter 18, section 3

Seeing the Mercy of God in Our Trials

Hardships and Trials
in the Fulfilling of Our Duties of State[5]

It is impossible to go to heaven by any other way than that which Jesus went by, the way of the Cross. You will meet with this Cross daily in one manner or another. The great thing is to accept it *in union with Jesus*. For it is that which gives it all its merit.

This life is not given by God as a Paradise. It is a time of trial followed by an eternity of joy and rest. Christ suffered all His life, for the shadow of the Cross ever hung over Him, and those who love Him share His Cross to some extent all their life long. The contrarieties, the misunderstandings, the sufferings of heart and body, household difficulties, all these things form the portion of your cross, and when you accept these trials they become holy and divine by their union with those of Jesus Christ. The virtue that I want to find in you on our next meeting is above all *patience*. Patience unites us exceedingly with Jesus suffering, as Mary was united with Jesus at the foot of the Cross.

May God bless you for having endured for His love, the pains, the lassitude and cares of motherhood in order to give Him souls to praise Him for all eternity. Mary will bless you because you have shared with her the divine maternity.[6] St. Bede tells us that each time we teach a soul to know and love Jesus, we beget Christ within it. You will thus be mother of your dear children by a twofold claim.

It is quite normal that you should feel forsaken and in a state of dryness and tedium from time to time. All souls that aspire to union with Jesus Christ must pass through that. This sense of incapacity, of weakness, of tedium is needful in order that our pride may not attribute to ourselves what comes to us from God. The sense of almost unconscious peace that you feel in the depth of your heart is a sign of the presence of the Holy Spirit in the depth of your soul.

---

5. So as not to lengthen this section excessively, we limit it to a consideration of the duties of state of people living in the world.
6. These lines were penned with Christmas wishes, hence the allusion to the maternity of the Blessed Virgin Mary.

Jesus is *the Lamb of God* and His immolation consists in this, that He *yielded* Himself up like a gentle lamb to all the sufferings that His Father willed to permit for Him. He did not turn His face away from those who spat upon Him. He did not open His mouth. If we wish to be united to this Divine Lamb, we must yield ourselves up in *bare faith* to God's hand that strikes us, to all the sufferings that His love and wisdom permit. That is the best and highest of immolations. Jesus has known weariness, fear, fatigue. He understands all that.

Union with God, chapter 3, section 2

I have the conviction that a woman like you, a faithful wife and the mother of a numerous family, is very dear to the Heart of Jesus. He is the faithful Friend Who thoroughly knows all your difficulties and Who, in His love, loves to supply for what is wanting in your actions.

We are full of miseries, but we have the signal honour of being members of Christ; that is why our Heavenly Father dotes upon us. Live united to Jesus Christ, and, in Him, yielded up to the Father.

Your soul is in God's hands; He loves it, He looks upon it unceasingly and He makes it pass through the states that, in His wisdom, He sees to be necessary for it. As the ground has to go through the death of winter and the grain of wheat to die before bearing the fruits of harvest, so your soul needs to go through the wine-press of temptation and weakness that Christ may make it bear His virtue and divine life. The more understanding we have of our wetness and of that depth of wickedness that lies in our heart, the more we honour God in believing in the greatness of His goodness and mercy.

I see more and more, my dear daughter, that no virtue is solid if not built upon the foundation of compunction and the *true* knowledge of our misery. According to the divine plan, God must be glorified by the power of His grace. Those who do not *feel*, who do not *see* their misery, do not know the need they have of grace. Therefore St. Paul rejoices in the knowledge of his weakness in order that all his strength may come to him from Christ. "I glory in my infirmities, that the power of Christ may dwell in me." That is why the Good God leads us by this path.

Union with God, chapter 4, section 2

Seeing the Mercy of God in Our Trials

Your kind letter gave me so much pleasure because I see you are seeking God with sincerity. I tell you in all simplicity that I believe God loves you dearly and that the little worries of this life form that portion of the Cross of Jesus which is to unite you to Him. God does not ask a married woman of the world for the austerities and mortifications that may be practised by those living in the cloister. But He sends them other trials adapted to their state and which render them so agreeable to His Divine Majesty.

Our Lord asks of you:

1.—To accept daily the sufferings, the duties, and the joys that He sends you, as Jesus accepted all that came to Him from His Father. When St. Peter wanted to turn Him away from His Passion, on account of his great affection for Him, Jesus answered him, "The chalice *which My Father hath given Me*, shall I not drink it?" There, my daughter, is the answer you ought to give when you seem to be overwhelmed with suffering.

2.—The perfect fulfilment of your duties:

a) *Towards God.*—Prayer, Mass, Holy Communion, not too many prayers, but great fidelity in saying those which it is a duty to offer to God, above all, family prayers.

b) *Towards your neighbour.*—Towards your husband. Marriage, says St. Paul, is the image of Christ's union with the Church, and the Sacrament of marriage gives you a *continual participation* in the union of Jesus and His Church. Jesus so loved His Church that He died for her, and she, in return, loves Him as her God and her Bridegroom. Thus you should love your husband as representing Christ for you.

Towards your children. The grace of motherhood has its origin in the Heart of God and He puts it in the mother's heart in order that she may love and guide her children according to the divine good pleasure.

c) *Towards yourself.*—At present no other mortifications are necessary for you than those which God sends you daily. But you must sanctify them by uniting them to the sufferings of Jesus Christ.

Be joyful and gay, natural and straightforward as you are, and God will bless you.

Union with God, chapter 2, section 5

I am always more and more crushed under the burden of work, but I cannot leave my poor daughter in sadness and anguish. Sadness is bad for the body, for the heart, and for the soul. So come, my daughter, you must take your courage in both hands.

Trials help us find God and show us that the world is a falsehood, a trifling bauble. You must profit by trials and turn ever more towards God; still, since you are called to be the mother of a family living in the world, you must not enfold yourself in black melancholy but begin to face the future. Every morning at Holy Mass I pray that our Lord may give you the grace to realize the ideal of Christian perfection.

Jesus is the Model of all His disciples. Now, Jesus is perfect God and perfect man. So that you may imitate Him, the divine life must reign in you through grace and union with God. Your humanity must become perfect through the practice of all the virtues which adorn human nature. Those virtues are human in their expression, but divine in their root and origin.

My poor child, I feel your sorrows; but I know that hardship often throws us into the arms of the Heavenly Father, Who alone loves us effectively.

I desire you to abandon yourself blindly into the hands of God. He will lead you to Himself by a sure path and He will arrange everything for the best, according to the fidelity of your trust in Him.

With all my heart I pray that Jesus may find in your home the image of His union with His Spouse, the Church. This will draw down upon you His protection and all the graces and favours you need.

I see that our Lord is giving you the light and the courage to consider the sacred work of motherhood from the correct point of view. Your sufferings are the surest pledge of the divine blessing on

Seeing the Mercy of God in Our Trials

the child which you bear, and a plentiful source of merit and sanctification for you.

Your very good letter was a real joy to me, because I saw that you had the true happiness which can be had here below: surrendering to the divine will and finding one's joy in the performance of one's everyday duties. Yes, life is serious, because it reaches even into eternity; and very sad is the spectacle of those who seem to live only for pleasure. I am happy that you have found in ... the companion of your life, your joys, and your sorrows. There is no unalloyed joy here below. If your health sometimes tries you, it is because God does not want you to become too attached to this world, since our true home is in heaven with our Heavenly Father.

I thank God for granting you blessed fertility and the honour of preparing for Him pure hearts to praise Him for all eternity.

I was so very, very happy in your happiness—and now this trial has come. All God's great works are built on the Cross, and thus your life as spouse and mother must begin with the Cross.

Our perfect rest is Paradise. Here below we must stay near Jesus, and upon earth, Jesus presents Himself above all upon the Cross. That is His official portrait. He gives us little joys so that we may be able to endure life and merit our heaven, but He blends a portion of the Cross with them. He will *certainly* give you the grace to manage your affairs if you confide yourself to His love. Don't think too much of the future. Live in the present. The future will bring its own grace when the trial comes.

> Extracts from various letters written
> over a period of time to the same person.

Humiliations

Christ Jesus wants us to learn of Him especially that He is "meek and humble of Heart." In Him there was no moral shortcoming or imperfection which could serve as a reason for His abasement. Quite the contrary! His humanity is the humanity of a God: *Non rapinam arbitratus est esse se aequalem Deo*—"He did not think it robbery to be equal to God." In that humanity are amassed "all the treasures of wisdom and knowledge" because "the Divinity dwells corporeally" therein. Its perfection is admirable: not only could no one convict our Lord of sin, but He always accomplished what was pleasing to the Father. What perfection will ever come near that? No moral weakness whatever taints this holy and immaculate High Priest elevated in holiness above the heavens.

But that humanity was created, and, as a creature, it annihilated itself before God with infinite reverence. In order to acknowledge the sovereign rights of His Father, Jesus offered Himself to Him in perfect submission which went even unto death: *Exinanivit semetipsum factus obediens usque ad mortem*—"He emptied Himself, becoming obedient even unto death, unto the death of the Cross." For us He suffered every humiliation: the Jews said He was possessed by the devil; they accused Him of working His miracles by obeying the inspiration of Beelzebub, the prince of darkness; they tried to stone Him. Then came the hour of the Passion. He Who is the Eternal One, the Son of God, the Almighty, Infinite Wisdom, He was "filled"—or, to use Bossuet's expressive term, "intoxicated"—with opprobrium; *saturabitur opprobriis*. Handcuffed like a malefactor, He was besieged with false witnesses, struck by a servant during a court session, and covered with spittle. Led before Herod, He was covered with a robe that called down insult upon Him; surrounded by a crude and brutal soldiery, He stood before a man who felt for Him nothing but "scorn," *sprevit illum*. Who would ever have thought of such humiliations? The God Who, by His wisdom and power, governs heaven and earth treated like a fool, like a play king being made fun of.... Suppose the least of these humiliations had been levelled at us, what would we say? Would we have the nobility of soul necessary to "embrace patience and keep silence"? In writing those words, Saint Benedict surely had in mind the example of Christ laden with insults during His Passion: *Jesus autem tacebat*. Exteriorly Christ kept silence; but in His Heart He repeated the prophetic verses which the Psalmist had sung of Him: "But I am a worm and no man: the reproach of men and the outcast of the people"—*Ego autem sum vermis et non homo, opprobrium hominum et abjectio plebis*.

Seeing the Mercy of God in Our Trials

Why suffer all these humiliations? Why descend to such depths? To expiate our pride and our self-love. To show us what our humility should be. "Christ did not say: 'Learn humility from the Apostles or from the Angels.' No; he said: 'Learn it from Me. My majesty is exalted enough for My humility to be abysmal.'"

I have been praying from the bottom of my heart that God and His Holy Spirit might give you light and strength to find in the trial which He has sent you, not bitterness, but a holy joy in union with that of Jesus in His Passion. It is certain that our Heavenly Father loves us so much that not a hair falls from our head without His permission. I am convinced that He knew and willed everything that has happened to you, even in its minutest details.... I earnestly desire that you should unite yourself to Jesus in His acceptance of the humiliations which He endured for us—"He was filled with opprobrium": *saturabitur opprobriis*. You will not be *entirely His* and you will not be able to taste His peace and His joy until you have embraced not only His Cross but also His humiliations. He reached the very bottom of the abyss and He felt the humiliation more than any mortal ever could feel it (He was so noble, so true!), but He welcomed suffering and loved it, because such was His Father's will. That is what I desire of you—what *He* desires of you. May God bless and love you.

Mélanges Marmion, pp. 111–112

The hour of sacrifice has struck. You already feel that it is not a small thing to aspire to the dignity of being the bride of the Crucified. Already He is associating you with His sufferings and ignominies. Herod treated Him, Eternal Wisdom, as a fool; Pilate treated Him as a seducer, the people preferred Barabbas to Him. And you, who aspire to very close union with Him, are beginning to be scorned and misunderstood by this world which would have surrounded you with adulation if you had chosen to smile upon it. Take courage, my child, these are certain signs that our Lord wishes to unite you very closely to Himself and to associate you with the works which He does for His Father's glory. What if people do treat you as selfish or ungrateful—let it suffice that Jesus sees your heart. As for you, my child, God leaves you your little miseries. You have need of them:

> 1.—To keep you in that abasement where you often find yourself and where the Good God will always seek you;

> 2.—That you may glorify Jesus acting in you and that you may not attribute to yourself the little good you might think you do of yourself.

For what regards your weaknesses, your failings, the Good God permits them in order to keep you in humility and in the sense of your nothingness. God can always draw good from our miseries, and when you have been unfaithful and have failed in confidence and abandon to His holy will, if you humble yourself deeply, you will lose nothing but, on the contrary, you will advance in virtue and in the love of God. If everything happened to you just as you could wish, if you were always in robust health, if all your exercises of devotion were performed to your satisfaction, if you had no doubts or uncertainties for the future, etc., with your character you would quickly become full of self-sufficiency and secret pride; and instead of exciting the bounty of the Father of Mercies and of drawing down His compassion on His poor weak creature, you would be an abomination in God's eyes. *Abominatio Domino est omnis arrogans.* "Every proud man is an abomination to the Lord." You must therefore set to work. Our Lord loves you, He sees into the depths of your soul, even into recesses hidden from yourself, and He knows what you need; leave Him act, and don't try to make our Lord follow your way of seeing things, but follow His in all simplicity.

Uncertainty, anguish, disgust are very bitter remedies necessary to the health of your soul. There is only one road that leads to Jesus, namely, that of Calvary; and whosoever will not follow Jesus upon this road must give up the thought of divine union. "If any man will come after Me, let him deny himself, and take up his cross, and follow Me."

Take courage! I have as much need myself of these considerations as you have, for nature does not like sacrifice, but the reward of sacrifice, namely, the love of God, is so great, that we ought to be ready to bear yet more in order to attain to it.

Union with God, chapter 3, section 2

Interior Sufferings

When God wills to lead a soul to the heights of perfection and contemplation, He makes her pass through great trials. Our Lord has said that when a branch united to Him, Who is the Vine, bears fruit, His Father purges it: *Purgabit eum.* And why? "That it may bring forth more fruit": *Ut fructum plus afferat.* Spiritual darkness falls upon the soul. She feels forsaken by God Who thus tries her in order to make her worthy of a closer and higher union with Himself.

Christ in His Mysteries, Part II, chapter 9, section 3

If I did not know that your soul is in the hands of Jesus Christ, and that *nothing* can befall you without having passed through His Sacred Heart I should be in anguish after having received your card. For our souls are so much one in Christ that your sufferings are mine, and I know *by experience* what cruel suffering is that through which you are passing. Saint Teresa had similar trials and so had Sister Mary of the Incarnation and many others. I have the conviction that it is a part of that crucifixion through which our Lord wills that you should pass.

It is by successive detachments that He ends by becoming *our All,* and at times this separation from all human solace is almost like death. I have gone through it, and know that poor human weakness could not bear it, were it to last; but little by little God becomes our *All,* and in Him we find again what we seem to have lost.

I have been praying much for you, first because I believe God has given you to me to cultivate and prepare for perfect union with Him, and then again because I *feel* how you are suffering. Such trials are often for souls like yours *le point de départ* of a very perfect life. For souls like yours God wants to be *all, Deus meus et omnia,* but as long as they could lean on any human aid, how legitimate and holy soever it might be, He could not be their *all*. This is the perfection of the virtue of poverty, it is perfect hope, to have lost all created joy, and to lean on God alone.

Abbot Columba Marmion, chapter 11

You have given yourself entirely to our Lord and He has taken you at your word. It is not a small thing to give oneself unconditionally to our Lord. He sees right down to the bottom of our heart. He sees within miseries, weaknesses, the possibility of falls which you do not suspect, and in His infinite mercy and wisdom, He makes you follow a treatment which produces great results in your soul, although it be bitter to the taste. You must never look back, but abandon yourself absolutely into God's hands. It is impossible to arrive at intimate union with our Lord without passing through these interior trials. So don't be discouraged in feeling such a great repugnance to suffering. Our Lord Himself felt this same repugnance, and the Holy Spirit inspired the Evangelists to describe to us at length this terrible agony of our Lord in the Garden of Olives, so that those who are sorely tried may be consoled by the sight of their God overwhelmed with sorrow and weariness. This is why St. Paul tells us, "We have a High Priest Who cannot have compassion on our infirmities: but one tempted in all things like as we are, without sin."

So have good courage! I tell you in the name of God that you are in the right path, and that in suffering with patience and love, you are glorifying our Lord and doing His holy will at present.

Union with God, chapter 3, section 2

I do feel intense pity for you and pray for you with *all my heart*, as I know what you are going through. No, dear, it is not pride—of course there is pride in us all—but that is not the reason of the awful isolation and *want* and hunger for God's love; no, it is God's doing. He is purging your soul in order to prepare it for union with His Divine Son. "If anyone bear fruit, My Father will purge him—

Seeing the Mercy of God in Our Trials

that he may bear more fruit." Now I want you to have confidence in me and believe my word. It is not our perfection which is to dazzle God, Who is surrounded by myriads of angels; no, it is our misery and wretchedness which draw down His mercy. All God's dealings with us are a consequence of His mercy (mercy is Goodness touched by the sight of misery), and that is why the great St. Paul says, Let others go to God leaning on the perfection of their life (as the Pharisee), "for me, I take glory in my infirmities that my strength may be His virtue." If you could once understand that you are never dearer to God, never glorify Him more than when, in the full realization of your misery and unworthiness, you gaze at His *infinite* goodness and cast yourself on His bosom, believing in faith that His mercy is *infinitely greater* than your *misery*. St. Paul tells us that God has done all in *laudem et gloriam gratiae suae*, "for the praise and glory of His grace." Now the triumph of His grace is when it raises up the miserable and impure and renders them worthy of divine union. See Mary Magdalen. She was a *sinner by profession*, she had seven devils in her whom Jesus expelled, and yet He not only allowed her to touch His divine feet, but it was to her He appeared first on Easter morning. He is a Spouse infinitely rich and powerful, and when He chooses a poor little child like you to be His bride His joy is to enrich her poverty, and clothe her with His own beauty. You are now passing through a period of trial, but Jesus loves you *dearly*. He is so happy to see you *want* to be loved by Him. That is not self-love, it is wishing for what God wants you to wish. If I could only get that into your head, and keep your eyes fixed on Him—on His goodness—and not on your little self. Seek the Lord, seek His face continually.

You are just going through what all souls called to close union with the Crucified must suffer. God sometimes allows sufferings of all sorts—bad health, weariness, temptation, difficulties, etc., to swoop down at once on the soul to purify her. She must *feel* her utter *dependence* on Him. Souls united as yours is with our Lord, whose whole life comes from Him, suffer more than others when He leaves them. This winter is only to prepare for a more fruitful summer. All you can do is to bow your head and accept the trial, and bear with the Lord till He come back. Jesus gives us the example. In the Garden of Olives it is said: "He began to fear, and to be weary, to be heavy and sad." I pray for you with all my heart.

Union with God, chapter 4, section 2

I pity you with all my heart in your interior trial. I know what it is by experience. It is *very painful.* Sometimes God leads us to the edge of the precipice; it seems to us we are on the point of uttering hateful blasphemies. It is the devil working on the *surface* of the soul. Jesus Himself was given over to the devil's fury. *Haec est hora vestra et* POTESTAS TENEBRARUM. From that moment the heart and soul of Jesus were the object of hell's terrible attacks. *Vere languores nostros ipse tulit.* Nothing purifies the soul like this inmost trial. It prepares for divine union. Then the *virtus Christi* becomes the soul's only strength.

On reading your letter, I saw that your soul is passing through the fire of *love in darkness.* St. Francis de Sales paints your state perfectly, while describing his own during the last years of his life. A prince had a musician who was most devoted to him. His joy was to rejoice the heart of his prince by his beauteous singing and the sweet harmony of his music. However at the same time, he himself took a vast pleasure in listening to his melodies. At last he became absolutely deaf. He could no longer find any pleasure *for himself* in his music and chant, but he continued to play and to sing with *all his heart* just to give pleasure to his beloved prince.

This is your case. I know your heart, and I know that you love God dearly, but just as Jesus on the Cross, He alone must see and feel the fragrance of that love. You must be immolated in the darkness of this Calvary. Take this as *certain.*

I know you are to such a degree in God's arms that I can wish nothing better for you than the perfect accomplishment of His holy will in you. I pray much for you, but solely that you may lend yourself without reserve to God's action.

Your soul is very dear to God, but He wants a more perfect *abandon*

Seeing the Mercy of God in Our Trials

into His hands, and allows you to feel all your impotency, as long as you fail to look for all things from Him.

Your present state is due in part to physical weakness and in part it is a trial; when it is past, you will find that you had been getting nearer God, though it seemed you were drifting from Him.

The sign that your present state is not due principally to your infidelities—though of course it is likely they are not wholly foreign to it—is that you feel deep down in your soul a great want of God, which is a real torment, as you seem so hopelessly estranged from Him. It is He Who gives this double and seemingly contradictory sentiment, He wants you to *long* for Him, and at the same time to *see* that of yourself you are quite incapable of finding Him. He will come in the end: *Desiderium pauperum exaudivit Dominus.* You are one of these poor ones just now.

Union with God, chapter 4, section 3

God wants of you great poverty and *nudity* of spirit, it is the spirit of Carmel. Jesus stripped of *everything*, separated from everything, lifted upon the Cross and living and dying for His Father, there is your model. The more God unites you to Him, the more your whole life will be Jesus Christ—the greater too will be your poverty and your suffering at the moments when God withdraws Himself.

The soul immolated to God in the nudity of pure faith, of hope and perfect union does more for the Church in an hour than others (more mediocre and less generous) do in their whole life.

Union with God, chapter 4, section 1

Ask for nothing, refuse nothing, desire nothing except what God desires for you, that is to say, your perfection. All the rest is not *He Himself*. One thing is necessary: It is He.

Place *all* your consolation in God, not in the sense that you should reject all other joy, but that no human consolation should be *necessary* for your peace.

Union with God, chapter 3, section 2

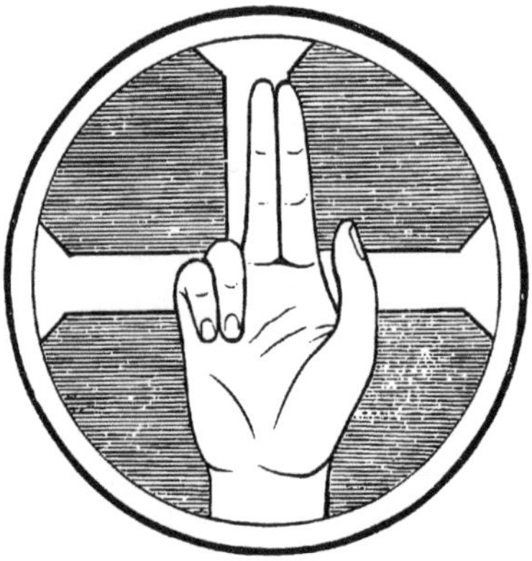

PART IV

The Fecundity of Suffering
Accepted in a Christian Spirit

How Suffering Leads to Life

Christianity is a Doctrine of Life

IN CHRISTIANITY, death is the prelude of life. Our Lord Himself says that the grain of wheat must first die in the ground before it can germinate and bring forth the fruit of the harvest which the householder will gather into his barns. This life will become so much the more fruitful, grace will so much the more abound, in proportion as abnegation has reduced, weakened and diminished the obstacles opposed to its free growth. For, always remember this important truth, holiness is for us of an essentially supernatural order, and God is its source; the more our souls, by means of mortification, free themselves from sin and are detached from self and creatures, the more the divine action is powerful within us. Christ tells us so; He even tells us that His Father makes use of suffering to render the life of the soul more fruitful: "I am the Vine, and My Father is the Husbandman; you are the branches. Every branch that beareth fruit, My Father will purge that it may bring forth more fruit. In this is My Father glorified, that you bring forth very much fruit." *Omnem palmitem qui fert fructum purgabit eum* UT *fructum plus afferat. In hoc clarificatus est Pater meus* UT *fructum plurimum afferatis.* When the Eternal Father sees that a soul, already united to His Son by grace, resolutely desires to give herself fully to Christ, He wills to make life abound in her and to increase her capacity for receiving it. To do this, He Himself enters into this work of renunciation and detachment, because that is the preliminary condition of our fruitfulness. He prunes away all that could prevent the life of Christ from producing its full effects; all that is an obstacle to the divine sap. Our corrupt nature contains roots that tend to produce evil fruits; by the repeated and deep sufferings He permits or sends, by humiliations and contradictions, God purifies us, digs and ploughs up the ground of our souls, as it were, detaches us from creatures, and empties us of self that we may produce numerous fruits of life and holiness: *Purgabit eum ut fructum plus afferat.*

Christ, the Life of the Soul, Part II, chapter 4, section 6

Let us no longer be discouraged by trials and disappointments. They will be so much the greater and deeper according as God calls us higher. Wherefore this law?

Because it is the way by which Jesus passed; and the more we wish to remain united to Him, the more we ought to resemble Him in the deepest and innermost of His mysteries. St. Paul, as you know, sums up all the inner life in the practical knowledge of Jesus, "Jesus Crucified." And our Lord Himself tells us that the Father, Who is the Divine Husbandman, purges the branch so that it may bear more fruit: *Purgabit eum ut fructum plus afferat.* God has a powerful hand, and His purifying operations reach depths that only the saints know; by the temptations that He permits, by the adversities that He sends, by the desolations and terrible loneliness that He sometimes produces in the soul, He tries it so as to detach it from all that is created; He digs deeply into it so as to empty it of itself. He pursues it, He "persecutes it in order to possess it"; He penetrates it to the marrow, He "breaks its bones," as Bossuet somewhere says, "so as to reign alone."

Happy the soul that thus yields itself into the hands of the eternal Husbandman. By His Spirit, all of fire and love, Who is the Finger of God, the Divine Artist engraves in it the features of Christ, so as to make it resemble the Son of His love according to the ineffable design of His wisdom and mercy.

Christ in His Mysteries, Part II, chapter 20, section 5

There are some people who have a great deal of activity; they pray, mortify themselves, and give themselves up to good works; they advance but rather limpingly, because their activity is partly human. There are others whom God has taken in hand, and they advance very quickly, because He Himself acts in them. But before reaching this second state, there is much to suffer, for God must

How Suffering Leads to Life

first make the soul feel that she is nothing and can do nothing; she must needs be able to say in all sincerity: *Ut jumentum factus sum apud te: ad nihilum redactus sum et nescivi.*

My dear child, it is this that the Good God is about to do in you, and you will have much to suffer before arriving at this result; but do not be alarmed if you feel everything is boiling over in you; don't be discouraged if next you feel your incapacity, for God after having as it were annihilated your human activity, your natural energies, will Himself take your soul and bring it to union with Him. When you make the Way of the Cross, unite yourself to the sentiments that our dear Saviour had; it cannot fail to please the Eternal Father, if we offer to Him the image of His Son. At the fourteenth station, we see our Lord's body *exinanitum*, but after three days, He comes forth from the tomb, full of life, of splendid life. It will be the same for us too; if we let God act in us, after He has destroyed all there is that is human and natural in us, we shall be filled with His life; it will then be the realisation of these words, *Christus mihi vita.*

This is what you must arrive at; the Eternal Father wishes to see in you only His Son. Remember St. Paul's words: *Ut inveniar in illo*, that is your way, my child. Your personality is still too strong; keep before the eyes of your soul the ideal that is to be found in Jesus Christ, where all comes from the Word without there being a human personality in Christ. I recommend you to take each of your faculties every morning and lay them down at Christ's feet, that all may come from Him and that you no longer act except out of love for Him.

Union with God, chapter 2, section 4

Beyond the shadow of a doubt, your interior sufferings are a great part of God's very merciful plan for the sanctification of your soul. We have all gone through that *winter*, because "if the grain of wheat falling into the ground *die* not, itself remaineth alone; but if it die, it beareth much fruit." It was *necessary* that your soul be harrowed by suffering and that you realize that the feeling of being totally abandoned by God is the greatest of all sufferings—"My God, My God, why hast Thou forsaken Me?" Without these trials, you would never be anything but a weak creature. Because you were pleasing to God, it was necessary that you be tested by hardship.... After the winter, spring will come, and then summer....

Mélanges Marmion, p. 114

Suffering Purifies and Frees the Soul

In confession, after the priest, Christ's minister, has imposed the necessary satisfaction, and, by absolution, has washed our souls in the divine blood, he repeats these words over us: "May whatever of good thou dost, and evil thou bearest, be to thee for the remission of thy sins, the increase of grace, and the reward of everlasting life." This prayer is not essential to the sacrament, but as it has been ordained by the Church, besides containing teaching that the Church assuredly desires to see us put into practice, it has the value of a sacramental.

By this prayer, the priest gives to our sufferings, to our acts of satisfaction, of expiation, of mortification, of reparation and patience which he thus links and unites with the sacrament, a special efficacy which our faith should not neglect to consider.

"For the remission of thy sins." The Council of Trent teaches on this subject a very consoling truth. It tells us that God is so munificent in His mercy that, not only the works of expiation that the priest imposes on us, or that we ourselves choose, but even all the sufferings inherent to our condition here below, all the temporal adversities which God sends or permits and we patiently support, serve, through Christ's merits, as satisfaction with the Eternal Father. That is why—I cannot too often recommend it to you—it is an excellent and most fruitful practice when we present ourselves to the priest, or rather to Jesus Christ, in order to accuse ourselves of our sins, to accept in expiation all the pains, all the annoyances, all the contradictions which may befall us; and still more, to resolve at this moment on such or such a special act of mortification, however light it may be, which we will accomplish until our next confession.

Fidelity to this practice, which enters so well into the spirit of the Church, is very profitable.

To begin with, it removes the danger of routine. A soul that, by faith, thus plunges itself again into the consideration of the greatness of this sacrament in which the blood of Jesus is applied to us, and with an intention full of love, offers to bear patiently, in union with Christ on the Cross, all that happens that is hard, difficult, painful or disappointing in life, such a soul is impervious to the rust which with many persons accompanies frequent confession.

Secondly, this practice is an act of love extremely pleasing to our Lord because it is a mark of our willingness to share the sufferings of His Passion, the most holy of His mysteries.

Christ, the Life of the Soul, Part II, chapter 4, section 6

Lastly, there are the renunciations that, under the guidance of Providence, we must expect in the course of life, and accept as true disciples of Christ Jesus: there are sickness and suffering; the loss of those dear to us, adversities, the oppositions and contradictions that thwart the realisation of our plans; the failure of our undertakings; our disillusionments; moments of weariness, hours of sadness, the burden of the day that weighed so heavily on St. Paul till, as he says himself, he was weary even of life: *Ut etiam taederet vivere*—all those miseries that detach us from ourselves and creatures by mortifying our nature and making it die in us little by little: *Quotidie morior.*

"I die daily." Those are St. Paul's words; but if he died daily, it was that he might the better live the life of Christ.

Christ, the Life of the Soul, Part II, chapter 4, sections 4 and 5

I feel the greatest compassion for you in the trial that the Good God is sending you at this present moment. It is a martyrdom. However, I am entirely conformed to the holy will of our dear Lord Who sends you this cross from His inmost Sacred Heart. Believe me, and I say this to you on the part of God: this trial has been sent to you by the love of our Lord, and it is to do a work in your soul that nothing else could have done. It will be the destruction of self-love, and when you come forth from this trial you will be a thousand times dearer to the Sacred Heart than before. So although I feel great pity for you, I would not for anything in the world have it otherwise, because I see that Jesus, Who loves you with a love a thousand times greater than that with which you love yourself, permits this trial to befall you. You may be sure that during all this time I shall recommend you to the Good God in my prayers and sacrifices, asking Him to give you the strength to profit greatly by this grace.

You know that God chooses to lead us along the path of perfection by the light of obedience, and often He deprives us of all other light and leads us without letting us understand His ways. During this kind of trial you must keep yourself in complete submission and have an unshaken confidence—despite all that the devil or your reason may suggest to the contrary—that He will know how to draw His glory and your spiritual advantage from it in quite a different way from that which you would have chosen for yourself. I tell you in the name of God that this trial is a *great grace* for you, and I am so convinced of it that as soon as I saw its beginning I knew that it would continue some time; it is most painful, it is the greatest cross that God can lay upon the soul He loves, but as long as you are obedient, there is no danger.

Union with God, chapter 3, section 2

Submission to God in Suffering is a Source of Peace

When we thus submit ourselves entirely to Christ Jesus, when we abandon ourselves to Him, when our soul only responds, like His own, with a perpetual *Amen* to all that He asks of us in the name of His Father; when, after His example, we abide in this attitude of adoration before all the manifestations of the divine will, in face of the least permissions of His Providence, then Christ Jesus establishes His peace in us: His peace, not that which the world promises, but the true peace which can only come from Himself: *Pacem meam do vobis; non quomodo mundus dat, ego do vobis.*

Indeed, such adoration produces in us the unity of all desires. The soul has but one thing in view: the establishing in her of

How Suffering Leads to Life

Christ's kingdom. Christ Jesus, in return, satisfies this desire with magnificent plenitude. The soul possesses the perfect contentment of her deepest tendencies because the satisfaction of her supernatural desires has been reduced to one; she is in the right order of things; she lives in peace.

Happy the soul who has thus understood the order established by the Father, that soul who seeks only to be conformed by love to His admirable order, where all leads up to Christ Jesus: she tastes peace, a peace of which St. Paul says that it surpasses all understanding and defies all expression. Doubtless, here below, peace is not always sensible; upon earth we are in a condition of trial and, most often, peace is won by conflict. Christ has not restored to us that original justice which established harmony in Adam's soul, but the soul that lays hold on God alone participates in the divine stability; temptations, sufferings, trials touch only the surface of our being; the depths where peace reigns are inaccessible to disturbance. The surface of the sea may be violently agitated by the waves during the tempest; the deep waters remain tranquil. We may be slighted, opposed, persecuted, be unjustly treated, our intentions and deeds may be misunderstood; temptation may shake us, suffering may come suddenly upon us; but there is an inner sanctuary which none can reach; here is the sojourn of our peace, because in this innermost secret of the soul dwell adoration, submission and abandonment to God. "I love my God," said St. Augustine, "no one takes Him from me: no one takes from me what I ought to give Him, for that is enclosed within my heart. . . . O inward riches which no one or anything can take away!"

In the centre of the soul that loves God there rises up the *civitas pacis* which no noise of earth can trouble, that no attack can surprise. We may truly say that nothing which is exterior, outside us, can, unless we so will, touch our inward peace: this essentially depends on only one thing, namely, our attitude towards God. It is in Him that we must trust. "The Lord is my light and my salvation, whom shall I fear?" If the wind of temptation and trial arises, I have only to take refuge with Him. "Lord, save me, for without Thee, I perish." And our Lord, as formerly when in the ship tossed about by the waves, will Himself calm the tempest with a single gesture; and there will come "a great calm": *Et facta est tranquillitas magna.*

If we really seek God in everything, by following in the footsteps of Christ, Who is the sole way that leads to the Father; if we strive to be detached from all, that we may only desire the Master's good pleasure; if, when the Spirit of Jesus speaks to us, there is in us no inflexibility of soul, no resistance to His inspirations, but only docility and adoration, we may be assured that peace, deep and abundant, will reign in us; for, O Lord, "much peace have they that love Thy law": *Pax multa diligentibus legem tuam.*

Christ, the Ideal of the Monk, Part II, chapter 18, sections 2 and 3

Christian Acceptance of Suffering Honours God, Draws Down Grace upon Souls and the Church, the Mystical Body of Christ

God showers singular blessings upon a soul which has the spirit of abandonment. We can never repeat often enough how sovereignly God acts in such a soul and how it advances in holiness. He leads it by sure ways to the height of perfection. Sometimes, it is true, these ways appear to go quite in a contrary direction, but God attains His ends, ordering all things with strength and sweetness: *Attingit ergo a fine usque ad finem fortiter, et disponit omnia suaviter.* "All things," said Christ Jesus again to His faithful servant Gertrude, "are ordered by the wisdom of My Providence."

Christ, the Ideal of the Monk, Part II, chapter 16, section 6

Happy are those souls whom God calls to live only in the nudity of the Cross. It becomes for them an inexhaustible source of precious graces.

Sufferings are the price and the sign of true divine favours.... Works and foundations built upon the Cross and upon sufferings are alone lasting.

How Suffering Leads to Life

The sufferings you have endured are for me a sign of the special benediction of the One Who, in His wisdom, chose to found all upon *the Cross*.

Union with God, chapter 7

In your letter there is a phrase which pleases me very much, because I see in it the source of great glory for our Lord. You say, "There is nothing, absolutely nothing in me upon which I can take a little security. Therefore I do not cease to cast myself with confidence into the Heart of my Master." That, my daughter, is the true way, for all that God does for us is *the result of His mercy* which is touched by the avowal of this misery; and a soul that sees her misery and presents it continually to the gaze of divine mercy, gives great glory to God by leaving Him the opportunity of communicating His goodness to her. Continue to follow this attraction, and let yourself be led, in the midst of the darkness of trial, to the nuptials of the Lamb to which He destines you.

Our Lord urges me to pray much for you that you may remain with great generosity on the altar of immolation with Jesus. A soul, even a very miserable one, thus united to Jesus in His agony, but like Abraham, "hoping against hope," gives immense glory to God and helps Jesus in His work in the Church.

Union with God, chapter 4, section 2

I have *seen* that you have been suffering, I have suffered with you. We are so much *one*! Yet I could not have wished it otherwise. I have placed you with Jesus like His *Amen* deep in the Father's bosom. He loves you infinitely more and infinitely better than I do. I yield you up to Him as Mary yielded up Jesus, and if He wills to fasten you on the Cross with your Spouse, if He wills for you shame, suffering, and misunderstanding, if He wills for you even *immolation*, I will it too as I will it for myself. We are not made for enjoyment down here, our happiness is on high, *Sursum corda.* In the divine plan all good comes from Calvary, from suffering. St. John of the Cross says that our Lord scarcely ever gives the gift of contemplation and perfect union except to those who have laboured *much*, suffered much for Him. Now my ambition for you is this perfect union, so fruitful for the Church and souls. St. Paul tells us, *Libenter gloriabor in infirmitatibus meis* UT *inhabitet in me* VIRTUS *Christi*. I wish to see you quite weak in yourself but filled with the *virtus Christi*. Jesus has promised that through Holy Communion not only shall we abide in Him but also that *He will abide in us*. That is the *virtus Christi*. The more our life flows from Him, the more we have the *virtus Christi*—the more it glorifies the Father. *In hoc clarificatus est Pater meus* UT FRUCTUM PLURIMUM *afferatis; qui manet in me et ego in eo, hic fert fructum multum*. "In this is My Father glorified, that you bring forth very much fruit; he that abideth in Me, and I in Him, the same beareth much fruit."

Union with God, chapter 3, section 2

Our Lord is Master of His gifts and, *without any merit on their part*, He calls certain souls to more intimate union with Him, to share His sorrows and sufferings for the glory of His Father and the salvation of souls: *Adimpleo in corpore meo quae desunt passionum Christi pro corpore ejus quod est Ecclesia*: "I fill up those things that are wanting of the sufferings of Christ, in my flesh, for His body, which is the Church." "We are the body of Christ and members of His members." God could have saved men without them having to suffer or to merit, as He does in the case of little children who die after baptism. But by a decree of His adorable wisdom, He had decided that the world's salvation should depend upon an expiation of which His Son Jesus should undergo *the greater part* but in which His members should be associated. Many men neglect to supply their share of suffering *accepted* in union with Jesus Christ, and of prayers and good works.

That is why our Lord chooses certain souls to be associated with Him in the great work of the Redemption. These are elect souls, victims of expiation and praise. These are dear to Jesus beyond all one can imagine. His delight is to be in them. Now, my dear daughter, I am convinced that you are one of these souls. Without any merit on your part, Jesus has chosen you. If you are faithful, you will attain

How Suffering Leads to Life

close union with our Lord, and once united to Him, lost in Him, your life will bear much fruit for His glory and the salvation of souls. On the day of your mystical nuptials one sees only the flowers of the crown that Jesus places upon your head. But, my daughter, never forget that *the spouse of a Crucified God is a victim*. I say this to you, for I foresee that you will suffer, and you have need of much courage, much faith, much confidence. There are deserts to be traversed, you must pass through darkness and obscurity, days when you feel powerless and forsaken. Without that, your love would never be deep nor strong. But if you are faithful and abandoned to Him, Jesus will always hold you by the hand. "Though I should walk in the midst of the shadow of death, I will fear no evils, for Thou art with me."

So, my dear daughter, give yourself without stinting, yield yourself up without fear. Do not *ask* for suffering, but *yield yourself up* to the wisdom and love of your Spouse that He may operate in you all that the interests of His glory demand. He will come to you every day in the Holy Sacrament *in order to change you into Himself*. Let this eucharistic life of Jesus be a continual model for you. There, Jesus is a Victim immolated to the glory of His Father, and given over as food to His brethren, even to those who receive Him with coldness and ingratitude, or to those who outrage Him. You, too, my daughter, be every day more and more a *victim* immolated *to the glory* of the Blessed Trinity in prayer, Divine Office, and mortification, and a *victim of charity* immolated to souls by expiation, and to your sisters by patience, kindness, indulgence. Be a *great soul* who forgets herself to think of the interests of Jesus and of souls. Do not be stayed by the trifles which occupy the thoughts and the life of so many consecrated souls. Let us help one another to arrive at this sublime ideal which I desire for myself as I do for you.

Union with God, chapter 3, section 2

It is not only over works which the Lord performs in it that the soul can rejoice: its life of complete union with Jesus extends that influence over the entire Church.

Our Lord explained this truth to Saint Catherine of Siena: "Oh, how sweet is this dwelling of the soul in Me—sweeter than all sweetness—through perfect union with Me! The will itself is no longer really an intermediary in this union between the soul and Myself, since it has become one and the same thing with Me." And as if, having posited the premise, He would immediately draw the conclusions, He added: "The fruit of its humble and constant prayers spreads like a perfume throughout the whole world. The incense of it desires rises towards Me in unceasing supplication for the salvation of souls. It is a voice which, without human words, forever cries forth in the presence of My Divine Majesty."

Shall we who live by faith be astonished at such widespread power? Is not God the sole guardian of the city of souls, and the sole support of the edifice of the Church? Does not He hold the eternal destiny of souls in His hands? And is not Christ the only Way, the unique Truth, the true Life of every man who comes into the world? But what credit with Him, what power over Him, does the soul possess when it belongs entirely to Him? It is all-powerful over the Sacred Heart, and its whole life is a constant calling down of the Lord's graces and blessings on behalf of His people.[1]

Therein lies one of the most profound aspects of the dogma of the communion of saints. The nearer one comes to God, the Author and Principle of every gift that adorns and rejoices hearts, the more truly does he become the benefactor of his brethren. How many graces it can implore, obtain, and wrest from Christ for the entire Church. How powerfully it co-operates in the conversion of sinners, the perseverance of the just, the salvation of those in agony, and the entrance of suffering souls into the blessedness of heaven! How admirably productive it is! Nature's fecundity is limited; the soul's is unlimited. A radiant beam shines forth from such a soul; those who draw near to it breathe "the good odour of Christ." A sort of divine virtue emanates from it to touch souls, obtaining pardon for them;

---

1. Pope Saint Gregory the Great says that, by their tears and their life of renunciation, the holy virgins of Rome—singlehandedly, so to say—protected that stricken city from the invading Lombards for several years. *Harum talis vita est, atque in tantum lacrimis et abstinentia stricta, ut credamus quia, si ipsae non essent, nullus nostrum jam per tot annos in loco hoc subsistere inter Longobardorum gladios potuisset.* (*Epistol.* 26, *lib.* VII)

How Suffering Leads to Life

helping, consoling, strengthening them; giving them a helping hand, bestowing peace and joy on them, and making them grow for the glory of Christ. The reason is that Christ lives in that soul; since He is always living and therefore never inactive and since, again, His action is love, He uses that soul to enlighten, vivify, and save others. It really co-operates with Him in the redemption. Its action and fecundity cannot be measured. It is like the snow on mountaintops which, nearer the warm rays of the sun, melts and flows down as living water to irrigate the valleys and plains below.

Sponsa Verbi, chapter 7

PART V

Facing Death, the Supreme Trial

Life is Not Taken Away, but Transformed

UPON THE VERY EVE of His death, Jesus said to His disciples: *Vos estis qui permansistis mecum in tentationibus meis*: "You are they who have continued with Me in My temptation," and He immediately adds: "and I dispose to you, as My Father hath disposed to Me, a kingdom": *Et ego dispono vobis sicut disposuit mihi Pater meus regnum*.

This divine promise likewise concerns us. If we "continue" with Jesus in His "temptations," if we often contemplate His sufferings with faith and love, Christ will come, when our last hour strikes, to take us with Him that we may enter into the kingdom of His Father.

The day will come, sooner than we think, when death will be near. We shall lie motionless upon our bed; those who will then surround us will look upon us, silent in their powerlessness to help; we shall no longer have any vital contact with the outer world. The soul will be alone with Christ.

We shall then know what it is to have continued with Him in His temptations; we shall hear Him say to us, in this supreme and decisive agony, which is now our own: "You did not forsake Me in My agony, you accompanied Me when I went to Calvary to die for you. Behold Me now; I am near you to help you, to take you with Me. Fear not, have confidence, it is I"! *Ego sum, nolite timere!* We shall then be able to repeat the words of the Psalmist with all assurance: *Et si ambulavero in medio umbrae mortis, non timebo mala; quoniam tu mecum es*: O Lord, now that the shadows of death already surround me, I am not afraid "for Thou art with me."

Christ in His Mysteries, Part II, chapter 13, section 5

Death cannot trouble the soul that has sought only God. Has it not confided itself to the One Who says: "He that believeth in Me, although he be dead, shall live," *Qui credit in Me, etiamsi mortuus fuerit, vivit?* Our Lord is the Truth; He is also the Life; and He brings us, He restores to us, the life that is unending. Even though the shadow of death falls upon it, this soul will abide in peace: *Nam etsi ambulavero in medio umbrae mortis, non timebo mala, quoniam tu mecum es.* Does it not know in Whom it has trusted: *Scio cui credidi?* And this presence of Jesus reassures the soul against every terror.

In one of her "Exercises," St. Gertrude allows her assurance, which the infinite merits of Jesus give her, to overflow. At the thought of the divine tribunal of which the image rises up before her mind, she makes the most moving appeal to these merits. "Woe, woe unto me, if, when I come before Thee, I had no advocate to plead my cause! O Love, stand Thou forth on my behalf, answer for me, sue out my pardon. If Thou undertake my cause, I know that I still have hope of life. I know what I will do, I will take the chalice of salvation, even the chalice of my Jesus. I will lay it upon the empty scale of the balance of Truth. So shall I supply all that is lacking, and outweigh all my sins. That chalice will raise up again the ruins of my hope, for therewith I shall infinitely overbalance all my unworthiness.... Come Thou with me to judgment," says St. Gertrude to our Lord; "there let us stand together. Judge me, for the right is Thine; but remember Thou art also my Advocate. In order that I be fully acquitted, Thou hast but to recount what Thou didst become for love of me, the good Thou hast decreed to do unto me, the price wherewith Thou hast purchased me. Thou hast taken my nature to this very end, that I might not perish. Thou hast borne the burden of my sins, Thou hast died for me, that I might not die an eternal death. Thou hast willed to make me rich in merit, and so hast Thou given me all. Judge me, then, at the hour of my death according to that innocence and that purity which Thou didst bestow on me in Thee when Thou didst pay all my debts, when Thou wast Thyself judged and condemned in my stead; that, all poor and destitute as I am in myself, I might have all and abound."

For souls moved by such sentiments, death is but a transition; Christ comes Himself to open to them the gates of the heavenly Jerusalem, which, much more so than that of old, deserves to be called the "blessed vision of peace": *Beata pacis visio.* There will be

Life is Not Taken Away, but Transformed

no more darkness, trouble, tears, or sighs; but peace, infinite and perfect peace. "Peace first becomes ours with the longing and seeking for the Creator; it is in the full vision and eternal possession of Him that peace is made perfect": *Pax enim nostra ex desiderio Conditoris inchoatur, ex manifesta autem visione perficitur.*

Christ, the Ideal of the Monk, Part II, chapter 18, section 3

I am told that you have received extreme unction. Your whole body was sanctified and consecrated to God by this sacrament, and you were placed in His fatherly hands that He may guard and console you. The grace of this sacrament lasts during all the illness, and obtains fresh graces for you at each instant.

My dear child, it is very painful and very hard for *nature* to be thus, at your age, so suffering, so powerless. And yet, if one could see you as the angels see you, how one would envy you! Having been baptised and having received Holy Communion, you are the image of Jesus Christ, and now that you are stretched upon your bed of suffering, you are the image of Jesus Christ upon the Cross. Every time you unite yourself to our Lord Crucified by acts of patience and conformity to God's holy will, you become dearer and dearer to the Heart of Jesus. Your state of suffering accepted lovingly and in union with Jesus Christ is as pleasing to God as that of a nun, and if you are faithful, if you lose none of the graces you are receiving at present, you may even surpass your sister, in spite of her alpargates [sandals] and Carmelite togue.

Union with God, chapter 3, section 2

I have just been celebrating the Holy Sacrifice for you and for myself this morning, without knowing if you were yet in life or already *in sinu Patris.* I have been praying *much* for you since receiving your letter telling me that the last sacraments had been administered to you. As I love you in the Father, it is in His Heart that I place you, knowing that He loves you more and better than I do. I can only want and ask for you what He desires.

Although everything seems to tell that the end is near, and although I have already committed you into the hands of the Heavenly Father Who loves you, I cannot persuade myself that it is the end: *Deducit ad inferos et reducit.* We are nothing in His hands and He can use us as He chooses. If He chooses to unite us to His Son like victims (*hosties*) that He breaks, it is too great an honour for us. Remain in a state of complete self-surrender full of faith and love, and if anguish wrings your heart, say with Job: "Though He kill me, yet will I trust in Him."

Abbot Columba Marmion, chapter 11

I cannot tell you what it is to come to such a moment; experience alone can make one understand what one feels on seeing oneself about to appear before God. When I thus saw myself on the threshold of eternity[1] I felt possessed by fear, and I resolved, if God left me longer to live, to be such at the moment of death that I could no longer have this fear.

Death is a great thing; it is a solemn hour. Our Blessed Father Saint Benedict tells us to have it ever before our eyes: *Mortem quotidie ante oculos suspectam habere.* As for me, I confess to you that I have it continually present to me.

By God's grace I am entering today on my sixtieth year; that is to say, the eternal hills begin to cast their shadow over my life. I ask your prayers that I may worthily spend for God the years that remain to me, if years there are.

We are journeying together towards that eternity where all will be consummated in the love of God.

God is very good to me. He tries me in every way, but at the same time unites me more and more to Himself. The thought of God, of eternity, of death, hardly ever leaves me, but it keeps me in joy and

---

1. This paragraph was written in 1915, when, in the course of a serious illness, Dom Marmion was at death's door.

Life is Not Taken Away, but Transformed

in great peace. I have a great fear of God's majesty, of His holiness and justice, and at the same time a certainty based on love that our Heavenly Father will arrange all *for the best.*

I, too, have a great fear of death. It is the *divine* punishment of sin: *merces peccati mors,* and this fear of death honours God; and if it is accompanied by hope it honours God very much. Often those who have most dreaded death during their life have no longer this fear when death comes. For myself, when making my Way of the Cross each day, I recommend myself to Jesus and to Mary for the moment of my agony and the judgment, and I have the conviction that they will be there to help me.

I feel a great longing for heaven. Yet I don't feel as if my work was done. I fear the judgment, and yet I cast myself on God's bosom with all my miseries and my responsibilities and hope in His mercy. Nothing else can save us, for our poor little works are not fit to be presented, and only His fatherly affection deigns to accept them. *Non aestimator meriti sed veniae quaesumus largitor admitte,* as we pray at Mass.

Let us think what will happen to us when we enter into eternity, what will then be granted to us. There are some words in Holy Scripture which have much struck me these days: *Denudabit absconsa sua illi.* We should meditate on these words. God will show Himself to the soul "without secret," as He is: *denudabit,* He will disclose to her, will "unveil" to her, the *absconsa,* the depths of His divinity, He will be all open to her, He will show Himself in the light, in the full day of His essential truth.

We are filled with miseries, with weaknesses, but Christ has willed to take upon Himself all these infirmities, in order to bestow upon us His strength. In the measure in which we acknowledge our miseries, in which we accept to share in the Passion of Jesus and in the weakness with which He deigned to clothe Himself, in that same measure we shall share in His divine strength: *Gloriabor in infirmitatibus meis.... Dum infirmor tunc potens sum.* We then become the object of the divine mercy and of the delight of the Heavenly Father Who beholds us in His Son.

It is at the hour of death above all that we experience this mystery and benefit by it. Christ has destroyed the penalty of death; our death has been swallowed up in His. Henceforward His death cries for mercy on us, and the Father sees in our death the image of the death of His Son. This is why the death of the just is precious in the sight of the Lord. *Pretiosa in conspectu Domini mors sanctorum ejus.* For some time past I have been imploring Christ each morning at holy Mass and asking Him to lend His own death to all the dying. In offering this prayer we can be sure that Christ will do for us, at the moment of our agony and death, what we have asked Him to do for others.

Abbot Columba Marmion, chapter 19

PART VI

Our Sharing in
the Eternal Glory of Christ

We Shall Be Glorified With Christ

Glorification Follows upon the Passion of Jesus

Having obtained for us the grace to bear our cross with Him, Christ Jesus likewise grants us to share His glory, after we have been associated with His sufferings: *Si tamen compatimur, ut et conglorificemur.* For us as for Him, this glory will be measured by our "passion." The glory of Jesus is infinite, because in His Passion, He, being God, reached the lowest depths of suffering and humiliation. And it is by reason of His deep self-abasement that God has given Him such glory: *Propter quod et Deus exaltavit illum.*

Indeed the Passion of Jesus, important as it was in His life, necessary as it is to our salvation and our sanctification, does not terminate the cycle of His mysteries.

We notice in reading the Gospel, that when our Lord speaks of His Passion to the Apostles, He always adds that "the third day He will rise again": *Et tertia die resurget.* These two mysteries are likewise linked together in the thought of St. Paul, whether he speaks of Christ alone, or whether he alludes to His mystical body. Now, the Resurrection is for Jesus the dawn of His glorious life.

This is why the Church, when she solemnly commemorates the sufferings of her Bridegroom, mingles her accents of compassion with those of triumph. The liturgical ornaments of black or purple, the stripping of the altars, the "lamentations" borrowed from Jeremias, the silence of the bells, attest the bitter desolation that oppresses the heart of the Bride during these anniversary days of the great drama. And yet she breaks forth into accents of triumph and glory:

> *Pange, lingua gloriosi*
> *Lauream certaminis...*

"Exalt, O my tongue, the laurels of a glorious combat! Upon the trophies of the Cross, proclaim the great triumph; Christ, the Redeemer of the world, comes forth as Victor from the combat in delivering Himself up to death." *Vexilla Regis prodeunt*: "The standard of the King advances, the mystery of the Cross shines forth.... Thou art beautiful and glorious, tree decked with royal purple.... Happy art thou to have borne the world's Ransom, suspended in thy arms...." Christ is Conqueror through the Cross: *Regnavit a ligno Deus*. The Cross represents the humiliations of Christ; but since the day when Jesus was fastened to it, the Cross occupies the place of honour in our churches. The instrument of our salvation has become for Christ the price of His glory: *Nonne haec oportuit pati Christum, et ita intrare in gloriam suam?* It is the same for us. Suffering is not the last word in the Christian life. After having shared in the Passion of the Saviour, we shall also share in His glory.

Christ in His Mysteries, Part II, chapter 13, section 5

One reason of this supreme glorification is its being a recompense for the humiliations that Jesus underwent out of love of His Father and charity for us.

I have often said that in entering into this world, Christ yielded Himself up entirely to the will of the Father. *Ecce venio ut faciam, Deus, voluntatem tuam.* He accepted to accomplish to the full all the abasements that had been foretold, to drink to the dregs the bitter chalice of sufferings and of untold ignominies; He annihilated Himself even to the malediction of the Cross. And why was this? *Ut cognoscat mundus quia diligo Patrem.* "That the world may know that I love the Father," His perfections and His glory, His might and His good pleasure.

"For which cause," *propter quod* (remark these words, borrowed from St. Paul: they show the reality of the motive), God has glorified His Son, and has exalted Him above all things: *Propter quod et Deus exaltavit illum.*

After the combat, it is with joy that earthly princes reward the valiant captains who have defended their prerogatives, won the victory over the enemy, and by their conquests widened the boundaries of the kingdom.

We Shall Be Glorified With Christ

Was it not this that took place in heaven on the day of the Ascension, though with an incomparable glory? With supreme fidelity, Jesus had accomplished the work that His Father had given Him to do: *Quae placita sunt ei facio semper.... Opus consummavi*; abandoning Himself to the action of divine justice, as a holy Victim, He had descended into an incomprehensible abyss of sorrows and humiliations. And now all was expiated, the price was paid and redemption accomplished, the powers of darkness were defeated, the perfections of the Father were acknowledged and His rights avenged, and the gates of the kingdom of heaven were opened to all the human race. If we may thus lisp about such mysteries, what joy for the Heavenly Father to crown His Son after the victory gained over the prince of this world! What divine gladness to call the sacred humanity of Jesus to the enjoyment of the splendour, the beatitude and power of an eternal exaltation!

And what still further enhanced this divine gladness was that Jesus, when about to consummate His sacrifice, had asked of His Father that glory which was to extend that of the Father: "Father, the hour is come: glorify Thy Son, that Thy Son may glorify Thee."

Yea, Father, the hour is come. Thy justice has been satisfied by expiation; may it be so likewise by the glory that comes to Thy Son Jesus, because of the love that He has manifested to Thee in His sufferings. O Father, glorify Thy Son! Establish His reign in the hearts of those who love Him; bring under His sceptre the souls that have turned away from Him; draw to Him those who, sitting in darkness, do not yet know Him. Father, glorify Thy Son, so that in His turn, Thy Son may glorify Thee in manifesting to us Thy Divine Being, Thy perfections, Thy will! *Pater, clarifica Filium tuum ut Filius tuus clarificet te.*

But the Father has already answered to us: "I have glorified it and I will glorify it still"—*Clarificavi et iterum clarificabo.* And we hear Him repeat to Christ Himself the solemn words spoken beforehand by the Psalmist: "Thou art My Son.... Ask of Me, and I shall give Thee the nations for Thy inheritance... and for Thy dominion the ends of the earth.... Sit Thou at My right hand until I have made Thy enemies Thy footstool."

The works of God are full of ineffable and secret harmonies which ravish faithful souls.

Where was it that the Passion of Jesus began? At the foot of the Mount of Olives. There, during three long hours, His blessed soul—foreseeing in the divine light, the sum of afflictions and outrages which were to constitute His sacrifice—was a prey to sadness, weariness, fear, and anguish. We shall never know what poignant agony was undergone by the Son of God in the Garden of Olives: Jesus suffered there in anticipation all the sorrows of His Passion: "Father, if it be possible, let this chalice pass from Me."

And where was it that our Divine Saviour entered into the joys of His Ascension? Jesus, Eternal Wisdom, Who, let us not forget it, makes only one with His Father and the Holy Spirit, chose the summit of this same mountain that had witnessed His sorrowful abasements from whence to ascend to heaven. There, in the same place where it fell upon Christ like a vengeful torrent, divine justice crowns Him with honour and glory; there, where in the horror of darkness, were preluded mighty combats, now arises the radiant dawn of an incomparable triumph.

Is not the Church, our Mother, justified in extolling as "admirable" the glorification of her Divine Head? *Per admirabilem ascensionem tuam.*

Christ in His Mysteries, Part II, chapter 16, section 2

The Everlastingness of our Glory

Our glory and our beatitude, participations in that of Christ, will be immense. "For which cause we faint not," writes St. Paul; "but though our outward man is corrupted, yet the inward man is renewed day by day, for that which is at present momentary and light of our tribulation, worketh for us above measure exceedingly an eternal weight of glory." *Id enim quod in praesenti est momentaneum et leve tribulationis nostrae, supra modum in sublimitate aeternum gloriae pondus operatur in nobis.* He writes again: "And if sons, heirs also; heirs indeed of God and joint heirs with Christ; yet so, if we suffer with Him, that we may be also glorified with Him," and he adds: "For I reckon that the sufferings of this present time are not worthy to be compared with the glory to come, that shall be

We Shall Be Glorified With Christ

revealed in us." Therefore in the same measure in which "you partake of the sufferings of Christ, rejoice that when His glory shall be revealed, you may also be glad with exceeding joy." *Communicantes Christi passionibus, gaudete, ut et in revelatione gloriae ejus gaudeatis exsultantes.*

Courage, then! I repeat with St. Paul. "Know you not," he says, in allusion to the public games, the races in the arena, that took place in his time, "know you not that everyone that striveth for the mastery, refraineth himself from all things so as to bear off the prize?" And what was the prize? A crown of a day, while it is for an imperishable crown that we deny ourselves, and this crown is to share forever in the glory and beatitude of our Head.

Christ, the Life of the Soul, Part II, chapter 4, section 6

Again when our Lord speaks of this beatitude, He tells us how God bids His faithful servant enter into the joy of his Lord. This joy is the joy of God Himself, the joy that He possesses in the knowledge of His infinite perfections, the beatitude that God has in the ineffable society of the Three Persons; the infinite repose and satisfaction wherein He dwells. His joy will be ours: *Ut habeant gaudium meum impletum in semetipsis.* His beatitude and His repose will also be ours; His life, our life—perfect life in which all our faculties will be perfectly satisfied.

There we shall find that "entire participation in the unchanging good," as St. Augustine excellently calls it: *Plena participatio incommutabilis boni.* Even to this extent God has loved us. Oh! if we knew what God has reserved for them that love Him! . . .

And because this beatitude and this life are those of God Himself, they will be eternal. "Death shall be no more," says St. John, "nor mourning nor crying nor sorrow shall be any more . . . and God shall wipe away all tears," from the eyes of those who enter into His joy. We shall be always with the Lord: *Semper cum Domino erimus.* There where He is, we shall be.

Hear in what forcible terms Jesus has given us this assurance. He says of those who are His sheep: "I give them life everlasting; and they shall not perish for ever, and no man shall pluck them out of My hand. That which My Father hath given Me is greater than all; and no one can snatch them out of the hand of My Father. I and the Father are one." What confidence Jesus Christ gives us! "You now indeed have sorrow," He said to His disciples, "but I will see you again and your heart shall rejoice; and your joy no man shall take from you": *Et gaudium vestrum nemo tollet a vobis.*

O divine promise, given by the Uncreated Word, by the Word in person, by the infallible Truth; promise full of sweetness: "I will come Myself! . . ." We shall belong to Christ, and through Him to the Father, in the bosom of beatitude. "In that day," says Jesus, "you shall know"—no longer *in umbra fidei,* in the shadows of faith, but in the full radiance of eternal light, *in lumine gloriae*—"you shall know that I am in My Father, and you in Me, and I in you." You shall see My glory as the only-begotten Son, and this vision shall be for you an ever living source of ineffable joy.

Let us say to Him: "O Lord Jesus, Divine Master, Redeemer of our souls, Elder Brother, give us of this divine, life-giving water, that we may never thirst; grant to us here below to remain united to Thee by grace so that one day we may be where Thou art, to behold the glory of Thy humanity, as Thou didst pray the Father for us, and enjoy Thee for ever in Thy kingdom!"

Christ, the Life of the Soul, Part II, chapter 13, section 1;
Christ in His Mysteries, Part I, chapter 3, section 6

The Measure of our Eternal Happiness

We shall enjoy God according to the same measure of grace to which we have attained at the moment of our going out of the world.

Do not let us lose sight of this truth: the degree of our eternal beatitude is, and will remain, fixed for ever by the degree of charity we have attained, by the grace of Christ, when God shall call us to Himself. Each moment of our life is then infinitely precious, for it suffices to advance us a degree in the love of God, to raise us higher in the beatitude of eternal life.

We Shall Be Glorified With Christ

And let us not say that one degree more or less is a small matter. How can anything be a small matter when it concerns God, and the endless life and beatitude of which He is the source? If, according to the parable spoken by our Lord in person, we have received five talents, it was not that we might bury them, but that we might make them bear increase. And if God measures the reward according to the efforts we have made to live by His grace and increase it in us, do not think it matters little what kind of a harvest we bring to our Father in Heaven. Jesus Himself has told us that His Heavenly Father is glorified in seeing us abound, by His grace, in fruits of holiness, which will be fruits of beatitude in heaven. *In hoc clarificatus est Pater meus ut fructum plurimum afferatis.* This is so true that Christ compares His Father to a vine-dresser Who prunes us by suffering in order that we bear much fruit: *Ut fructum plus afferat.* Can it be that our love for Jesus Christ is so weak that we account it a small thing to be a more or less resplendent member of His mystical body in the heavenly Jerusalem? The holier we become, the more we shall glorify God during all eternity, the greater will be our part in that song of thanksgiving sung by the elect to Christ the Redeemer: *Redemisti nos, Domine.*

Let us then be vigilant ever to put away from us the obstacles that might lessen our union with Jesus Christ; to let the divine action penetrate us deeply, and the grace of Jesus act so freely within us that we may "come to the fulness of the age of Christ." Hear the pressing exhortation that St. Paul, who had been caught up to the third heaven, made to his dear Philippians: "For God is my witness how I long after you all in the Heart of Jesus Christ. And this I pray that your charity may more and more abound . . . that you may be sincere and without offence unto the day of Christ; filled with the fruits of justice, through Jesus Christ, unto the glory and the praise of God": *Et hoc oro ut caritas vestra magis ac magis abundet ut sitis . . . repleti fructu justitiae per Jesum Christum, in gloriam et laudem Dei.*

And, above all, see what a wonderful example he sets in the fulfilment of this precept. The great Apostle has reached the end of his career; the imprisonment he is enduring in Rome has suspended the course of the numerous journeys undertaken to spread abroad the good news of Christ: he has arrived at the term of his struggles and labours. He is so deeply imbued with the mystery of Christ which he has revealed to so many souls that he can say to these same Philippians: "For me, to live is Christ, and to die is gain."

However, he continues: "And if to live in the flesh, this is to me the fruit of labour, and what I shall choose I know not. But I am straitened between two; having a desire to be dissolved and to be with Christ, a thing by far the better. But to abide still in the flesh, is needful for you ... for your furtherance and joy of faith.... Our conversation is in heaven, from whence also we look for the Saviour, our Lord Jesus Christ, Who will reform the body of our lowness, made like to the body of His glory, according to the operation whereby also He is able to subdue all things unto Himself." And the Apostle at last ends with this moving and pressing salutation: "Therefore, my dearly beloved brethren, and most desired, my joy and my crown, so stand fast in the Lord."

Christ, the Life of the Soul, Part II, chapter 13, section 3

The dearer one is to God, the more one suffers in this world. Jesus, God's beloved Son, suffered as man has never suffered. Mary, our Mother, is the Mother of Sorrows. Why? Because God is so good, He gives to unbelievers and to the wicked who will not have the happiness of enjoying His beautiful Paradise, the good things of this world, things which will last a few years and then pass away forever. But to His friends He gives *eternal* good things, for each little suffering borne for God and in union with Jesus will have an *ineffable* reward for all eternity. That is why Mary was so poor; that is why she suffered martyrdom all her life, ever after the holy man Simeon foretold to her the sufferings of her Son.

Try then, my dear child, to unite all your sufferings of body and of *heart* to the Sacred Heart of Jesus, for it is this union which gives them all their merit.

You have been so *suffering.* If there were only this poor world with its trials, separations and sorrows, I should be very grieved at this news, for I love my dear child. But I keep my eyes fixed on that beautiful

We Shall Be Glorified With Christ

Paradise where we shall all be one day and where each day of suffering here below endured *with Jesus* and *for Him* will have an eternal reward, joy and rest. Yes, my dear child, Jesus is treating you as He treated His Mother, and as He treats those whom He especially loves. Courage then! I pray daily for you that our Lord may give you *entire* submission to His holy will. . . . A single day of weakness and illness borne joyfully for Jesus counts as months (in ordinary health).

This life is certainly full of sadness and tears, for we have constantly to see those we love suffer and to be separated from those who are dearest to us. But there is a fatherland on high, the Home of our Heavenly Father. In that land there will be no tears, no separation, there we shall be forever with those we love. But for that, we must suffer here below, and this is why the greatest friends of God suffer much upon this earth so that they may not be attached to the things of this world since they will have *infinite* happiness for all eternity.

Thanks for your very kind letter. I should have written sooner, but I was not too sure where you were. I pray for you *very much* and every day. I rejoice in your joys and suffer with your sorrows as if they were my very own. However, lift your eyes up to God and look at things in the light of eternity and truth. This world is not our home. Heaven is our true fatherland, and our Heavenly Father arranges matters in such a way that we may not become too attached to what *must* pass. He grants us some joy so that our going through this stage, this life, may be endurable; but He also sends the Cross to everyone because, to go to heaven, we *must* carry the Cross with Jesus.

 I thank God from the bottom of my heart for the protection and the graces He gives you. I know that you have suffered much, and each day I ask God to keep you, to console and to help you. The closer I come to the eternal hills, however, I *see* that our life here below is but a journey and a test, and that all who are united to Jesus Christ must expect to share in His Cross. To accept that Cross just as it presents itself—that is *true holiness*.

The older I get, the more I see that this life is but a brief apparition framed by two eternities, one which precedes it, and another which follows. This life is a test which precedes eternity, a time of expiation, a sharing in the Passion of Jesus Christ. God is so good that, in order to make our life bearable, He pours into our cup a few drops of highly evanescent joy; but it is not at all His will that we should cling to such joy. Saint Benedict has a saying which teaches us the right attitude with regard to the happiness which God sends us: *Delicias non amplecti*—we must not *embrace* it or become *too wrapped up in it*. He does not say that we should not rejoice. God Himself grants us pleasures and allows us—nay, at times even wants us—to accept them; but He does not want us to plunge ourselves into them, for then we should be in danger of leaving God and cleaving to creatures. The various and most difficult trials you have been going through in these past few years are lessons which your Heavenly Father gives in order to detach you from creatures.

Correspondence

The Resurrection of the Body

God is so magnificent in what He does for His Christ, that He wills that the mystery of His Son's Resurrection should extend not only to our souls but also to our bodies. We too shall rise again. That is a dogma of faith. We shall rise corporally, like Christ, with Christ. Could it be otherwise?

Christ, as I have often repeated, is our Head; we form with Him a mystical body. If Christ is risen—and He is risen in His human nature—it is necessary that we, His members, should share in the same glory. For it is not only in our soul, it is likewise in our body, it is in our whole being that we are members of Christ. The most intimate union binds us to Jesus. If then He is risen glorious, the faithful who, by grace, make part of His mystical body, will be united with Him even in His Resurrection.

Hear what St. Paul says on this subject: "Christ is risen from the dead, the firstfruits of them that sleep"; He represents the firstfruits of a harvest; after Him, the rest of the harvest is to follow. "By a man came death, and by a man the resurrection of the dead. And as in Adam all die, so also in Christ all shall be made alive." God, he says

We Shall Be Glorified With Christ

more energetically still, "has raised us up together . . . through Jesus Christ": co*Nresuscitavit nos . . . in Christo Jesu*. How is this? It is that, by faith and grace, we are the living members of Christ, we share in His states, we are one with Him. And as grace is the principle of our glory, those who are, by grace, already saved in hope, are already also, in principle, risen in Christ.

This is our faith and our hope.

But now "our life is hidden with Christ in God"; we now live without grace producing those effects of light and splendour which will have their fruition in glory; even as Christ, before His Resurrection, held back the glorious radiance of His divinity and only allowed a reflection of it to be seen by the three disciples on the day of the Transfiguration on Tabor. Our inner life here below is only known to God; it is hidden from the eyes of men. Moreover, if we try to reproduce in our souls, by our spiritual liberty, the characteristics of the risen life of Jesus, it is a labour which is still wrought in a flesh wounded by sin, subject to the infirmities of time; we shall only attain this holy liberty at the cost of a struggle incessantly renewed and faithfully sustained. We too must suffer so as to enter into glory, as Christ said of Himself to the disciples of Emmaus, on the very day of His Resurrection: *Nonne haec oportuit pati Christum et ita intrare in gloriam suam?* "We are the sons of God," says the Apostle, "and if sons, heirs also; heirs indeed of God, and joint heirs with Christ; yet so if we suffer with Him, that we may be also glorified with Him."

May these thoughts of heaven sustain us during the days we have yet to pass here below. Yes, the time will come when there shall be no more mourning, nor crying, nor sorrow; God Himself will wipe away the tears of His servants become the co-heirs of His Son; He will make them sit down at the eternal feast which He has prepared to celebrate the triumph of Jesus and of those whose Elder Brother Jesus is.

Christ in His Mysteries, Part II, chapter 15, section 6

A Parting Word

Stand fast in the faith in Jesus Christ; keep an invincible faith in His merits, live in His love. By ardent faith, holy desires, and a charity which causes you to yield yourself without reserve to the generous and faithful accomplishment of the divine good pleasure, do not cease, as long as you are here below, "absent from the Lord," as St. Paul says, to augment your capacity of seeing and loving God, of enjoying Him in eternal beatitude, of living of His own life. The day will come when faith will give place to vision, when hope will be succeeded by the blessed reality, when love will fully unfold in God's eternal embrace. Sometimes it seems to us that this beatitude is so far off; but no, each day, each hour, each minute brings us nearer to it.

I would say to you again, with St. Paul: "Seek the things that are above, where Christ is sitting at the right hand of God. Mind the things that are above, not the things that are upon the earth," such as fortune, honours, pleasures; "for you are dead" to all these passing things; "your life," your true life, that of grace, "is hidden with Christ in God." But "when Christ," your Head, "shall appear" triumphant at the last day, "you also shall appear with Him in glory," that glory which you will share with Him because you are His members. *Cum Christus apparuerit vita vestra, tunc et vos apparebitis cum ipso in gloria.*

Therefore, let no pain, no suffering cast you down; "for that which is at present momentary and light of our tribulation, worketh for us above measure exceedingly an eternal weight of glory." Let no temptation hold you back, for if you are found faithful in the hour of trial, the hour will come when you will receive the crown which will be given to you on entering into the true life "which God hath promised to them that love Him." Let no senseless joy seduce you, "for the things which are seen are temporal, but the things which are not seen are eternal." Time is short, and the world passes away. That which does not pass away is the word of Jesus Christ: *Verba autem mea non transibunt.* These words are for us the principle of divine life: *Spiritus et vita sunt.*

Christ, the Life of the Soul, Part II, chapter 13, section 3

We Shall Be Glorified With Christ

Until we rejoin Jesus in Heaven, or rather until He takes us there Himself, since He has gone to prepare a place for us, let us live there, by faith in the boundless power of His prayer and of His mediation, by hope of one day partaking of His felicity, by the love that yields us up joyously and generously to the faithful and entire fulfilment of His will and good pleasure: it is thus that we shall prepare ourselves to participate fully in the admirable mystery of the glorification of Jesus.

Christ in His Mysteries, Part II, chapter 16, section 6

*Blessed are they that mourn
for they shall be comforted*